HERMAN MELVILLE:
Reassessments

HERMAN MELVILLE:
Reassessments

edited by
A. Robert Lee

VISION
and
BARNES & NOBLE

Vision Press Limited
Fulham Wharf
Townmead Road
London SW6 2SB

and

Barnes & Noble Books
81 Adams Drive
Totowa, NJ 07512

ISBN (UK) 0 85478 365 2 ⎫ (cloth)
ISBN (US) 0 389 20376 9 ⎭
ISBN (UK) 0 85478 036 X ⎫ (paper)
ISBN (US) 0 389 20471 4 ⎭

Printed and bound in Great Britain by
Unwin Brothers Ltd.,
Old Woking, Surrey.
Phototypeset by Galleon Photosetting,
Ipswich, Suffolk.
MCMLXXXIV

Contents

Introduction

by A. ROBERT LEE

> Compass, quadrant and sextant contrive
> No farther tides. . . . High in the azure steeps
> Monody shall not wake the mariner.
> This fabulous shadow only the sea keeps.
> —Hart Crane, 'At Melville's Tomb' (*White Buildings*, 1926)

> I am willing to ride Melville's image of man, whale and ocean
> to find in him prophecies, lessons he himself would not have
> spelled out. A hundred years gives us an advantage. For
> Melville was as much larger than himself as Ahab's hate. He
> was a plunger. He knew how to take a chance. . . .
> Melville took an awful licking. He was bound to. He was an
> original, aboriginal. A beginner. . . . Beginner—and interested
> in beginnings. Melville had a way of reaching back through
> time until he got history pushed back so far he turned time into
> space.
> —Charles Olson, *Call Me Ishmael* (1947)

> There was the handwriting:
> Columbus, the early Columbus, man of the ocean-sea and the
> Indes, confident, level, forward-flowing, the touch light, the
> form disciplined. . . .

> And Melville: harder, more incised (the Yankee) and crabbed,
> but like Christopher, leaning forward against the restraints,
> and on a level line. . . .
> —Paul Metcalf, *Genoa* (1965)

All three of these extracts express the tribute of fellow writers
to Herman Melville (1819–91), a profound sense of imaginative
affinity and debt. For Hart Crane, Melville figures as 'this

fabulous shadow' who, though buried inland (at Woodlawn Cemetery in the Bronx), remains always a voice of ocean boldness and of mysteries 'beneath the wave' according to an earlier line in the poem—no small twist of irony in retrospect that Crane himself should die a suicide at sea in 1932. For Charles Olson, whose *Call Me Ishmael* and other essays pioneered the links between Melville and Shakespeare, he ranks among the great 'archaeologists of morning', to adapt the title of one of his own collections of poems,[1] an 'aboriginal' and 'plunger' whose prophetic spirit probed with almost nervous intensity the outer edges of human awareness. For Paul Metcalf, great-grandson through the line of Melville's daughter (and in turn her daughter Mrs. Eleanor Melville Metcalf, author in 1953 of *Herman Melville: Cycle and Epicycle*) and a novelist and poet in his own right, Melville serves as a double-progenitor, blood-relative and an exemplary figure of philosophic quest. However elliptical and individual, taken together these tributes pay Melville handsome modern due. They also confirm his emergence from the painful obscurity of his own later nineteenth-century years—which continued through to the 1920s—and the appropriate perception of him as having struck out more boldly even than in his agreed centre-piece, *Moby-Dick* (1851), his 'wicked book' as he told Hawthorne, estimable and capacious as is that narrative.

Nor would one be hard put to encounter other recent American testimony to Melville's powers, whether in the form of a Norman Mailer war novel, a Robert Lowell poem, or a latterday essay by John Updike.[2] Further, with the issue of each volume of the definitive Northwestern-Newberry Edition (1968–)[3] and the unabating critical effort which has followed Melville's recovery, any past scantness of attention has been amply rectified, indeed excessively so for those who begin to see him as the victim of modern academic overkill. But whether well or ill served by scholarship, the reasons Melville continues to fascinate (even his failings) are not hard to discern. His work draws unmistakably upon a prodigious energy of imagination, a creativity if at times wayward always full of engagement and life. To employ one of his own favoured terms, he saw himself unremittingly the 'diver', attentive, enquiring, and never willing to settle for less than a reckoning with First Causes, the absolute condition of things. He expresses the ambition, no doubt a very American one, of wanting to confront Truth whole, Truth a term he always capitalized and which appears and reappears in his writing like a beckoning obsession. Not that so large an ambition does not come accompanied by a great fund of irony, playful, dry Yankee humour which takes its origin in his own tough mariner years and the grasp of those discrepancies which exist between man's attainments and aspirations.

Yet, in both art and life, he did indeed suffer, as Charles Olson says, 'an awful licking': among other things his failure to secure a sympathetic nineteenth-century readership; his need in 1866 to take on the post of New York Customs Inspector (fellow literary Customs men like Chaucer and Hawthorne at least did things the other way round) which he was forced to pursue for an income during nearly two decades; the deep trauma in 1832 of his father's death which he tried to understand in *Pierre* (1852) and then of having to live with the deaths of his own two sons (Malcolm in 1867 and Stanwix in 1886); and the non-publication in his own lifetime of his late masterpiece, *Billy Budd, Sailor*, written in the years 1888–91 but destined not to appear in print until 1924 and then in a faulty text. For a writer who had on his record not merely *Moby-Dick* but five earlier narratives, *Typee* (1846), *Omoo* (1847), *Mardi* (1849), *Redburn* (1849) and *White-Jacket* (1850), stories as momentous as 'Bartleby, the Scrivener' (1853), 'The Encantadas' (1854) and 'Benito Cereno' (1855), an astonishing 'masquerade' like *The Confidence-Man* (1857) and a poem the length of *Paradise Lost* in *Clarel* (1876), obloquy could hardly have been crueller than in the obituary which appeared in the *New York Daily Tribune* in September 1891:

> He won considerable fame as an author by the publication of a book in 1847 entitled 'Typee'. . . . This was his best work, although he has since written a number of other stories, which were published more for private than public circulation.[4]

But due restitution has been made. Today he cannot be thought other than a cornerstone not only of the American Renaissance—that busy, collective literary flowering of the American 1840s and 1850s and for which his encomium of

Hawthorne as fellow Truth-seeker and New England contemporary in 'Hawthorne and his Mosses' (the *Literary World*,
17 and 24 August 1850) ranks alongside Ralph Waldo
Emerson's *Nature* (1836) and 'The American Scholar' (1837)
as an essential clarion call—but of all American literature and
literary tradition far beyond. In this latter respect, too, we
have the valuable early witness of Britishers like the sea-
novelist William Clark Russell (1844–1911), who in a letter to
the now forgotten American poet Augustus Allen Hayes in
1883 called Melville 'the greatest genius your country has
produced', and like James Billson (1858–1932) who corre-
sponded directly with Melville and sent him copies of English
poetry. To these, latterly, can be added the impressive European voices of D. H. Lawrence, Cesare Pavese and Albert
Camus, to name three from among many—though not of
Joseph Conrad who thought *Moby-Dick* 'a rather strained
rhapsody with whaling for a subject and not a single sincere
line in the 3 vols of it'.[5]

The essays which appear in this collection—newly com-
missioned and from both sides of the Atlantic—reaffirm
Melville's continuing hold as a major literary force (Conrad
notwithstanding) and seek to open up a number of fresh
avenues into the overall range of his writing. So plural and
carefully self-masking a writer perhaps unsurprisingly has not
sponsored any single orthodoxy of response; indeed, so much
to the good, for he offers each subsequent reader a chance to
take aim and undergo his own 'shock of recognition', in
Melville's memorable phrase from 'Hawthorne and his
Mosses'. In no case has this been truer than *Moby-Dick*, high
adventure (as any child will testify), yet equally, and no less
than, a massive parable about Truth's languages and enigmas.

In the opening essay Herbie Butterfield re-argues the extraordinary vitality and engaging good ease of *Typee* and *Omoo*,
evidence by any standard of unlikely precocity in a Yankee
mariner newly back from the South Seas and an unsought
early manhood spent whaling and beachcombing in Polynesia.
Harold Beaver seeks to unlock some of the contrary imaginative tensions which lie behind and within *Mardi*, by general
consent Melville's least successful narrative yet one which
Hawthorne believed contained depths to 'compel a man to

10

swim for his life'.[6] In his account of *Redburn* and *White-Jacket*, James Justus examines the vexed issue of authoriality in the two narratives, both seemingly pitched in a single, encompassing voice yet both strangely incomplete and revelatory of psychological and sexual anxieties only hinted at in the adventuresome ship stories they ostensibly put on offer.

Moby-Dick, as legendary a fable now as *Don Quixote* or *Huckleberry Finn*, receives two essays, a right measure of its centrality in Melville's *oeuvre*. My own examines the text as a species of 'anatomy', a great Grammar-book of the world's codes which plays into and through the surface story of Ahab's and the *Pequod*'s pursuit of the rolling, elusive, mammalian white whale. Eric Mottram develops another perspective: he approaches *Moby-Dick* as a Lawrentian fable about the sexual and resonantly mythic origins of power, the ancestral urge to find identity (and manhood) in the subduing of Nature and its dynamic, titular expression in the form of the whale.

Pierre Richard Gray approaches as a Chinese-box narrative, a story whose 'Ambiguities', its half-title, refers in layer upon layer of equivocation to the act itself of making literary fiction, an achievement which even where it risks solipsistic awkwardness uncannily anticipates the whole current of postmodernist debate. William Wasserstrom takes a selective look at Melville's short fiction—'The Town-Ho's Story', 'Benito Cereno' and *Billy Budd* especially—analysing its designed fissures and paired likes and unlikes and linking them to the larger historical currents of nineteenth-century cultural debate. *The Confidence-Man* has always been something of the wild card in Melville's fictional pack, a Mississippi river story yet also and tauntingly 'a metaphysical masquerade', dexterous and highly devious in tone and overall direction. The analysis I offer does not lay open every aspect of its equivocation, but attempts to explore the play of its voicing, a crucial dimension I suggest of its audacity as satire.

Melville as poet has always had his proponents, notably (and honourably) Robert Penn Warren,[7] and in his essay Andrew Hook argues for yet further revaluation of the achievement, beginning from the Civil War poems *Battle-Pieces and Aspects of The War* (1866) and moving on to *Clarel* (1876) as a massive, linear meditation about nineteenth-century religious

11

doubt and search. By contrast, H. Bruce Franklin in the concluding essay and on the basis of the posthumous *Billy Budd, Sailor* proposes a 'political' Melville, whose bitterest indictment goes beyond the 'outside' narrative of a Midshipman's accusation, trial and execution aboard an eighteenth-century British man-of-war into a judgement about militarism at large and the hidden agenda of colonialism and the power play of Empire.

The magnanimity Melville once showed Hawthorne—'this Portuguese diamond in our Literature' as he calls him in 'Hawthorne and his Mosses'—has properly redounded to himself, as Crane, Olson, Metcalf and others have emphatically underlined. Hawthorne's own nineteenth-century view of him in his Journal for November 1856 as 'a very high and noble nature, and better worth immortality than most of us' also shrewdly points to the rehabilitation it has taken our own century fully to establish (and this of a Melville who at the time alleged himself ready to be 'annihilated'). Which is not to evade the fact that Melville has not always satisfied completely. Even his warmest admirers can see flaws, slips of judgement and design. To those especially given to Jamesian canons of form, he has been tasked with lacking a steadying sense of proportion, a saving disinterestedness. Whatever the merit of these charges, for others, not least the contributors to this volume, he embodies quite different qualities, broadness of scale and inquisitiveness, a willingness to take genuine imaginative risk. And as the contour of his career becomes yet clearer there can be little doubt that he had at his command an art—an artfulness—to test the ingenuity of his most up-to-date critic. In achievements of this order, if nothing else, he laid the groundwork for his own kind of immortality.

It is a great pleasure to acknowledge a number of debts which lie behind the making of this book: firstly, to the American Council of Learned Societies and its Executive Director for American Studies, Richard Downar, for the award of a Research Fellowship during 1981–82; to Eric Mottram of King's College, London University, who kindly oversaw my first interests in Melville and has been an example since; to the Department of English at Northwestern University who have welcomed me on several occasions—and most especially Harrison Hayford, doyen of Melville scholarship and to whom I owe warmest personal and academic gratitude, and to Gerald Graff, its recent Chairman; and to the Art Department at Santa Rosa Junior College, California, from whose version of the Rockwell Kent engraving the front-cover illustration for this volume has been taken, and to Jim Styles of the Photographic Unit at the University of Kent at Canterbury who made the adaptation.

NOTES

1. Charles Olson, *Archaeologist of Morning* (London: Cape Goliard Press, 1970).
2. I have in mind Norman Mailer, *The Naked and the Dead* (New York: Holt, Rinehart and Winston, 1948); Robert Lowell, 'The Quaker Graveyard in Nantucket' in *Lord Weary's Castle* (New York: Harcourt Brace, 1946); and John Updike, 'Melville's Withdrawal', *The New Yorker*, May 1982 (reprinted in *Hugging the Shore*, New York: Alfred A. Knopf, 1983).
3. *The Writings of Herman Melville*, The Northwestern-Newberry Edition (Evanston: Northwestern University Press, 1968–). Edited by Harrison Hayford, Hershel Parker and G. Thomas Tanselle.
4. Extracted and reprinted in Jay Leyda (ed.), *The Melville Log: A Documentary Life of Herman Melville, 1819–1891* (New York: Harcourt, Brace and Co., 1951), Vol. 11, p, 837.
5. See D. H. Lawrence, *Studies in Classic American Literature* (New York: T. Seltzer, 1923); Cesare Pavese: 'The Literary Whaler', *Sewanee Review*, LXVII (Summer, 1960), 407–18; Albert Camus, *Théâtre, Récits, Nouvelles et Essais* (Paris: Pléiade, 1963, 1965); and Joseph Conrad, Letter to Sir Humphrey Milford, 15 January, 1907.
6. Letter from Nathaniel Hawthorne to Evert Duyckinck, 29 August 1850.
7. Robert Penn Warren, 'Melville the Poet', *Selected Essays of Robert Penn Warren* (New York: Random House, 1958), pp. 184–97.

1

'New World All Over': Melville's *Typee* and *Omoo*

by HERBIE BUTTERFIELD

The pertinent, biographical facts are these: with behind him in 1839 a voyage to Liverpool and back as a deckhand, on 3 January 1841, at the age of 21, Herman Melville shipped out of Fairhaven, Massachusetts, on board the *Acushnet*, a whale ship that would serve him as a maritime university, 'my Yale College and my Harvard'. Eighteen months later the *Acushnet* anchored in Nukuheva Bay in the Marquesas Islands, where on 9 July 1842, in the company of Toby Greene, Melville deserted and headed inland. Having become separated from Greene, he arrived back at the coast exactly a month after-wards and on 9 August signed on as an able seaman on the trading vessel the *Lucy Ann*. This month's residence on Nukuheva was to be the stuff of *Typee*, with *Omoo* opening 'in the middle of a bright tropical afternoon', that 9 August, as he boarded his new ship. On 29 September, while the *Lucy Ann* was anchored off Tahiti, he joined ten others in refusing further duties and with them was held in custody on the island on a charge of revolt. After eluding his native warders in the middle of October and working briefly as a plantation labourer, he joined another whaler, the *Charles and Henry*, and, one day in early November, as *Omoo* concludes, 'by noon, the island had gone down in the horizon; and all before us was the wide Pacific.' Thence, by May 1843, he went to Hawaii; and thence, after a three months' stay, he was bound for home, as an ordinary seaman on the naval frigate, the *United States*. However, it was not until the autumn of the following year, 1844, that he reached Boston, to be discharged on 14 October, after five years off and on at sea, a 25-year-old graduate in all its ways.[1]

Back in the family home, Melville quickly established a local reputation as an accomplished story-teller around the fireside, and within a short time had decided also to try his hand at writing up some of his experiences. Having neither professional training nor business aptitude, no other means of income readily presented itself. Throughout the early months of 1845 he worked on *Typee*, the story of two young sailors, Tommo, the narrator, and Toby, who jump ship and, for several months in Tommo's case, 'live among the cannibals'.[2] In the summer he submitted it to a New York publisher, only to have it turned down on the grounds that 'it was impossible that it could be true and therefore was without real value.' His brother Gansevoort, a rising young diplomat (though doomed to an early death the following year), then took the manuscript with him to London, where he showed it to John Murray. Like his American counterpart, Murray too was at first interested chiefly in the matter of the book's authenticity, but after receiving further chapters he became sufficiently convinced in that regard to publish it on 27 February 1846, in his Colonial and Home Library, a series devoted to supposedly true accounts of exotic, foreign travel. Two weeks later it was published in the United States.

Encouraged by the success of its publication and wide, mainly favourable notice, Melville was soon at work on *Omoo*, which he completed later that year. Here, that same sailor, now signing himself Typee, voyages on a badly captained ship, on which he strikes up a close friendship with the ship's disaffected doctor, Long Ghost, and later takes part in a general revolt for which he is imprisoned on Tahiti. Together with Doctor Long Ghost he escapes his flimsy prison and goes to work for a couple of longer and better established deserters on a neighbouring island, before picking up another ship and sailing on. *Omoo* was published by Murray on 30 March 1847, and a month later in New York. With two books behind him, Melville's literary career was now well under way.[3]

15

It was necessary, if only to ensure publication, for Melville in correspondence and in the prefaces to the two books to insist upon their factual rather than fictional character, to proclaim his 'earnest' or his 'anxious desire to speak the unvarnished truth', and to emphasize that what might appear 'incomprehensible' was only thus because so very 'strange' to American and European eyes. With respect to this require-ment of credibility, he was indeed fortunate when shortly after the publication of *Typee*, Toby Greene reappeared, ready in the face of sceptics, 'to testify to the entire accuracy of the work, so long as I was with Melville'. 'Accurate reports', 'true accounts' the books in large part evidently are, at the same time as they are also works of narrative invention (*Typee*'s time-scale considerably extends the month spent on Nukuheva), character creation (*Omoo*'s robust comedian, Doctor Long Ghost, in particular surely owes far more to Melville's creative powers than to his original, John B. Troy), erotic and romantic imagination, and of anthropological information sometimes gleaned from other South Sea journals rather than from personal experience.

Autobiographical romance is probably the best composite term for them, works of autobiography that simply permit themselves the licence of romance in their desire to eschew the unromantic ordinary. In this context we may note that when talking of the romantic aspects of *Typee* in the preface Melville uses exactly the same word as those other slightly senior American romancers, Irving, Cooper and Hawthorne, to characterize in contrast the everyday experience of an American—that word being 'commonplace'.[4] To the American 'commonplace' present, Irving, Cooper and Hawthorne opposed the romance either of Europe or of the past, European or American, or of the receding American wilderness; and Melville, here, the romance of the South Pacific, based though it might be closely upon his own real experience.

'Mr. Melville's manner is New World all over', wrote Henry Chorley, *Typee*'s earliest reviewer.[5] And in no way was he more 'New World' than in finding in the South Seas pristine New Worlds, whose prelapsarian sweetness and light (one dark culinary custom apart) were threatened chiefly by the loom-ing, lowering encroachments of Christian civilization. At the time of writing, the time of recalling and recreating, Melville's philosophical inclinations were largely naturalist and primitivist, and in consequence effectively anti-Christian and anti-European.[6] Of the two great citizens of Geneva, it is very much Rousseau's star that at this point is in the ascendant.[7] Absent, or nowhere directly expressed, is 'that Calvinistic sense of innate Depravity and Original Sin' which he was soon to acknowledge, and 'from whose visitations' he was further to observe, 'in some shape or other, no deeply thinking mind is always and wholly free.'[8] Although there is depression in *Typee* (after Toby's departure, Tommo was alone amongst strangers), and although there is anxiety (he was alone amongst reputed cannibals, and his friend had mysteriously disappeared), what there is not is either pervasive guilt or cosmic gloom.

Before all else, before any human is encountered, the islands have the visual appearance of paradise. On Tahiti, 'such enchantment . . . breathes over the whole, that it seems a fairy world, all fresh and blooming from the hand of the Creator', a very 'Garden of Eden', as a previous much-travelled visitor, de Bougainville, had found it.[9] Likewise is Nukuheva in its 'hushed repose' an 'enchanted garden' while its 'blooming valleys, deep glens, waterfalls, and waving grass' make up 'the loveliest view I ever beheld.' In such paradises an almost ideal life is lived, has been lived for centuries, for ages outside Western time. (The adverb, 'almost', is of course crucial, and we shall return to it.) Nature and the elements accord to offer bodily sustenance and comfort for the smallest of efforts. Here, more is supplied:

> A poor European . . . is put to his wits' end to provide for his starving offspring that food which the children of a Polynesian father, without troubling their parent, pluck from the branches of every tree around them. (*Typee*, 112)

Here, less is demanded:

> In these genial regions, one's wants are naturally diminished; and those which remain are easily gratified; fuel, house-shelter, and, if you please, clothing, may be entirely dispensed with. (*Omoo*, 253)

(Note that teasing 'if you please', so quiet and inconspicuous, but nicely, naughtily calculated to affront or titillate a buttoned-up New England readership.)

17

Well fed and adequately protected from the weather, the Typees scarcely know sickness, and this general good health is one of the two bases of their characteristic way of life and mind. The other is the absence of any sexual guilt. The girls especially are 'gay', 'frolicsome', free 'from care and anxiety', in a state of 'perpetual hilarity' and possessed of an 'artless vivacity and unconcealed natural graces'. Fayaway, Tommo's 'peculiar favourite', is erotic perfection, every cultivated Christian's dream-girl, with 'hands as soft and delicate as those of any countess', yet 'a child of nature . . . nurtured by the simple fruits of the earth'. She is an idyllic fantasy, or a fantastic memory, whose evocation must have warmed the author, writing in his New York winter. In her company and amongst her scarcely less exquisite playmates, restraints of the kind usual to Tommo are few, so that what he relishes is undoubtedly an exhilarating freedom from previous bondage. Yet to be free in some respects, he learns, is not at all to be formless, for unfamiliar conventions are many, sexual rôles are strictly demarcated, and by the taboo women are forbidden various places and activities on pain of death. At the same time, nowhere are women 'better appreciated as the contributors to our highest enjoyments; and nowhere are they more sensible of their power' (*Typee*, 204), one measure of this power and of the Typee men's agreeable passivity being the polyandrous relationships which are the rule. In this and other areas of social life, mutual confidence and understanding reign, together with a 'universally diffused perception of what is *just* and *noble*' since a 'spirit of unanimity' infects a society whose members are not so much programmatically equal as incidentally not very unequal.

Thus with Nature easily taking care of the body, custom and tradition lightly secure the psyche; so that, pleasure-loving and pleasure-giving, carefree, delightful and trusting, the Typees enjoy an 'infinitely happier' existence than the Europeans, as do the inhabitants of any place so far incompletely converted or colonized, like the fortunate inland villagers of Tamai in *Omoo*. These are indeed natural paradises, the gardens of the children of Nature, the parks of Nature's noblemen[10]; the life lived here is perfectly comfortable, enjoyable, just and orderly. It is also almost entirely physical. Religion, such as it is, seems to be taken with scant seriousness or respect: neither is spiritual consolation sought, nor metaphysical speculation pursued. All is 'merry' and 'godless', happy, lively bodies with light-travelling, feather-weight souls.

Upon this Edenic, Pacific world, the Atlantic breaks with irresistible, destructive force. The effects of white incursion, whether European or American, whether naval, commercial or missionary, are portrayed as universally damaging, ubiqui-tously malificent. In this context, Melville produces in *Typee* what amounts to Nukuheva's swansong, where *Omoo* is Tahiti's epitaph. The difference lies in the fact that the world of the Typees is as yet undisturbed—albeit for precious little longer, as over the mountain which Tommo and Toby had scaled to reach the Typees' valley, in the bay beneath French warships are at anchor, from which two months previously Rear-Admiral Du Petit Thouars had claimed possession of the Marquesas Islands for France. Nevertheless, at the time of Tommo's visit, the Typees are still unfallen, intact, unenlight-ened. In *Omoo*, however, Tahiti has many years since suc-cumbed to a succession of Spanish, English and French interests, whilst in both books there is frequent reference to the awful example of the Hawaiian (here Sandwich) Islands, of late hopelessly subject to the attentions and advances of New England missionaries.

In every respect, physical and psychological, political and cultural, colonization brings disaster upon the island peoples, casually scattering communal tragedy across the Pacific. With 'self-complacent' arrogance the interlopers ignore what should be unquestioned human rights, and their 'unprovoked atrocities' inevitably provoke in retaliation further atrocities, thus in-augurating a morally chaotic reign of retributive violence. The white man 'taints' and 'contaminates' what before was naturally wholesome, his sailors and traders introducing sickness and the causes of sickness—mosquitoes, alcohol, smallpox, venereal disease, and 'other bodily afflictions . . . unknown before the discovery of the islands by the whites' (*Omoo*, 127). Upsetting the natural economic balance, he has brought to Tahiti, as a further 'distressing consequence of civilization', hunger and permanent destitution. Weakened and demoralized, the

Tahitians have soon become reliant upon unsolicited, superflu-
ous and inferior European and American goods, and have
neglected their ancient crafts, so that even the most important,
canoe-building, 'like all native accomplishments, has greatly
deteriorated' (*Omoo*, 160), while their 'original national cos-
tume . . . graceful in the extreme' is exchanged for 'ridiculous
. . . foreign habilments' (*Omoo*, 182). As for their 'many
pleasant and seemingly innocent sports and pastimes', in case
these are not quickly enough abandoned, the new authorities
and their missionary advisers soon see to it that they are
forbidden:

> Among their everyday amusements, were dancing, tossing the
> football, kite-flying, flute-playing, and singing traditional
> ballads—*now*, all punishable offences. (*Omoo*, 183)

Diseased, pauperized and deculturated, the Polynesians
are offered in return the material and spiritual benefits of
Christianity and white civilization. It is a civilization characterized here for Melville's polemical purposes by incarceration
and torture of the body, by desiccation of the spirit, or at its
mildest by lifelong sentence to the economic treadmill. In
terms soon to be taken up by Thoreau, whose two years'
sojourn by Walden Pond coincided with the writing and publication of *Typee* and *Omoo*, Melville specifies 'those thousand
sources of irritation that the ingenuity of civilized man has
created to mar his own felicity'. He points, for instance, to the
'foreclosures of mortgages . . . bills payable . . . assault and
battery attorneys . . . destitute widows with their children
starving . . . beggars . . . debtors' prisons'. These and other
essential elements and familiar details of 'civilized' American
life are absent from the Typee world because it has managed
to escape one great modern vice—'to sum up all in one
word—no Money! That "root of all evil" was not to be found
in the valley' (*Typee*, 126).

If Melville's native country is trademarked by the tyranny
of money, Europe is branded by blood-lust and authorized
sadism. The Typees may be cannibals,

> Very true; and a rather bad trait in their character it must be
> allowed. But they are such only when they seek to gratify the
> passion of revenge upon their enemies; and I ask whether the

20

mere eating of human flesh so very far exceeds in barbarity that custom which only a few years since was practised in enlightened England—a convicted traitor, perhaps a man found guilty of honesty, patriotism, and such-like heinous crimes, had his head lopped off with a huge axe, his bowels dragged out and thrown into a fire; while his body, carved into four quarters, was with his head exposed upon pikes, and permitted to rot and fester among the public haunts of men! (*Typee*, 125)

Better to die in battle and be consumed as 'long pig' than thus to be dispatched and waste as carrion.

As for that civilization's spiritual gift-bearers, the missionaries, the best that the islanders can expect from them, in the way of a particular, personal fate, is simply to survive, alive at least, though humiliated and dehumanized, 'civilized into draught horses, and evangelized into beasts of burden . . . literally broken into the traces, and . . . harnessed to the vehicles of their spiritual instructors like so many dumb brutes'. The general result of missionary intervention is that 'no sooner are the images overturned, the temples demolished, and the idolaters converted into *nominal* Christians, than disease, vice, and premature death make their appearance' (*Typee*, 195). Thus are the savages civilized, thus are the pagans converted. And thus 'is the term "savage" incorrectly applied', for 'the hospitality of the wild Arab, the courage of the North American Indian and the faithful friendship of some of the Polynesian nations, far surpass any thing of a similar kind among the polished communities of Europe' (*Typee*, 202–3), home of 'the white civilized man', who with his 'death-dealing engines . . . and the misery and desolation that follow in their train', is 'the most ferocious animal on the face of the earth' (*Typee*, 125). The judgement is sonorously definitive: outraged, prejudiced, of course, and partial; but as partial history undeniable. Melville begins his literary career in the middle 1840s, holding the various strands, age-worn or new-plaited, of the American radical heritage—the fibres of cleansing Protestant, broad-sweeping democrat, romantic primitivist, libertarian, Transcendentalist, and Utopian dreamer.

To feel the pity and the pathos in *Typee* and *Omoo*, to experience the books with a full sympathy, we must both

21

recognize the reality of the ills and insults visited upon the islanders and believe in the reality of the precolonial Polynesian world that Melville recreated for us: this is a real good over which evil is triumphing, or at least which numerous wrongs are eroding. But while the wrongs are always and wholly real—unwelcome gifts, in the first instance from those ships whose rough and often brutal reality Melville depicts, fleetingly here, elsewhere at length, with such a vivid, purposeful realism—by contrast the island paradises partake also of the quality of dreams. They are places where 'every object strikes him like something seen in a dream' (*Omoo*, 66), and where events have 'all the strangeness of a dream' (*Omoo*, 7). Thus would it seem to that other great sailor-turned-writer when he too would journey backwards in time, as it were, amongst remote peoples—to Conrad and his Marlow, 'trying to tell you a dream' in *Heart of Darkness*. That dream would end as nightmare, just as nightmare, not much differently compounded, hovers always on the edge of Tommo's Typee paradise, as a shiver in the shadows of his otherwise enchanted mind.

The nightmare is of course cannibalism, the rumour of which chills the spine of *Typee*, from the time of uncertainty early on as to whether it will be the reputedly friendly Happars or the reputedly ferocious Typees that the two adventurers first come upon, to Tommo's increasingly fearful anxiety in the later pages about Toby's disappearance and his own prospective fate, being as he is, with his wounded leg, effectively a prisoner in the valley. At the time of writing *Typee* it does not serve the Rousseauistic Melville's ideological intention to dwell too closely upon the extent to which cannibalism negates, or at least thoroughly complicates, the essential innocence of the South Seas, but it does very much serve his narrative intention to have it ever ready as an exciting threat, a source of horror and suspense. It can be treated lightly, turned as a joke against the islanders: 'I verily believe the poor creatures took us for a couple of white cannibals who were about to make a meal of them' (*Typee*, 69). It can be observed quite dispassionately as a Typee custom, 'a very bad trait in their character it must be allowed', a rather serious flaw in paradise, something of an original stain upon Eden, it might be thought, were it 'not half so horrible as it is usually described!' (*Typee*, 295). But finally it must be the ultimate terror, and a terror felt precisely at the moment when it leaps out of an anthropological world of customs amongst natives, amongst distant others, to be something heartstoppingly nearer: 'Two of the three heads were of the islanders; but the third, to my horror, was that of a white man' (*Typee*, 233).

The Typee valley that Tommo flees in desperate haste in the last chapter is of course before all else this revealed cannibal world, in which white heads are unwrapped from what have long been sinisterly mysterious packages and in which suddenly it must appear only too likely that he also is being fattened for some eagerly awaited feast. Leaving behind his perfectly devoted attendant, Kory-Kory, and the wondrous Fayaway, 'speechless with sorrow', he must escape by whatever means, ready even to kill, feeling 'horror at the act I was about to commit' (in the final tally another white atrocity, after all), yet knowing 'it was no time for pity or compunction' (*Typee*, 252).

There is another sense, though, in which it is not only from the actively dangerous world of cannibalism that he breaks free, in which it is not only from the nightmare that he bursts, but from the very paradisaic dream itself, from the whole dreamy lotus-world[11] of happy, healthy bodies in easy, incurious souls. Just as in *Heart of Darkness* Kurtz's 'horror' hints not only at cannibal nightmare but also at abandoned sexual dream, so here cannibal hell and sexual paradise merge into the composite other that must finally be rejected. As so often in his essays on American writers, D. H. Lawrence expresses it vividly and lightly to the point:

> But Paradise. He insists on it. Paradise. He could even go stark naked like before the Apple episode. And his Fayaway, a laughing little Eve, naked with him, and hankering after no apple of knowledge, so long as he would just love her when he felt like it. Plenty to eat, needing no clothes to wear, sunny, happy people, sweet water to swim in: everything a man can want. Then why wasn't he happy along with the savages? . . . .
> Because he wasn't.
> Well, it's hard to make a man happy.
> But I should not have been happy either. One's soul seems under a vacuum, in the South Seas.[12]

23

Cannibalism apart, Melville could no more have remained content as Tommo in the valley of the Typees than as Ishmael he could have stayed safe at home in the 'pitiful port' that 'is safety, comfort, hearthstone, supper, warm blankets, friends, all that's kind to our mortalities'.[13] Neither beside a Southern Sea, nor beside a Northern hearth, neither in languid glade nor cosy nook, could there be for Melville a comfortable resting-place in a happy 'vacuum'. So, leaving Typee, he reappears in *Omoo*, whose title 'is borrowed from the dialect of the Marquesas Islands, where, among other uses, the word signifies a rover, or rather, a person wandering from one island to another' (*Omoo*, xiv). In that book's closing chapters no anxieties about cannibals ruffle the pleasant ease of life on Imeeo, where Doctor Long Ghost, the narrator's previously inseparable companion, has decided to 'tarry awhile'; but the rover, the restless wanderer, heads out again into the far Pacific. However delicious was Eve, or however delightful was Paradise, there could be no happy home there, one light-hearted and light-spirited, for the strenuous, energetic, heavy-weight soul of that South Pacific waif, that ship's deserter, who would become the creator of Ahab.

Typee and *Omoo* are often taken and considered, as here, in tandem; and with good reason, since they have much in common that differentiates them from all Melville's later work, beginning with the book that was essayed while *Omoo* was still at the printer's, *Mardi*, which was to develop into an altogether more ambitious kind of book and to express an altogether more complicated view of life. The two books have, nevertheless, their distinctive and separate characters, to which it is their very titles that at first point, *Typee*'s to the name of a people and a place, to a society, *Omoo*'s to a particular kind of single person, a free individual, a rover, a wanderer, loose from society. Broadly speaking, we can say that the structural lynch-pin of each book is to be found in its title: the first, *Typee*, is primarily about a people called the Typees; the second, *Omoo*, chiefly concerns a rover's wanderings. *Typee*, therefore, contains rather more detailed and substantial anthropological information, and with its frequent, lengthy comparisons of 'savage' and 'civilized' life is the more polemical and ideological, and for this reason has tended in

this century to receive the more attention. It is also a book of
sharper contrasts, for if there is no figure in *Omoo* as bright and
joyous as Fayaway, neither is there any shade as dark as that
cast by the fear of cannibalism. The latter is a cheerful, cheeky,
roguish book, humorous, good-humoured, and, off the subject
of the despoliation of Tahiti and Hawaii, even-tempered, a
book of escapes and escapades and of the ridicule and dis-
comfiture of inept or puffed-up authorities, a book of characters, idiosyncratic and unrepresentative, such as Cockney
Shorty and Yankee Zeke; such as Doctor Long Ghost, with his
'light, unscrupulous grey eye, twinkling occasionally with the
very devil of mischief'; such as Father Murphy, rosy and
glowing, whose brandy flasks 'always contained just enough to
need emptying' and who as a consequence 'sometimes was
perceptibly eccentric in his gait'; and such as the sailor so
'excessively ugly' that he could only be nicknamed Beauty. It
is a thoroughly amiable book, with its author in jovial mood,
making altogether good, broad, entertaining company: Melville
as Falstaff or Pickwick, rather than as Faust or Raskolnikov.

Doubtless because of the exoticism of its Pacific setting and
because of the notoriety of its cannibal subject-matter, on
publication *Typee* was widely noticed in both England and the
United States; and, profiting from this celebrity that attached
itself to *Typee*, *Omoo* was yet more frequently reviewed. The
British reviewers tended to be more sceptical of *Typee*'s
authenticity than their American colleagues, some of them
finding it hard to believe that a gentleman of evident education and literary culture would readily submit himself to the
undignified life of an ordinary seaman, and an often errant or
mutinous one at that. But the most hostile responses came
from the American religious press, specifically from such
journals as the *Evangelist* and the *Christian Parlor Magazine*,
whose reviewer found 'the worst feature' of *Typee* to be 'the
undisguised attempt to decry the missionary work in every
feature'.[14] *Omoo* suffered (or perhaps benefited) from similar
treatment, Horace Greeley deeming it 'positively diseased
in moral tone'. The author might be 'a born genius, with few
superiors either as a narrator, a describer, or a humorist', but
he betrayed 'a penchant for bad liquors' and 'a hankering after
loose company not always of the masculine order'.[15] Generally,

25

however, the receptions of both books were enthusiastic and highly favourable, and Melville's 'clear', 'lively', and 'brilliant' style was commended even by those who on other grounds were disapproving; while, inspired by *Omoo* in particular, several readers launched into passionate anti-Colonialist tirades, as highly charged as Melville's own. Indeed, the angriest and the most melancholy denunciation of all appeared in *The Times*.[16]

Having established Melville's reputation, the two books kept their popularity, and, to the author's later very mixed feelings, remained throughout his lifetime the relatively light and simple works by which the public preferred to remember this extraordinarily dark and complex writer. At a time, in the early years of this century when, incredible though it may seem to us now, Melville was largely forgotten, they were nevertheless two of the first books to appear in Dent's Everyman library.[17] Only with his rise to literary-historical predominance from the 1920s onwards, as one of the greatest of all American writers, and as the author of perhaps the greatest of all American books, have *Typee* and *Omoo* receded from view.

With *Typee*'s delectable Fayaway and with *Omoo*'s venturesome mischief the two books belong to the roving, bachelor days of Melville's imagination. (Indeed, they are the only books to be written and published before his marriage on 4 August 1847, to Elizabeth, daughter of Judge Lemuel Shaw, to whom *Typee* had been dedicated.) Although he would soon become an altogether greater artist, we may cherish and return to *Typee* and *Omoo*: for their qualities of impish, rebellious vitality; for the moral sprightliness ever alert to matters of individual and communal justice; and for the spontaneous, democratic generosity that naturally aligns Melville with the powerless and the underling against the powerful and the overbearing—specifically here the ordinary seaman against the officer and the native against the invader. Out of the young romantic's vigorous indignation grew in a very few years the mature man's tragic wisdom.

NOTES

1. For the information contained in this paragraph, see Jay Leyda (ed.),
   The Melville Log: A Documentary Life of Herman Melville, 1819–1891 (New
   York, 1951), Vol. 1, pp. 86–96 and pp. 113–86. See also Leon Howard's
   historical note to *Typee*, Vol. 1 in The Northwestern-Newberry Edition
   of *The Writings of Herman Melville* (Evanston and Chicago, 1968), pp.
   277–78; and Gordon Roper's historical note to *Omoo*, Vol. 11 in the same
   edition, 1968 also, pp. 320–21.
2. 'Think of it!' wrote an exasperated Melville to Hawthorne in 1851, 'To
   go down to posterity . . . as a man who lived among cannibals.'
3. See Leyda, op. cit., pp. 196–207 and pp. 226–43; Howard, op. cit., pp.
   278–85; and Roper, op. cit., pp. 322–34.
4. See Washington Irving, 'The Author's Account of Himself' in *The
   Sketch-Book*; James Fenimore Cooper, 'Learning and Literature' in
   Notions of the Americans; and Nathaniel Hawthorne, the preface to *The
   Marble Faun*.
5. Leyda, op. cit., p. 204.
6. Lawrence Thompson, *Melville's Quarrel with God* (Princeton, New Jersey,
   1952), pp. 47–8, is of course right to stress Melville's 'deeply-ingrained
   Puritanism' but surely wrong to claim that at this time Melville's
   viewpoint was 'dominantly Christian'.
7. Rousseau is mentioned in *Typee*, Northwestern-Newberry Edition, p.
   127.
8. From Melville's essay, 'Hawthorne and his Mosses'.
9. *Omoo*, Northwestern-Newberry Edition, p. 66. Henceforth all references
   to *Typee* and *Omoo* will appear in the text, and will refer to the two
   standard editions cited in the first footnote.
10. The ubiquitous romantic-primitive figure makes his appearance in
    Typee, p. 78: 'The warrior, from the excellence of his physical proportions,
    might certainly have been regarded as one of Nature's noblemen. . . .'
11. 'Arva' rather than the Lotus tree was the source of Typee's narcotic. See
    p. 165.
12. D. H. Lawrence, *Studies in Classic American Literature*. The essay is also
    available in Richard Chase (ed.), *Melville: A Collection of Critical Essays*
    (Englewood Cliffs, New Jersey, 1962).
13. *Moby-Dick* (1851; Everyman edition, 1907), p. 95.
14. Watson G. Branch (ed.), *Melville: The Critical Heritage* (London, 1974),
    p. 88.
15. Ibid., pp. 121–22.
16. Ibid., pp. 134–38.
17. *Moby-Dick* was also an early Everyman.

2

Mardi: A Sum of Inconsistencies

by HAROLD BEAVER

J. M. Barrie, that master of dream worlds, followed Melville to the South Seas. Peter Pan flits from Kensington Gardens to that magical ocean, plagued by Captain Hook and the pursuing crocodile, which is the playground of his Lost Boys. For Melville too had been a lost boy. He had been there before him, with an imaginary historian and philosopher and poet in tow. Instead of Tinkerbell, he had been pursued by Hautia, the enchantress queen; instead of Wendy, he had pursued the fair Yillah. Such was the world of Mardi, whose very name, read backwards, seems to spell 'I dream'.

'Dreams! Dreams! golden dreams: endless, and golden, as the flowery prairies, that stretch away from the Rio Sacramento. . . .'[1] The trouble with such dreams is precisely their endless drift. Another is that one rarely wakes up laughing. (Melville, in his late twenties, aimed at outsoaring the rôle of a mere raconteur, a master of tall tales.) On and on he scribbled, piling chapter on chapter for his wife or sisters dutifully to copy and assemble. The result was a farrago, a mess. His mind was not trained enough; his style not yet sufficiently subtle or muscled; the flotsam and jetsam of his literary ocean not sufficiently dense to furnish material for 195 chapters. It is always dangerous to share one's dreams. Their langorous procrastinations, however fascinating to the dreamer, usually bore his audience. How gravely Melville must have retired

28

each morning to write of Bardianna and Babbalanja, of Ohiro-Moldona-Fivona and the groves of Pimminee! How marvellously easy it must have seemed to write with Spenser and Burton and Sir Thomas Browne jumbled in one's head! If anything, his fiction began to resemble the fantastic and anguished nonsense of his contemporary, Edward Lear. At wearisome length he presented himself, after *Typee* and *Omoo*, as a kind of American Jumbly who had been to sea in a sieve. *Mardi*, it must be said at the outset, remains largely unreadable to this day.

This is partly a matter of rhetoric. The same tropes and far-fetched comparisons are piled up as in *Moby-Dick*:

> In me, many worthies recline, and converse. I list to St. Paul who argues the doubts of Montaigne; Julian the Apostate cross-questions Augustine; and Thomas-a-Kempis unrolls his old black letters for all to decipher. Zeno murmurs maxims beneath the hoarse shout of Democritus; and though Democritus laugh loud and long, and the sneer of Pyrrho be seen; yet, divine Plato, and Proclus, and Verulam are of my counsel; and Zoroaster whispered me before I was born. (367–68)

Yet the effect is that of a catalogue, of a book-crazed youngster simultaneously displaying all his wares. Melville's spell depends on a Wagnerian control of theme balanced against theme, of phrase dissolved into phrase. When Tommo first glimpses the valley of the Typees, transfixed with surprise and delight, 'a single syllable might dissolve the spell'.[2] But *Mardi* is almost all such enchantments. The overblown rhetoric is thus peculiarly harmful. That moment of trance, to which Melvillean narratives inevitably lead, is here the very subject of pursuit; which is almost to say that the act of writing itself is the object of its own pursuit. Such self-perusals and literary mirrorings should have carried their own warnings. But for Melville, to the contrary, they carried their own Poe-like attractions. He was a best-seller. His first two narratives were being eagerly read in England and America. Not only could he afford, he felt, to indulge such infatuations; he had to, if his return from Polynesian isolation to the bustle of New York was to carry the weight of any responsible, speculative judgement.

Unlike Spenser, however, and certainly unlike Tolkien in

29

our day, he hardly had a story to tell. Melville was always reliant on the elaboration of other men's tales (be it of Amasa Delano or Mocha Dick) or those of his own adventures. But by 1848 he had almost exhausted his own adventures; and without the thrust of such narratives he was lost. Without a weather eye constantly open on real experiences—recalled however dazedly from his mast-head observations—he was doubly lost. Intoxicated by his discovery of mythopoeic form and the inventions of episodic yarn-spinning, Melville must have felt he was on to a good thing; and he was, if only in the sense that, by risking all, he had tapped the full and seemingly inexhaustible reservoirs of his literary being.

'Sailing On' (Ch. 169) expounds this mood of resolute drift:

> And, as the sun, by influence divine, wheels through the Ecliptic; threading Cancer, Leo, Pisces, and Aquarius; so, by some mystic impulse am I moved, to this fleet progress, through the groups in white-reefed Mardi's zone.
>
> Oh, reader, list! I've chartless voyaged. With compass and the lead, we had not found these Mardian Isles. Those who boldly launch, cast off all cables; and turning from the common breeze, that's fair for all, with their own breath, fill their own sails. Hug the shore, naught new is seen; and 'Land ho!' at last was sung, when a new world was sought. (566)

Every American must be his own Columbus. Like Emerson (whom he would one day lampoon in *The Confidence-Man*), Melville was not to sail by any common breeze, but with his own breath fill his own sails. There is not a hint of irony in this bombast. The writer, as transcendentalist, depends on inner resources that plunge him into a world of dream, where the spell and spelling become one. All are landlocked mariners plunging into that oceanic mind where each 'its own resemblance' finds.[3] For Melville, as for Rimbaud after him, this was an intoxicating task; and with romantic bravado he pushed off from all safe literary shores.

> That voyager steered his bark through seas, untracked before; ploughed his own path mid jeers; though with a heart that oft was heavy with the thought, that he might only be too bold, and grope where land was none.
>
> So I.

That voice was to become embodied in Bulkington, the suppressed mariner-hero of *Moby-Dick*; and 'Sailing On' is 'The Lee Shore' of *Mardi*:

> Know ye, now, Bulkington? Glimpses do ye seem to see of that mortally intolerable truth; that all deep, earnest thinking is but the intrepid effort of the soul to keep the open independence of her sea; while the wildest winds of heaven and earth conspire to cast her on the treacherous, slavish shore?
>
> But as in landlessness alone resides the highest truth, shoreless, indefinite as God—so, better is it to perish in that howling infinite, than be gloriously dashed upon the lee, even if that were safety![4]

But Bulkington is the self-imposed outcast, in perpetual flight from 'safety, comfort, hearthstone, supper, warm blankets, friends'. The narrator of *Mardi* is still intent on an ideal America, a new found land:

> But this new world here sought, is stranger far than his, who stretched his vans from Palos. It is the world of mind; wherein the wanderer may gaze round, with more of wonder than Balboa's band roving through the golden Aztec glades.

The glory was in the quest; and Melville was always at one with his questor heroes. All his novels, until he ceased to practise as a professional writer, were of physical or metaphysical quests. The conspicuous danger was 'to sink in boundless deeps'; and with youthful, suicidal abandon Melville almost welcomed 'an utter wreck, if wreck I do'.

That reckless note is central to *Mardi*. Rôles to be apportioned between Ahab and Ishmael are here given jointly to an impostor hero who claims to be Taji, the sun god. 'Call me Taji' might have been his opening challenge, but then the dialectic of his romance would have been quite different. For Taji is a pseudo-god, a pseudo-avatar. Despite his claims to have 'chartless voyaged', he may even have found his zodiacal chart (as Maxine Moore has argued) in *The American Almanac*[5]; or, as H. Bruce Franklin earlier argued, in Sir William Jones's theory of the 'Four Principal Sources of All Mythology'.[6] For the Mardian archipelago is also a constellation in the Milky Way; and *Mardi* is both a quest for an ideal religion and the questioning of that quest.

31

So, in the end, he cannot move in a circle with the zodiac; nor can he complete a circular unity. If Mardi evades him, so does a final landfall (called Serenia) where the philosopher, poet and historian, are saved by the gospel of love. Taji moves on like Ahab, pursued by the furies of sin and conscience and remorse: both glorious and damned and doomed. The Mardian quest had ended in Serenia under the rule of Alma (Christ). But Melville/Taji/Ishmael could never rest in spiritual allegiance (to Christ), nor in carnal bondage (to Hautia). Ever restless he moves on, forever pursued, 'over an endless sea'.[7]

For *Mardi* can have no resolution: this literary Columbus discovers no ultimate 'world of mind'. His only option, like Bulkington's, is for risk. His decision, melodramatically, is for instant chaos and doom. With final bravado, he cries: 'Now, I am my own soul's emperor; and my first act is abdication!' That must imply a symbolic suicide on launching into the endless sea, which is the precise point where *Moby-Dick* begins.

So suicide and dream become one. The very opening was, to say the least, odd. Why did the narrator desert his ship? From boredom, it seems; to escape stagnation; to pursue some vague transcendental kind of mast-head vision:

> I cast my eyes downward to the brown planks of the dull, plodding ship, silent from stem to stern; then abroad.
> In the distance what visions were spread! The entire western horizon high piled with gold and crimson clouds; airy arches, domes, and minarets; as if the yellow, Moorish sun were setting behind some vast Alhambra. Vistas seemed leading to worlds beyond. To and fro, and all over the towers of this Nineveh in the sky, flew troops of birds. (7–8)

Here is a pose midway between Tommo's pragmatic decision to desert and Ishmael as 'sunken-eyed young Platonist'.[8] Like Tommo, this anonymous seaman too will have to confront the horror of calms, of sharks, of isolation at sea. But, oddest of all, he has no idea where he may be going. He wants to be on the move, that is all. As long as he has a buddy (old Jarl, the heroic Skyeman) and a whaleboat to cover a thousand miles of Pacific, he is content. The opening is thus as self-destructive as the ending. It is as impetuously zany, in fact, as the opening chapter of Poe's *The Narrative of Arthur Gordon Pym*.

For all the Defoe-like details of their openings, then, both Poe and Melville are intent on other game. For all Taji's Odyssey through realms of gold—those many goodly states and kingdoms of the Mardi archipelago—he reaches no conclusion, no conceivable Penelope, no Ithaca. Omega is alpha; in the end is the beginning. The quest, as usual with Melville, is circular. What begins on the monotonous ocean ends on 'an endless sea'. Nothing has been resolved. The whole book merely reflects the pendulum stasis of 'Time's endless tunnel'. The opening lull proves everlasting. No soul is found to be 'a magnet', 'none with whom to mingle sympathies'. All is as repetitious as the overlapping fictions of Bill Marvel's stories or Ned Ballad's songs:

> Bill Marvel's stories were told over and over again, till the beginning and end dovetailed into each other, and were united for aye. Ned Ballad's songs were sung till the echoes lurked in the very tops, and nested in the bunts of the sails. (5)

Despite some apparent hue and cry, *Mardi*'s days will remain 'uneventful as cycles in space'.

This is the very pattern of dream, or rather (in this peculiar case) of the dreamer as artist, or of the artist as dreamer. The very structure of *Mardi* is that of a voyage from fact to fiction: to see (in the words of Melville's preface) whether 'the fiction might not, possibly, be received for a verity; in some degree the reverse of my previous experience'. But in thus advertising the fiction as fiction, Melville is playing the reverse of a Defoe-like trickster. No one could be taken in by *Mardi* as by *A Journal of the Plague Year*. *Mardi* is openly acknowledged to be 'a romance of Polynesian adventure'; and as romance, it is also a voyage from an outer to an inner world, 'a voyage to the very center of the writer's creative imagination'.[9]

Melville even introduces an author, Lombardo, whose *magnum opus* ('A curious work: a very curious work') is itself a paradigm of all creative labour. Lombardo is Melville's most obvious *alter ego*, just as 'his grand Koztanza' constitutes a fathomless *mise-en-abîme* within *Mardi*'s ferment. To Lombardo is assigned that archetypal romantic boast: 'I have created the creative'.

For genius, in this paradigm, moves forward gropingly like a

33

sleepwalker: 'it was a sort of sleep-walking of the mind.'
Moving with an instinctive energy that fuses past and present,
it is free from all constrictions of place and time:

> When Lombardo set about his work, he knew not what it would
> become. He did not build himself in with plans; he wrote right
> on; and so doing, got deeper and deeper into himself; and like a
> resolute traveler, plunging through baffling woods, at last was
> rewarded for his toils. 'In good time,' saith he, in his auto-
> biography, 'I came out into a serene, sunny, ravishing region;
> full of sweet scents, singing birds, wild plaints, roguish laughs,
> prophetic voices. Here we are at last, then,' he cried; 'I have
> created the creative.' And now the whole boundless landscape
> stretched away. (595)

Art, then, is reverie; it is spelled in trance. The creative act, it
follows, cannot be contained by the unities; 'they are wholly
wanting in the Koztanza', as in *Mardi*. But without unity,
coherence must be contrived by endlessly diverting digressions,
branchings, wayward gropings. As the narrator remarks in the
midst of the *Parki* story: 'But all this is an episode, made up of
digressions. Time to tack ship, and return' (92). But return
whither? By the time Melville wrote *The Confidence-Man, His
Masquerade*, no *terra firma*, no narrative core was left to which to
return. All was episode-within-episode, voices-within-voices-
within-voices. So Lombardo's *Koztanza* 'lacks cohesion; it is
wild, unconnected, all episode', as the Mardian archipelago
itself:

> —nothing but episodes; valleys and hills; rivers, digressing from
> plains; vines, roving all over; boulders and diamonds; flowers
> and thistles; forests and thickets; and, here and there, fens and
> moors. And so, the world in the Koztanza.

This mystery of universal digression implies a lack of centre.
All in *Mardi* is relative, all artificially composite. Again and
again the motion is from nothing to nothing, whose secret is
'Ineffable Silence'. 'Truth is in things', pronounces the
philosopher Babbalanja, 'and not in words: truth is voiceless'
(283). Or again:

> All Mardi's history—beginning, middle, and finis—was written
> out in capitals in the first page penned. The whole story is told
> in a title-page. An exclamation point is entire Mardi's auto-
> biography. (580–81)

Serenia's gospel of divine love, which amazingly satisfies Babbalanja and his comrades, cannot satisfy Taji. For Taji is an adept of quite another gospel, the Mardian gospel of mystic nihilism. Hivohitee, supreme pontiff of Maramma, reveals Alma's mystery as hollow. All mythical kings of Mardi are frauds, just as the demigod Taji (the runaway sailor who stepped out of a stolen rowboat) is himself a phantom who outlives his own death.

So Taji alone disclaims Alma as the Christ and Messiah of Mardi. But what is Taji but the assumed name of a sailor chasing a girl? Or, allegorically, a fake demigod chasing a phantom? The one thing that can be said with certainty of Taji is that he is a damned soul. The *Arcturion*, turning from the equator to arctic waters to hunt the cachalot, illustrated (according to the narrator) 'the Whistonian theory concerning the damned and the comets' (5). William Whiston (1667–1752) believed that the conditions on comets were such that comets must be the location of hell. But if anyone is damned, if anyone is hell-bound, if anyone represents a Whistonian comet circling the same situations, again and again jumping ship, again and again abdicating responsibility, abdicating even from Serenia and the worship of Alma, whose first and last act is 'abdication', it must be Taji. His very claim to supernatural status is a token of such abdications. 'But to split no hairs on this point,' he announces in the opening chapter, 'let me say, that were I placed in the same situation again, I would repeat the thing I did then.' Repetition, circling digression, abdication are the marks of this symbolic ritual on 'an endless sea'. Taji is bound to his past and doomed to repeat it. He both inhabits a world of romance and, as narrator, *creates* that world in circling subjection 'to the tyranny of time',[10] which can only be evaded in trance, in creative endeavour, or in dreams.

Still, a story of a kind is evoked by that playful title: *Mardi: and A Voyage Thither*. A Melvillean sailor, for a start, needs a chum: '*chummying* among sailors is like the brotherhood subsisting between a brace of collegians (chums) rooming together' (14–15). So Jarl, the Skyeman, becomes the Fidus Achates to the narrator's sun-god. They escape the *Arcturion*, as it were, in search of a quest, which develops incident by Poe-like incident.

A drifting brigantine, a hen-pecked Polynesian, the sea on fire are thresholds of mystery. With the slaughter of a high priest and the rescue of Yillah (a Disney-like creation of 'snow-white skin, blue firmament eyes, and Golconda locks') and her eventual disappearance (Ch. 64) at last a quest begins. It is a double quest; for as Taji pursues the fair Yillah, he is in turn pursued by the dark vampire Hautia, heralded by three hooded 'brunettes'. 'Yillah I sought; Hautia sought me' (643). Harry Levin was the first to remark how Taji's metaphysical quest becomes a domestic flight.[11] Goldilocks eludes him, while menacing Hautia, in her snaky bower, all but devours him.

What sort of sexual parable is this? Melville had married Elizabeth Shaw on 4 August 1847.[12] Like Lombardo, he began *Mardi*, it seems, with only the vaguest plan; but as he wrote, sleepwalking into his text, he 'got deeper and deeper into himself'. Interpret it how we will, Yillah, like *Typee*'s Fayaway, is a mirage. She may well have represented the charms of an idealized courtship, but what intervened (in Newton Arvin's phrase) were 'the fleshly realities of marriage'. *Mardi* flinches in circling flights from such realities into philosophy, satire, poetry, dream. *Mardi* celebrates male companionship (nautical chummies) at the expense of heterosexuality, now viewed with a kind of flustered hysteria. The searching sexuality of Hautia's version of a 'Bowre of Blis' was 'charged through and through for Melville with guilt and anxiety'.[13] Like Pierre, Taji yearns for a Dionysian intensity and complicity, while shying away from all closer contacts or social responsibility.[14] Hautia replaces Yillah; and it is from Hautia that Taji ultimately flees.

This splintering of consciousness is *Mardi*'s most constant mode. It is a symbolic mode; and despite many local allegories, the romance can hardly be called allegorical nor epic. Its models are Rabelaisian, Swiftian, Erasmian (on folly), and Johnsonian (on the vanity of human wishes). There are notable spoofs of war-games (the Isle of Diranda) and of fashion (Pimminee) and of organized religion (Maramma). There are political cartoons of the 1848 revolution in France (Franko) and in Europe at large (Porpheero), of the Chartists' march on Parliament (Dominora) as well as of American conventions and the California Gold Rush (Vivenza). Melville reserved his gloomiest criticism for Vivenza and its treatment of the 'tribe of Hamo'. 'These South Savannahs', he warned in 1849, 'may yet prove battlefields.' Yet nowhere on this chartless voyage is he intent on charting an ideal commonwealth or its antitype, a Utopia or an Erewhon. Despite the topical touches, Taji's travels, unlike Gulliver's, aim at some transcendental illumination.

Like Lombardo, too, Melville put his trust in instinct. He admitted as much to his English publisher, John Murray, in March 1848 when he explained that 'proceeding in my narrative of *facts* I began to feel . . . irked, cramped & fettered'; besides it was best to follow one's '*instinct*', for 'instincts are prophetic, & better than acquired wisdom—. . . .' Murray, like King Media, may well have spluttered: 'Incoherent again! I thought we were to have no more of this!' (597). But the coherence of the incoherent was Melville's whole point. Like Lombardo, he was intent on pulling down one gross world, and ransacking the etherial spheres, 'to build up something of his own—a composite'. Or as the philosopher Babbalanja put it: 'My lord Media, there are things infinite in the finite; and dualities in unities.'

Such as Samoa, the Polynesian on the drifting brigantine, the first man to be encountered on this chartless voyage:

> In his style of tattooing, for instance, which seemed rather incomplete; his marks embracing but a vertical half of his person, from crown to sole; the other side being free from the slightest stain. Thus clapped together, as it were, he looked like a union of the unmatched moieties of two distinct beings; and you fancy was lost in conjecturing, where roamed the absent ones. When he turned round upon you suddenly, you thought you saw some one else, not him whom you had been regarding before. (98–9)

This precursor and guide into the Mardian mysteries is himself a composite: a splintered duality, like Yillah and Hautia, Taji and Jarl. So on Juam, the first island encountered, an inner valley is 'cut in twain by masses of day and night', as shadows darken the west when the eastern half is lit by the afternoon sun. Its prisoner-king, Donjalolo, who may never leave his Happy Valley, rules over two villages, 'one to the west, the other to the east', between which he is carried each day. Moving from east to west, Donjalolo is another *roi soleil*, shunning the sun to live in shadow. Even his two dwellings are symbolically contrasted: his 'House of Morning' suggesting the male principle ('raised upon a natural mound'), while his 'House of the Afternoon' consists of a womb-like grotto fed by a spring.

From this emprisoned, divided and childless condition there is no hope of contact with the outside world, except by messenger. Donjalolo must travel vicariously to learn about foreign lands; he must send out 'special agents' and 'observers' to satisfy his curiosity even about his own realm. But the information that returns is either self-contradictory or else ambivalent. One man reports that the coral reef on the isle of Rafona is red (exhibiting a specimen of coral). Another reports that it is white (exhibiting a specimen of coral). In despair, Donjalolo dashes both specimens to the ground, crying: 'For me, vain all hope of ever knowing Mardi! Away! Better know nothing, than be deceived!' (250). It is left to Babbalanja to mediate, quietly observing to King Media: 'My lord, I have seen this same reef at Rafona. In various places, it is of various hues. As for Zuma and Varnopi, both are wrong, and both are right.'

It is the very nature of Mardi to be inconsistent. It is the very nature of a symbolic world, 'the world of mind' (verbalized in a fictitious language and nomenclature that Melville devised along with its Pacific geography), to be inconsistent. Donjalolo in his despair prefers ignorance to deception. For the whole world, for all its reported evidence, may well prove a hoax, a trick. 'Better know nothing', then, 'than be deceived.' For the ideal of knowledge, by this logic, is necessarily self-delusion. Donjalolo, in other words, is a self-conscious prisoner in Plato's cave. It is sceptics, like Babbalanja and Ishmael, who alone survive.

Between Babbalanja and Donjalolo there is a further need of mediation, which is King Media's rôle as he accompanies Mohi or Braidbeard, the historian, Yoomy, the poet, and Babbalanja on their travels. For this quartet strangely appropriates Taji's quest, as it moves west through the looking-glass of this ocean. Their search for a transcendent and blissful absolute (Yillah) ends with the acknowledgement of love as the supreme principle. 'This have I learned, oh! spirit!', cries Babbalanja at last: 'In things mysterious, to seek no more; but rest content, with knowing naught but Love' (633). But Taji, like Ishmael, like Melville himself, could 'neither believe, nor be comfortable in his unbelief' (as Hawthorne was to record in his English journal). Fiction for Melville was to become the very source and testing-ground of inconsistencies. Fiction was the one centre where all divergencies might converge and where all inconsistencies must necessarily consist.

That was to become Melville's task: not to resolve the dichotomies of love and hate, male and female, fact and fiction; but to calibrate their mutual tension. *The Confidence-Man* was to be his final and most complex analysis of such necessary and inevitable and composite inconsistencies. 'How many more theories have you?' King Media asks Babbalanja. 'You are inconsistent.' Babbalanja replies:

> And for that very reason, my lord, *not* inconsistent; for the sum of my inconsistencies makes up my consistency. And to be consistent to one's self, is often to be inconsistent to Mardi. Common consistency implies unchangeableness; but much of the wisdom here below lives in a state of transition. (459)

It was in *Mardi* that Melville for the first time explored the paradoxical truth of fiction: how alone in fiction we can look 'for more reality, than real life itself can show'.[15]

NOTES

1. *Mardi*, ed. Harrison Hayford, Hershel Parker and G. Thomas Tanselle, The Newberry-Northwestern Edition (Evanston and Chicago, 1970), p. 366. All subsequent page references are to this edition.
2. Melville, *Typee*, the last paragraph of Ch. 7.
3. Andrew Marvell, *The Garden*, lines 43–4.
4. Melville, *Moby-Dick*, Ch. 23, 'The Lee Shore'.
5. Maxine Moore, *That Lonely Game: Melville, 'Mardi', and the Almanac* (University of Missouri Press, 1975). Cf. also Merrell R. Davis, *Melville's 'Mardi': A Chartless Voyage* (New Haven: Yale University Press, 1952).
6. I.e. distortion of natural and human history; adoration of astronomical events; poetic invention; and metaphysical invention. H. Bruce Franklin

argues that by 'dramatizing the identity of Sir William Jones's four sources of mythology, Melville rejects the mythological basis of religion. In a world in which history, poetry, and philosophy offer mere myths, the only safe basis for religion seems to be intuitive, psychological and moral truth.' *The Wake of the Gods: Melville's Mythology* (Stanford: Stanford University Press, 1963), p. 52.

7. *Mardi*, Ch. 195, the final words.
8. *Moby-Dick*, Ch. 35, 'The Mast-Head'.
9. Edgar A. Dryden, *Melville's Thematics of Form: The Great Art of Telling the Truth* (Baltimore: The Johns Hopkins University Press, 1968), p. 47.
10. Dryden, *Melville's Thematics of Form*, p. 57.
11. Harry Levin, *The Power of Blackness: Hawthorne, Poe, Melville* (London: Faber and Faber, 1958), p. 137.
12. On 5 May 1848, Elizabeth wrote to her stepmother in Boston telling her that 'The book is done now . . . and the copy for the press is in far progress'; and on 6 June she reported that she was 'nearly through—shall finish this week' making a fair copy of the manuscript for the printer. Finally, on 27 January 1849, Melville's sister Augusta wrote Elizabeth, who was visiting the Shaws in Boston, that 'The last proof sheets are through. "Mardi's" a book!'
13. Newton Arvin, '*Mardi, Redburn, White-Jacket*', in *Melville: A Collection of Critical Essays*, edited by Richard Chase (Englewood Cliffs: Prentice-Hall, 1962).
14. Cf. Warwick Wadlington: 'This is the dark truth incorporated most significantly in the allegory of Hautia's association with and covert substitution for the quest-object, Yillah. The protagonist, as hero and as narrative presence, ultimately wants commitment without civility.' *The Confidence Game in American Literature* (Princeton: Princeton University Press, 1975), p. 69.
15. Melville, *The Confidence-Man: His Masquerade*, Ch. 33.

3

Redburn and *White-Jacket*: Society and Sexuality in the Narrators of 1849

by JAMES H. JUSTUS

1

The pairing of *Redburn* (1849) and *White-Jacket* (1850) begins with Melville himself, almost as if the prodigious energy that resulted in the composition of both books in the summer of 1849 was its own justification for their author's seeing them as an unbroken effort in the same enterprise—making money.[1] As in *Typee* (1846) and *Omoo* (1847), Melville mined his youthful sea experiences for *Redburn* and *White-Jacket*, but unlike his first two works, these of 1849 are conceptually complex. Whether he really thought *Redburn* 'beggarly' or that both works were merely hackwork that would put 'money into an empty purse', certainly he assiduously undertook them as books that might retrieve a reputation that was suffering from the unfavourable reception of *Mardi*, his third novel and the first in which he discovered his bent toward metaphysical fancy and an expressive rhetoric to articulate it.[2] Neither *Redburn* nor *White-Jacket* shows the extravagance of genius that we see in the speculations that so engaged him in *Mardi*

41

(1849), and the works of 1849 betray little of his penchant for allegory that erects yet another barrier to the accessibility of that romance. Despite their more conventional appearance, they are generically more sophisticated than *Mardi*. *Redburn*, with its unresolved *Bildungsroman* structure, and *White-Jacket*, with its unnovelistic guise as first-hand reportage, mark perhaps the furthest advance then taken by an American novelist in the manipulation of first-person narrating techniques.

Enveloping a simple structure that in each book propels the protagonist forward in a straight-line sequence of 'first-time' adventures is a retrospective narrator who systematically interrupts the chronology with reminders of present time, when he is writing his account, a perspective that also occasionally permits Melville to merge the ruminations of the narrator with his own voice. M. F. K. Fisher, a skilful memoirist as well as a celebrated gourmet, has observed that 'nobody but a child can write what has just happened to him', that it is nearly impossible 'for an older person to report such things without coloring them, twisting, invading the story, to make a more vivid or more self-flattering report'.[3] In *Redburn*, the maturing of the *naïf* is so extraordinarily rapid that on the return trip the tone of his observations often seems identical to that of the retrospective narrator—indeed, to that of the 'invading' author himself. Since the protagonist in the more complex *White-Jacket* is a more experienced mariner, the narrator and author may be closer, inviting speculation that we should see the views of the admirable White-Jacket as Melville's own.[4] It is of course more tempting to identify his creator with the stalwart democrat of the *Neversink* than with the priggish cabbagehead of the *Highlander*, but in either book the precise equation of protagonist-narrator and Melville is finally not subject to critical verification.

Certain formal links between the two books, however, are clear. In both the convenient structure of the voyage allows Melville the kind of flexibility that we see in the stuttering levels of discourse often awkwardly joined to the primary narrative: personal tribulation, meditation both genial and melancholy, scene-painting, technical information for its own sake, anecdotal digressions, characterization and caricature leisurely introduced and then forgotten. But what is most interesting formally about the works of 1849 is the extent to which we can see the conceptual continuities in the central characters, both explicit and covert, that fuel their actions and structure their observations on the meaning of those actions.

The two protagonists would appear to be strikingly different persons, as of course formally they are, and most readers have seen few links between them and the larger purposes of their separate stories: Redburn is a comic hero, a Peter Simple who on his road to maturity must experience the cold charities of the world; White-Jacket is a responsible mariner whose common sense reliably ratifies his exposé of the inequities and vices of the U.S. Navy.[5] If one is a foolish young man who brings much of his mistreatment upon himself, the other is an ordinary seaman whose unordinary intelligence penetrates the institutional usages that protect inept and tyrannical officers. If the heritage of the first prevents social assimilation with ordinary crewmen, the other is an overt defender of the rights of all. But these are finally superficial differences.

Although Redburn's social gracelessness has been expediently corrected in the older protagonist, White-Jacket still betrays an awkward, incomplete integration with his fellows, deriving in part from an ingrained snobbery that surfaces often enough to mar his ringing endorsements of equality. Both are attracted to those few who are blessed with physical beauty, social status, or personal flair; and both possess a sense of humour and a gift for wit, often whimsically self-directed, even during crises. Each protagonist establishes his identity in his opening chapter by an incongruous garment that sets him apart from his more appropriately attired mates. Though it is sometimes the source of pride as well as chagrin, its presence invites derision, alienation, even danger. The garments must be trimmed, retailored, and finally maimed in order for their wearers to survive; the steady shrinking operation on Redburn's shooting-jacket is paralleled by the ripping away and harpooning of White-Jacket's coat. Badges of difference, the garments suggest that much accommodation will be needed to transform the 'scourings of the earth' and a 'rabble rout' into fellow seamen and brothers. Both protagonists attack social wrongs while privately nourishing a sense of their superiority; even though both are provided with the perspective of experience seen from a later time, their original bias is not notably changed.

It is not necessary to assert, as has been done, that Redburn and White-Jacket are literally the same sailor separated only by time and the maturity it inevitably brings.[6] It is sufficient only to see them as linked personae, both born in that spurt of creative energy so intense that it would be surprising if they were not imaginative brothers. Conceptually, White-Jacket is Redburn projected beyond those 'far more perilous scenes than any narrated' in the story of his first voyage.[7] Wellingborough Redburn has a past that he painstakingly recreates to give us sympathetic insights into why this snobbish young man should be worth listening to; in the entire course of his narrative, the anonymous democrat who aggressively preaches the rights of 'the people' and who is known only as White-Jacket supplies himself with virtually no past—allusions to his former experiences in a merchantman and a whaler are unobtrusively dropped, mostly to contrast with his life aboard a man-of-war. Compared to Redburn's, White-Jacket's is an uninterpreted life, an omission that allows the reader to duplicate the author's compositional shorthand and apply silently to the second reminiscences the facts and resonances absorbed from the first. What importantly connects the two protagonists, however, is a pair of related traits: an instinctive self-regard that is translated socially into a bias that radiates throughout their often difficult relationships aboard ship, insuring the perpetuation in their lives of a kind of spiritual orphanhood; and their ambivalent attraction to homoerotic sexuality that they must overtly reject.

2

One of the curiosities of *Redburn* is the discrepancy between the tale it tells and its tone. It is often noted that the voyage out is tonally different from the voyage back, that the chastened Redburn after his Liverpool experiences is no longer a comic hero and that the humour built into his pretentiousness, priggishness, and naïveté, is succeeded by serious social criticism.[8] But the disparity between the comic tone and the gritty factual realism of a world far removed from the bucolic Hudson Valley of Redburn's youth exists in the first half of the novel as well as the second. The acuity of the protagonist's observation in Chapter 2—'that this indeed was the way to begin life, with a gun in your hand!'—indicates a temperament already alert to the paradoxes of life, a sensibility that is capable of wry humour at his own expense. In the same chapter the paragraph on the bitterness of one on whom the 'mildew has fallen' long before middle age, of 'pangs' and 'scars' and 'blights' that plague the young victim, is not rodomontade directed against a country boy who is both yokel and fop; if its rhetorical burden seems excessive for the young Redburn whom we follow from countryside to city to sea, its truth is verified in the subsequent behaviour of the hero and in the final implications of his story. The entire first half of the narrative is a mixture of comedy and the psychological terror embedded in the old tale of the young man making his way in the world. The process of that mythic pattern inevitably pits the hero's sense of his innate worth against the world's image of him. That dramatized clash is the source of the humour. But however funny his experiences in the pawn shops, in his preparations for going to sea, in his financial miscalculations, in the stumbling familiarity with the captain and his bumbling efforts to ingratiate himself with his fellow sailors, the retrospective narrator never quite permits himself as protagonist to be *merely* an object of fun. The blighting effects are always there, tracing the outlines of the character. Prior even to his New York adventures, the narrator sketches an episode that is prototypical of many of the more crucial episodes that follow.

Vaguely conscious on the steamboat of his difference from other passengers ('I sat apart, though among them'), Redburn responds to their cold glances first by trying to hide his patched trousers; then, imaginatively anticipating his rebuff from one convivial group, he aggressively thrusts his patched legs into full view while fingering his gun. When his inability to pay his full fare predictably produces a scene, leaving 'every eye fastened' on him, he directs his gun at the hostile faces, clicking the trigger lock. Although in retrospect he is unable to account for his 'demoniac feelings', this astonishing episode, with its superbly rendered responses veering back and forth from defence to offence, is psychologically credible. It is also a self-actuating melodrama that establishes a pattern for Redburn's future difficulties in adjusting an extravagant belief

45

in his worth to the external image that belies it. The segment concludes with a ludicrously inadequate one-sentence paragraph: 'Such is boyhood.' That the retrospective narrator can find it adequate says something about the open-ended nature of this *Bildungsroman*, the tale of a young gump whose halting growth is not capped by the earned insights of the mature but the ongoing, incompleted pains of the maturing. The scars on the acting Redburn are still visible on the narrating Redburn.

Although the narrator gets much comic mileage out of his youthful self's struggle to adjust to Captain Riga's world, he is also shrewdly effective in suggesting the psychological pains of the misfit who is simultaneously complacent about his superiority to that world. As 'a sort of Ishmael in the ship', Redburn is a scorned alien, the experience of which hardens his heart. If he begins ignorantly enough, pleased to think of himself as 'naturally of an easy and forebearing disposition', he soon discovers depths in himself previously unknown. His compassion for his fellow sailors is childish and pretentious—he advises them to go to church and to read good books—and his moral smugness arouses their ire. Their goadings finally anger him, and his anger is their opportunity for further abuse. What begins as the class-conscious pity of a pretentious *naïf* ends with the frustration of an adolescent do-gooder spiritually stripped of all comforting supports: 'I loathed, detested, and hated them. . . .' Such self-revealing words structurally prepare for the introduction of Jackson, the epitome of one who is consumed with hatred, 'as if all the world was one person, and had done him some dreadful harm'. This man's magnetic malevolence jolts Redburn into a prayer that his own hatred 'might not master [his] heart completely, and so make a fiend' of him.

Despite occasional expressions of adolescent delight in exploring the world away from his village, what dominates in Redburn's account is what the later Ishmael will describe as a 'wolfish world'. Both at sea and ashore Redburn discovers a world of rapaciousness, uncertainty, suspicion, and unaccountable evil that overshadow the kinds of ordinary vice that his Sunday school training has armed him against. The impact of these experiences aboard the *Highlander*, including a suicide, the combustion of a corpse, and the death of Jackson, and of squalid scenes around the Liverpool docks, is never tonally counteracted by the few pleasant experiences, such as the social pleasures of going to church in England and having tea with a rural English family. Redburn's first sight of Britain, what he wryly calls 'a beautiful introduction to the eastern hemisphere', is that of a thieving Irish fisherman who makes off with fifteen fathoms of toeline that the mate miscalculatingly extends to him; his last sight of Liverpool is that of 'a police-man collaring a boy, and walking him off to the guard-house'. Between this Hibernian trickster and the casual tyrannizing of British officialdom comes a staggering array of rubbish-pickers, beggars, con men, starvelings, hardened widows, calloused policemen, crabby gentlemen, dissolute gamblers, mantrap-ping farmers, crimps, and—extending to the return voyage—improvident and dying emigrants, snobbish cabin passengers, and cheating captains.

Throughout his first voyage Redburn sees few examples of a generative brotherhood. Our indelible image of him is that of the lonely but resilient explorer of his world, a wanderer, the same young man who months earlier among the passengers on the Hudson boat said 'I sat apart, though among them.' He is quick to be insulted by uncivil behaviour of the mates and crude language of the crew, but even after he has more com-fortably mastered his job and expediently relaxed his moral strictures, he finds little camaraderie among the sailors. Though he is quick to locate what he guesses are the excep-tional sailors in order to make friends, they all turn out to be disappointing. So alien does he remain that, repudiating their idealization by romance writers, he agrees with the popular image of sailors as 'the refuse and offscourings of the earth'; simply being sailors points to 'a certain recklessness and sensualism of character, ignorance, and depravity', and the fact that they are necessarily separated from a 'respectable and improving society' and 'shunned by the better classes of people' is enough for Redburn to conclude that their case is 'not a very promising one'. Observing the custom-house officer who stays aboard the docked *Highlander* to prevent smuggling, he constructs an imaginary character for him, one that is emotionally consonant with his own case: 'he seemed to be a man of fine feelings, altogether above his situation. . . .'

47

His purely self-pitying observations of how his 'warm soul' has been 'flogged out by adversity' in a 'hard-hearted world', in which Redburn manifests a romantic melancholy worthy of Tom Sawyer, occur in the early portions of his narrative. After his immersion in the unprotected life at sea and the Darwinian world of the docks, the responses cease to be merely juvenile and assume the moods and manners that actual experience necessarily provides. Redburn's shock in Launcelott's-Hey stands as a watershed in his development. By the time the narrator relates the accruing deaths from plague among the emigrants, the story is only minimally dramatic and tonally matter-of-fact—the fitting psychological stance of an adolescent who has already travelled light years from the cheerful moralism of the Juvenile Total Abstinence Association.

What Melville does finally with his youthful hero is to cast him in the existential configurations of orphan. It is not surprising that, after about four weeks in England, Redburn should quickly spot Harry Bolton as a spiritual brother, equally alone, equally incongruous in the boarding-house street at the docks. His very appearance makes him, in Redburn's eager judgement, the 'incontrovertible son of a gentleman' in whose society he could have the 'kind of pleasure so long debarred' him. Though in time his vague and mysterious connections with English high life breeds a nagging distrust in the protagonist, there is never any question that Redburn considers him his only fit companion during his voyage. Unlike Bolton, Redburn is only a spiritual orphan, but his emotional deprivations aboard the *Highlander* and in Liverpool are clearly the natural extension of his paternal dispossession. His entanglements with Harry Bolton, which he resolves much less successfully than those involving his apprenticeship in the merchantman, provide him with his only sustaining, if ambiguous, relationship once he leaves home— and that ends with their farewells in New York.

Considering the lengthy personal background the narrator provides in his beginning chapters, it seems surprising that Redburn's return to his family is so anticlimactic. A mother, a brother, three sisters, and an unspecified number of 'kind uncles and aunts' remain to greet him, but his homecoming is passed over, tucked into a single perfunctory paragraph. Its casualness suggests that the maturing youth, now supposedly at home in the world, no longer needs that familial nourishment he required as a child; but, as in much of Melville, the sense of loss is more profoundly felt than any sense of alternative gains. The perfunctory homecoming also says that for the dispossessed, once expelled from the family hearth, no real return is emotionally possible. In its place is Redburn's account of his separation from and subsequent loss of Harry Bolton, as if that loss is now the crucial one for his future passage in the world. If the spiritual underlining of the relationship between Redburn and Bolton has been *we orphans must stick together*, the loss now of a brother orphan is considerably more serious, more potentially maiming, than the initial separation from the family, which the retrospective narrator treats as a painful but necessary educative stage.

As conventional moralist Redburn censures swearing, drinking, smoking, and the general abuse he calls 'dissipation'. But the fate of Jackson, in the latter stages of a wasting disease, comes to represent the course of human depravity, a fate linked with fornication; and because of his fearful fascination with Jackson, Redburn enters a more shadowy psychological region that the conventional moralist must shun. In Liverpool, where a relaxed shipboard discipline permits more freedom of movement, he observes what glories he can find, but he returns again and again to the spectacle of the vice-ridden dock area. He is especially harsh on landlords, barkeepers, and 'boarding-house loungers', all of whom are depicted as 'land-sharks' devouring helpless mariners; but for the rôle of prostitutes in this devouring he resorts to allusion ('denizens of notorious Corinthian huants') and heightened Sunday school rhetoric ('depravity . . . not to be matched by any thing this side of the pit that is bottomless'). In concluding his chapter on the Booble-Alleys, the lowest haunts of sailors, Redburn becomes as explicit as he ever does in citing the prevalence of sexuality in its manifold variousness. In these dens, whose very walls are 'begrimed', 'sooty', 'reeking', 'Sodom-like', and 'murderous', such vices as gambling and cursing seem only 'common iniquities'. Though generalized, it would be inaccurate to call the narrator's confrontation with sexual vice delicate in its indirection, since the passage fairly throbs with rhetorically inflamed language. 'Propriety forbids that I should enter into details', he says, but he hardly needs to. In this area 'putrid with vice and crime' the 'infected gorgons and hydras' comprise

> a company of miscreant misanthropes, bent upon doing all the malice to mankind in their power. With sulphur and brimstone they ought to be burned out of their arches like vermin. (191)

On the other hand, the narrator allows young Redburn's attraction to Harry Bolton (and both young men's fascination with the chestnut-haired, rich-cheeked Carlo and his marvellous organ) to be strongly and frankly homoerotic. Melville's invention of Bolton for presumably structural reasons—to replace Redburn's social difficulties on the voyage out with a parallel figure on the return—is also a brilliant device for coalescing the protagonist's character. The tattered rural dandy who begins his voyage with more social presumption than common sense ends it as an experienced sailor, proud of his skills learned in the tough testing grounds of the *Highlander*. But his own effeminacy has not been totally exorcized. Drawn to Bolton at first glance, captivated by his 'imperial reminiscences of high life', Redburn forges a friendship with Bolton that draws attention to his likenesses to the Englishman. That Bolton is an 'unseamanlike person' who performs in 'a gentlemanly and amateur way' is for Redburn a mark in his favour. When it turns out, however, that he is incapable of scampering about in the rigging as his duties require, the tone emphasizes the 'Bury blade' as androgynous dandy, a 'girlish youth' who, preparing to stand his morning watch, chooses from among his collection of silks, velvets, broadcloths, and satins 'a brocaded dressing-gown, embroidered slippers, and tasseled smoking-cap'. Bolton's conscious outrageousness becomes the fulfilment of the earlier unconscious dandyism of Redburn as he dressed for his projected call on the captain. When the narrator speculates on Bolton's passive 'reception of contumely and contempt' from the crew, he professes his inability to explain how his friend becomes 'an altered person'—an evasive disingenuousness, since Redburn seems to have forgotten their shared experiences in London.

The chapter on the couple's evening in the Palace of

Aladdin is the most sexually suggestive of all episodes. Nominally a gentleman's gambling club, the quarters are described in terms that make gambling one of the lesser iniquities. The club's exteriors glow with a purple light, and its interiors, a triumph of stylistic indirection, suggest that 'No. 40' is a male bordello as well as a gambling den.[9] Despite the lush extravagance of marble columns, frescoed ceilings, and Persian carpets, the narrator senses a hollowness about and below him, a 'magnificent spectacle' that is self-mocking in its 'subterraneous despair'. While Bolton attends to his pleasures, a *trompe d'oeil* reinforces Redburn's 'dismal forebodings' in a room that is metaphorically *twisted*: the damask of the lounges is 'interwoven' with tournament scenes; the warp and woof of ottomans are wrought into 'plaited serpents, undulating beneath beds of leaves'; 'Laocoon-like chairs' are draped in 'fringes of bullion and silk'; paintings of mythological erotica are suspended by 'tasseled cords of twisted silver and blue'. The setting, in short, invokes less the literature about private clubs than it does nineteenth-century pornography.

The narrator disallows his younger self any real initiation into such a world, first by making Bolton, his negative double, the active agent in the drama of the ongoing corruption of an already initiated young wastrel, and second, by making young Redburn's sensibility a recorder of ambivalent concern: he becomes 'mysteriously alive to a dreadful feeling' that he has experienced before only when 'penetrating . . . the lowest and most squalid haunts of sailor iniquity in Liverpool'. If in the Palace of Aladdin he feels like 'somebody else', so does Bolton seem 'almost another person', presumably because the 'whole place seem[s] infected', as if its 'foundations take hold on the pit'. On the most innocent level—Redburn's—it is a place to observe and, ambivalently, to judge, drinking glasses of 'pale yellow wine', assuming the careless posture of a young Prince Esterhazy, and noting an ever-shifting scene presided over by 'the Duke', a bald-headed, marble-mouthed old man with a 'mysteriously-wicked expression'. On the least innocent level— Bolton's—it is a place of desperate, obsessive pleasures which, because they occur behind doors closed to Redburn, must remain tantalizingly sinister.

His rural piety makes him uncomfortable with the trappings

of sin during his momentous thirty-six hours in London, but being superintended by the exotic Bury blade, who both is and is not like him, allows Redburn to have it both ways. To assert, as Redburn does, that Bolton was 'a very equivocal character' means more than that he is 'light-fingered gentry' (which the crew suspects) or a liar (which Redburn himself suggests). A calculated reticence accompanies the history of Bolton, but even before he relates how his friend 'got along as a sailor', Redburn telegraphs the unhappy death of 'Poor Harry!' in a lugubrious paean to his departed spirit in language that summons up classical rather than Christian antecedents ('strange forms', 'centaurs of fancy', 'half real and human, half wild and grotesque', 'wild', 'dryad'). And although the ornate diction conceals more than it reveals when the narrator describes how the usually buoyant Bolton ('my zebra!') is brought low by 'those ocean barbarians', pursuing him out of every retreat, Bolton in fact survives his persecution and probable assaults. His is to be a dramatic but relatively masculine death on another voyage—aboard a whaler.

The function of Bolton as a doubling figure, the objectification of unresolved sexuality that we see in the protagonist,[10] accounts for the rather truncated tale of Bolton's last days, an odd coda that veers awkwardly between intense concern and casual, almost playful, report. The narrative closure and emotional resolution of the last chapter are not harmonized—perhaps because they could not be without the addition of more revelatory information than either narrator or author was willing to divulge. Although we can normally detect the difference between Redburn the pious protagonist and the older Redburn who remembers and records, it is well nigh impossible, I think, to distinguish formally between some segments presided over by the retrospective narrator and Melville the maker of both personae. One suspects, however, that the sly gusto in the implanted sexual jokes comes from the same source that would in another two years take the opportunity to make sexual puns and double entendres a substantive and rhetorical part of the unity of his greatest work. Those in *Redburn* have none of the ebullience of those in *Moby-Dick* (1851), and they stand out a little awkwardly, as if neither the cabbagehead of a protagonist nor his maturer self has any clear notion of what he is saying. In one instance, when the appreciative and determined young Redburn has tea and muffins with 'three admirable charmers' in the country, he says, 'And there they sat—the charmers, I mean—eating those buttered muffins in plain sight. I wished I was a buttered muffin myself.' Though the episode of the nautical mooning, in which the crewmen display their backsides as a final contemptuous salute to Captain Riga, is in pace and syntax fully consistent with the style of the retrospective narrator, the final touch comes surely from Melville, who permits the sailors to retire for a final round of drinks at a bar called 'The Flashes'. And the rhetorical extravagance of Chapter 49 ('Carlo'), so conspicuously different from any other chapter, is so dithyrambic that it calls attention to itself as a set piece. Though often taken as a tonal mistake of Melville's, it is overtly mock-romantic and covertly sexual—a phallic tour-de-force in which the programmatic description of Carlo's playing his hand-organ becomes a stylistic exercise in describing masturbation.

Both the extended 'Carlo' and the scattered sexual jokes are not so much necessary aspects of characterization itself as tonal accretions to character, an indulgent, supplementary context that provides a subversive adult rating to a story its author referred to as a 'nursery tale'.[11] But the manipulation of sexual puns is tonally different from the fascinated but finical voice we hear in the passages dealing with the sheer social fact of homosexuality. The kind of charged atmosphere in which the subject generates the frisson may—or may not be—the expression of authorial anxiety; certainly it becomes an aspect of characterization, as Redburn emerges from his first experience in the world with disturbing implications for his psychological maturity.

During the final leavetakings in New York, Redburn and Harry follow the crew to a bar, but significantly do not participate in their mutual toasts. Redburn, who in Liverpool with his father's useless guidebook had discovered that the world 'is a moving world . . . and its sands are forever shifting', now comes close to voicing his belief in the brotherhood of the sea:

> If to every one, life be made up of farewells and greetings . . .
> then, of all men, sailors shake the most hands, and wave the most

hats. They are here and then they are there; ever shifting themselves, they shift among the shifting: and like rootless sea-weed, are tossed to and fro. (309)

But despite his actual experiences with these sailors, they remain 'they'; the rhetoric here is that of the Irvingesque observer, not a participant, and reinforces the fact of social alienation that Redburn experiences throughout his voyage. If participation in camaraderie is not emotionally possible, the convivial leavetaking touches a sentimental chord: 'It was a touching scene.' This response from the same young man who once suffered the derision of the old tars contrasts sharply with that of Harry Bolton, whose miserable life on the return voyage has been reckoned 'fair play for their worst jibes and jeers'. The two young men watch the crew stagger happily on their way:

> 'They are gone', said I.
> 'Thank heaven!' said Harry. (309)

The difference in this response not only points to Redburn's failure to find a satisfactory community among the men of the sea; it also suggests an emotional failure in maintaining an emotional relationship with one young man who is a landsman most like himself.[12] In his resolution of the Bolton connection, sketchily condensed out of the narrative future, the narrator is notably free of any but the most perfunctory expressions of regret. The stranger's question, 'Harry Bolton was not your brother?' is allowed to go unanswered.

3

Like *Redburn*, *White-Jacket* uses both protagonist and retrospective narrator, but unlike the previous work, it suffers from none of the tonal discrepancies necessary to distinguish actor from memoirist. The individual who boards the *Neversink* in Callao is not a *naïf* but already a mature man with sea experience—in both a merchantman and a whaler—behind him, and though the chronological gap between White-Jacket the protagonist and White-Jacket the narrator is vague, the emotional gap is clearly narrow. The voice we hear has none of the ponderous gravity of the early Redburn; the tones range from the skylarking vivacity of one who is comfortable with wit and paradox to sharp-eyed intensity of one with a gift for logic and common sense when faced with mean actions and meaningless traditions.

As readers sometime note, *White-Jacket* is perhaps the least novelistic of Melville's larger works because its substance is a mélange of factual reports, propaganda, philosophical meditations, scenic descriptions, melodrama, and set pieces reminiscent of the old seventeenth-century form known as the 'Character'.[13] Its integral unity depends upon the loose chronology of a voyage as it is paced by the narrator, who is given the intellectual, emotional, and forensic talents to construct and direct his account with full consciousness that those diverse segments must be joined to and balanced against the straight-line chronology. Whereas the matter of *White-Jacket* is thus marked by casual pace, variety, and flexibility, the narrator's choice of perspective—by restricting his account to a description and analysis of life aboard a man-of-war—lends it rigour and coherence. We are given no shore scenes. White-Jacket makes nothing of Callao, and he ends his account before arriving in Norfolk, indeed before sighting land. Despite twenty-six chapters devoted to ship life while the *Neversink* is anchored in Rio, the narrator depicts officers' ceremonial pleasures, the sailors' anticipation of shore leave and their sorry state when they return from it, and an impressive word-painting of the Bay of all Beauties as it appears to one on deck. The flavour of the place, rigidly spectatorial, is fully in keeping with the narrator's balance and self-control. The narrator is simultaneously character and consciousness, and though his voice is appropriately modulated to accord with the subjects that he sequentially introduces, it is an unwavering source of consistency.

The analytical White-Jacket we see as well as hear. One of the traits by which he most commonly characterizes himself is his penchant for emphasizing gradations of men; his account is structured by exercises in separating, classifying, dividing, enumerating, and placing men in juxtaposed relationships. This logical, systematizing White-Jacket is formally appropriate to the controlled manipulation necessary for the teller to fuse the varied segments, those different moods, topics, and genres that comprise his account. His systematizing—a

55

creative extension of Redburn's habit of categorizing people and then judging the categories they occupy—is also a trait of temperament through which we gain insight into a White-Jacket who is not merely a technical proxy for Melville, but a fully created character separate from the 'I' of the prefatory Note, who casually says that his experiences are 'incorporated' in the book.[14]

What unifies the character of the narrator and establishes the consistency of a voice despite its articulation in several registers is an ambiguity toward that sense of brotherhood found in ships. The attitudinizing dandy of the *Highlander* has been expelled from the deck of the *Neversink*, but his patrician bias remains. The dread of ostracism that dogs every crewman of the microcosmic world affects White-Jacket as well, but his fear of exclusion from the group—a select group—is balanced by an exclusivity that is almost obsessive. His sense of his proper place among other men and his sensitized feelings for classes of men are transformed into a hard-edged discrimination of innate values and human and social worth beyond the maritime functions for which classes on a frigate necessarily exist.

While White-Jacket can be both trenchant in his outrage at naval inequities and irrelevancies and wittily mock-heroic in his suffering, some of his pain, like Redburn's, comes from enforced socializing among those he instinctively finds inferior. He is blunt in his scorn for the waisters—those 'sorry chaps . . . with the hayseed yet in their hair' who tend the chicken-coops and pig-pens. But if he can dismiss these as the 'tag-rag and bob-tail of the crew', he can also be patronizing to those 'sea-dandies' or 'silk-sock-gentry' who serve as after-guardsmen, young gentlemen driven by circumstance into the 'hard-hearted Navy'. Though these refugees from respectable society are presumably the narrator's social equals as landsmen, he can be condescending because they spiritually remain landsmen, unchanged by their sea experiences (except for a broader range of love affairs in foreign ports), who read novels and romances and compare notes among themselves about the 'melancholy and sentimental' careers that none of them has chosen.

Rhetorically as well as functionally, White-Jacket, a 'looser of the main-royal' and one of the main-topmen, separates himself from the rest of the crew: the 'cross and quarrelsome' gunner's gang; the 'troglodytes' below the berth-deck; the cooks, steady-sweepers, and musterers throughout the frigate— a 'narrow-minded set . . . with contracted souls'. Even those sailors he admires for their 'mirthfulness' are admirable primarily because they are seen at a distance, usually from the perspective of 'the loftiest yard of the frigate'. The top-men, his select class, are such capital fellows because, according to White-Jacket's only half-whimsical theory, they always look out 'upon the blue, boundless, dimpled, laughing, sunny sea' and down upon 'the petty tumults, carping cares, and paltrinesses of the decks below'. The narrator draws his reportorial authority from this perspective, an enabling angle that metaphorically assures a

> free, broad, off-hand, bird's-eye, and, more than all, impartial account of our man-of-war world; withholding nothing; inventing nothing; nor flattering, nor scandalizing any; but meting out to all—commodore and messenger-boy alike—their precise descriptions and deserts. (47)

White-Jacket's excessive claims to objectivity may or may not be advanced with tongue-in-cheek; but his aloofness, what he himself calls his 'fastidiousness', can scarcely contribute to the unbiased picture he professes to be painting. He shuns 'indiscriminate intimacy', confesses that 'scores of men' remained strangers to him, and literally numbers those crewmen with whom he 'unreservedly consorted': the poet Lemsford, Nord, Williams, Jack Chase, and 'my comrades of the main-top'. If Redburn finally sees sailors as a shabby lot, White-Jacket is even harsher toward the 'mob' and 'rabble rout' of the Navy, which he in a burst of poetic condescension describes as 'the asylum for the perverse, the home of the unfortunate', which he then elaborates: 'Here the sons of adversity meet the children of calamity, and here the children of calamity meet the offspring of sin.'

Larry J. Reynolds argues persuasively that White-Jacket's 'undemocratic' bias compromises considerably his rhetorical affirmations of brotherhood and equality; his expressed sentiments blur his image as 'unconditioned democrat' forever championing 'the people', the common seamen who are paradoxically held in tyranny by an arm of republican America.[15] The narrator's democratic sentiments are clearly theoretical: giving voice to an idealism that in ethical and political terms can hardly be questioned. His undemocratic sentiments are just as clearly practical, social, and human— the kind of contradictory impulses that make him more, not less, credible as a character because they are born of human complexity rather than ideological necessity. The conflicts, contradictions, and unresolved urgencies of identity in White-Jacket affirm a state of actuality, not some ideal state of psychic health.

Like his idol Jack Chase, White-Jacket may be an admirable fellow, and it is obvious that he is humane, civilized, conscientious, and moral. But he is not particularly generous, and his critical eye surveys not merely the institutional abuses of the Navy and the Articles of War but his officers and fellow sailors who are locked into the system. For most of his narrative White-Jacket asserts his opinions with the kind of authority that comes from the happy knowledge that he is not alone, that he belongs to a like-thinking group of men assured of their superiority to the rest of the crew and most of the officers, those individuals whose only superiority derives from ranks arbitrarily attached to them. His snug place among the princes of the crew permits White-Jacket the luxuries of evaluation, judgement, bemused toleration, and condescension; it allows him to indulge in rhetorical flights, caricature, and his always ready wit; and it encourages the outright condemnation of institutional evils: the surgeon who kills rather than saves, the chaplain who represents peace aboard a vessel designed for war, the rigid hierarchy sanctioned by a government dedicated to the fluid mobility of classes of men.

White-Jacket is neither yokel nor fop, but some continuities from Redburn's kind of fastidiousness persist. Redburn's itch to become an instant interior decorator, to show how 'the dainty hand of taste' can spruce up the drab deck of the *Highlander*, is transformed by White-Jacket into a vocational theory on the necessity of surrounding oneself with pleasant objects and temper-soothing sounds (an Aeolian harp, a conch shell, a punch-bowl, a Dutch tankard, or a shelf of 'merrily-bound books'). Like Redburn, who has difficulty in finding examples of it, White-Jacket appreciates mannerly behaviour even aboardship. One of the functions of genial Jack Chase, as a kind of model elder brother, is in 'mending our manners and improving our taste'. The narrator's response to his messmates' hostility—which occurs when White-Jacket proves to be a maker of inedible 'duff'—is a tonal throwback to the naïve Redburn: 'I was shocked. Such a want of tact and delicacy!' He is offended at the sight of Shanks, who in warm weather fans himself with the front flap of his shirt, 'which he inelegantly wore over his trowsers'—a sartorially critical judgement that is echoed much later when he observes that the midshipmen's Professor wears 'uncommonly scanty pantaloons, exhibiting an undue proportion of his boots'.

A resolute sense of his own worth compels Redburn to dress and make a formal call on the captain; White-Jacket's sense of his own worth is no less, but his greater maturity has taught him the realistic expediency of keeping his place, however arbitrary that may be and however galling it is for him to see his inferiors in elevated positions. 'I can not say a great deal, personally, of the Commodore', he wryly observes; 'he never sought my company at all; never extended any gentlemanly courtesies.' Some of Redburn's effeminacy is distributed in *White-Jacket* to Selvagee, the 'genteel, limber, spiralizing exquisite' who looks at passing sights with opera-glasses and who proposes to the captain that a 'few drops of lavender' might help the offending mustiness of the furled sails. White-Jacket can be ruthless in his mockery of Selvagee and the displaced sea dandies of the after-guard, but he never perceives the possibility that his own attraction to and relationship with the manly Jack Chase might suggest some empathetic links with those figures of fun. What blocks that possible insight in White-Jacket is the psychological and political security of his place. The brotherhood that so eludes Redburn is for White-Jacket a potent palliative against the general abuses that all must endure. 'We main-top men' comes comfortably from his lips, and the liberal, easy references to 'esprit de corps', 'fraternity', and 'brothers' suggest the extent to which the security of place masks even to himself the homoerotic bonding it implies.

He is not blind to his social complacency, but insight comes selectively. As a self-congratulatory humanist, White-Jacket declares that the reimposition of discipline, once it is relaxed (as in the May Day festivities), is a cruel reminder of the power of a master over a slave: 'Methinks, if but once I smiled upon a man—never mind how much beneath me—I could not bring myself to condemn him to the shocking misery of the lash.' His difficulty in getting more 'swing' to his hammock becomes a little parable reminding him of the folly of 'striving to get either *below* or *above* those whom legislation has placed upon an equality with yourself'. The recurring spatial language—*above, below, beneath, on top*—to signify White-Jacket's pride in his professional place on the maintop serves also of course to signify his pride in what he fancies as his superior social rank. His occasional frankness about his assuming airs that set him apart from others allows him in his more meditative phases to mock his own pretentiousness. He perceives his complacency in pitying Rose-Water when the mulatto is scourged: 'Thank God! I am a white.' Even though all men, of whatever colour, are liable to the lash,

> there is something in us, somehow, that, in the most degraded condition, we snatch at a chance to deceive ourselves into a fancied superiority to others, whom we suppose lower in the scale than ourselves.

This latter moment of insight, however, calculatedly precedes White-Jacket's own arraignment at the mast, a scene dramatizing the ironies of condescension. What prevents the scene from becoming an exemplum on the *penalties* of condescension is the ineptness of the officers (who neglected to tell White-Jacket of his assigned station) and the intervention of Colbrook, the 'remarkably handsome and gentlemanly corporal of marines', and the always 'manly' Jack Chase (whose rare action serves to ratify the protagonist's real nature and thus to perpetuate his notion of himself as superior). As a summary scene of the internal dimensions of the narrative, it subverts the fleeting guilt for undemocratic impulses, rendering harmless an insight that momentarily linked Rose-Water and

White-Jacket; it reminds the reader once again that naval officers are arbitrary, tyrannical, and inept, while 'the people' are their victims; it establishes the protagonist's confirmed admiration for the most beautiful of 'the people', who in demonstrating their fairness and courage also reflect back onto White-Jacket his real worth—that is, his true links are with Colbrook and Chase, not Rose-Water. Shipboard scourging, symbolic rape, is both social and sexual; its purpose is the assertion of power and the preservation of the hierarchy of dominance. The terms the narrator most often associates with flogging are *humiliate, degrade, unman, insult* and their variants. If White-Jacket can say that he 'almost burst into tears of thanksgiving' when the captain accepts the intervention of Colbrook and Chase, we must suspect that it is not so much because of his explicit interpretation—that he has 'just escaped being a murderer and a suicide'—but because he sees that desperation to preserve 'my man's manhood so bottomless within me' mystically acknowledged by both 'the foremost man among the seamen' and 'the foremost man among the soldiers' whose intercession confirms his place in the select band.

Unlike flogging, the narrator perceives the threat in that other symbolic rape, 'The Great Massacre of the Beards', as *merely* symbolic, and his mock-heroic account can even include praise for Captain Claret whose order should have 'come near breeding a mutiny'. In a style elevated and hortatory this Irvingesque episode bristles with scriptural injunctions against the marring of beards, historical precedents for bearded warriors, parallels from natural history, mock liturgical absolution of the barbers, classical apostrophes to the holdouts, and rhetorical declarations of independent manhood. Ironically, all the upright exemplars of manhood who have previously been singled out succumb in the end to the instruments of 'the ruthless barbers'. Only old Ushant, the venerable Nestor of the *Neversink*, stands with his manhood firmly intact, even after his flogging and incarceration. In contrast to White-Jacket's case, no man steps forward to intercede. Jack Chase's impulse to do so cools notably when a top-mate reminds him of the harsh penalty that would surely result, and 'with moist eyes' he retreats to one side of the massed spectators.

The flogging of Ushant should be a more touching scene than it is, but the narrator de-emphasizes its seriousness. If 'most landsmen' view Ushant's treatment with abhorrence, 'the people', though they are indignant, do not denounce it because, being so habituated to excessive cruelties, 'they are almost reconciled to inferior severities.' That is, Ushant for his rebelliousness might have suffered more than twelve lashes or he might have been condemned to 'keel-hauling' or flogged 'through the fleet', the subject of the narrator's following chapter. Moreover, the narrator's parting salute to Ushant is a curious mix of admiration and drollery:

> I know not in what frigate you sail now, old Ushant; but Heaven protect your storied old beard, in whatever Typhoon it may blow. And if ever it must be shorn, old man, may it fare like the royal beard of Henry I, of England, and be clipped by the right reverend hand of some Archbishop of Sees. (367)

In these two narrative segments—White-Jacket's and Ushant's arraignments at the mast—the disparity both in treatment of incident and in tone originates in the character and temperament of the narrator, whose springs of action come from a complex of half-disclosed, half-understood, and unadmitted motives.

Without a firm sense of community Redburn at the end of his voyage stands emotionally naked, stripped of the psychological and political protection that might have rendered innocent his homoerotic impulses. But White-Jacket, who has a place in his social hierarchy, is almost too comfortably ensconced, too complacently moral, to permit self-inquiry into the sexual bases of his little society. Only in the curiously misshapen chapter, 'The Social State in a Man-of-War', does he come close to linking his concern for social ranks and the proper relationships among them and his unresolved feelings of emotional bonding and sexuality.

The narrator begins Chapter 89 by declaring that the varied evils that he has illustrated throughout his account—flogging, robbery, blaspheming, swearing, gambling, smuggling, and thimble-rigging—'by no means comprise the whole catalogue of evil' aboard ships; but the 'single feature . . . full of significance' that he chooses to specify turns out to be a nine-paragraph discussion of the mutual antagonism between sailors and the small contingent of marines housed on every naval ship. The argument is that the inclusion of soldiers on a man-of-war serves as a 'system of checks', another example of institutional distrust of 'the people' that inspires bitterness throughout the ship's complement. This 'single feature', though consistent with the range of criticism in other chapters, here seems displaced—even, given the dark introductory hints, anti-climactic. In a long paragraph beginning 'It is the same with both officers and men', the narrator continues his point about social animosities, only to end with an observation about incurable 'organic evils'. If the diction in the early passages of this paragraph—*sinister, sickening, unmanning*—seems excessive for its subject, it is appropriate for the narrator's real topic sentence: 'the worst facts touching the common sailor are systematically kept in the background. . . .' The final paragraph of Chapter 89 continues to keep the taboo subject of homosexual practices in the background, although by allusion and indirection the narrator touches on those 'sins for which the cities of the plain were overthrown'. After noting that the deck officer turns away 'with loathing' at complaints brought into the open, the narrator ends with references to the literature of incest; let landsmen remain ignorant of 'even worse horrors than these, and forever abstain from seeking to draw aside this veil'. But of course he has just drawn it aside—however skittishly— and the reader is no longer ignorant of the 'contagious' evils below deck. Do the officers turn away with loathing only because the subject is made public? Is such common sexuality among seamen another Naval vice that should be exposed? If so, how far exposed? Does the narrator, who draws aside the veil while telling the reader not to look, see any connection with this vice and the idealistic camaraderie among his own main-top men?

Such questions are of course never directly addressed, but the hesitant way in which the narrator draws aside the veil, his diffuse focus, and his indirections reveal a mind subliminally aware that the sexual practices he deplores suggest unpleasant connections to the impassioned celebration of his selective brotherhood. To acknowledge such connections would threaten that camaraderie along with the emotional and social certitude that such a select group spirit induces. White-Jacket's tonal uncertainty in Chapter 89 is the analogue of Redburn's nervous dispatching of Harry Bolton in his Chapter 62.

Redburn's seeming maturity at the end of his first voyage is belied by the awkward dénouement by which he seeks to resolve the emotional complications he has introduced in his 'Confessions and Reminiscences'. The financial failure— Redburn ends the voyage, according to the wily captain's bookkeeping, by owing Riga $7.75!—means that he is no more 'on his legs again' than the figurehead of *La Reine*, which still 'lies pitching head-foremost down into the trough of a calamitous sea'; and the brief glimpse into his future shows him once again at sea, this time among whalers. The narrative fact, sparse as it is, suggests a kind of continued restlessness in the protagonist that the *Bildungsroman* in its closure conventionally avoids. The projected future in his spiritual continuation as White-Jacket is more promising because of his surer tones of authority that derive from a firmer sense of place within a community of like-minded fellows. But his greater maturity, because it is socially derived, masks even more seriously the affective irresolution of his character. Despite the often trenchant attacks on the Navy throughout his account, the narrator's position in *White-Jacket* reasserts the claims of hierarchy and thus the social ranks upon which they are based. White-Jacket the acerbic observer and wit dies in his caesarean ripping of the shroud-like garment that has so long made him special among his mates; in his place is born a more resolute but conventional individual who preaches against mutiny and pleads for brotherhood. In his rebirth White-Jacket does not expunge his old alliance with his man-of-war world but expands it,[16] incorporating the whole earth as a man-of-war that 'sails through the air'; the shrill denunciations of discrete evils are replaced by a chastened vision of a brotherhood linked by general evils that are humanly inevitable.

The concluding chapter in effect reverses the general

emphasis of the book, whose burden has been the reiterated external evils catalogued and illustrated by an observer who thinks of himself as rational and objective. From attack, indignation, vituperation, and scorn the narrator turns in humility to a plea for general toleration. Unlike the buoyant spirit of the preceding chapter, with its imaginative ceremony of linked hands ('round our mast we circle, a brother-band, hand in hand, all spliced together'), the peroration of 'The End', with its elaborately extended metaphor, is sober and inward, a reminder of an ineradicable sickness holding sway in all lives. It asserts that despite its clean lives on the surface, the world is made up of the wicked, the inefficient, the sick; that they are we, 'the people', as well as they, the officers; that all souls, 'store-rooms of secrets', are below the waterline. The narrator never specifies 'the worst of our evils [that] we blindly inflict upon ourselves'; but in the face of 'the rest' of the evils, he suggests that an ideal brotherhood of mutual responsibility can nourish each man. In his last chapter Redburn's quick glimpse into his future assures the continuation of his own uncertain sojourn in the world. In his last chapter White-Jacket closes the gap between protagonist and retrospective narrator into a perspective that joins them in a single consciousness; its present tense signifies an existential Now, since 'our last destination', the future, 'remains a secret' to all mortals who travel 'with sealed orders' toward a final harbor 'predestinated' since Creation.

Technically, the manipulation of point of view in these two books points to the even greater complexities in the use of first-person in *Moby-Dick*, whose Ishmael is not only both actor and memoirist but a fluid consciousness that is forced to compete with other consciousnesses, modes, moods, and genres, all with their separate claims to authoritative perspectives. Substantively, the imperatives of brotherhood, which remain inchoate and fleeting in *Redburn* and too narrowly conceived and celebrated in *White-Jacket*, must wait for the comprehensive, inclusive spirit of *Moby-Dick*. White-Jacket's anti-mutiny and pro-brotherhood sentiments in his peroration may well anticipate the moral postures of Ishmael, whose values include submission to a communal order based on power ('Who ain't a slave?'); but they yet give little promise of Ishmael's mature acceptance of that non-ideological, non-threatening homoeroticism that would almost casually become so attractive a part of his 'genial, desperado' philosophy. Though conceptually there is emotional growth in Redburn/White-Jacket, the protagonists are so ungenially taxed by their unresolved sexuality that their breaking away as desperados must lie beyond the boundaries of their stories.

NOTES

1. *The Letters of Herman Melville*, ed. Merrell R. Davis and William R. Gilman (New Haven: Yale University Press, 1960), p. 91.
2. *Letters*, p. 95.
3. M. F. K. Fisher, *As They Were* (New York: Random House, 1982), p. 5.
4. Larry J. Reynolds, 'Antidemocratic Emphasis in *White-Jacket*', *American Literature* 48 (March 1976), 19.
5. Edgar A. Dryden, *Melville's Thematics of Form: The Great Art of Telling the Truth* (Baltimore: Johns Hopkins Press, 1968), p. 67.
6. See especially James E. Miller, '*Redburn* and *White-Jacket*: Initiation and Baptism', *Nineteenth-Century Fiction* 13 (March 1959), 273–93. Dryden also calls *White-Jacket* a 'sequel of sorts' to *Redburn*, p. 57.
7. All quotations from *Redburn* and *White-Jacket* are drawn from Volumes 4 and 5 of *The Writings of Herman Melville*, ed. Harrison Hayford, Hershel Parker, and G. Thomas Tanselle (Evanston and Chicago: Northwestern University Press and The Newberry Library, 1969, 1970).
8. William H. Gilman, *Melville's Early Life and Redburn* (New York: New York University Press, 1951), pp. 218–31.
9. Harold Beaver has characterized Aladdin's Palace as a 'Gomorrah to match the "Sodom-like" grime of Liverpool' in his edition of *Redburn* (London: Penguin, 1976), p. 25. See also Newton Arvin, *Herman Melville* (New York: William Sloan, 1950), p. 106.
10. Several critics have commented on this doubling device: Martin J. Pops, *The Melville Archetype* (Kent, O.: Kent State University Press, 1970), p. 57; William B. Dillingham, *An Artist in the Rigging: The Early Work of Herman Melville* (Athens: University of Georgia Press, 1972), p. 58. Merlin Bowen was the first to note the parallels between Redburn and Bolton in '*Redburn* and the Angle of Vision', *Modern Philology* 52 (November 1954), 107–8. As a corrective, James Schroeter added the equally significant parallels between Redburn and Jackson in '*Redburn* and the Failure of Mythic Criticism', *American Literature* 39 (November 1967), 293–96, and noted that the survival of Redburn depends upon his avoiding both aristocratic and plebeian excesses.
11. *Letters*, p. 93.
12. Dryden, p. 67.

13. There are probably more modes represented in *White-Jacket* than these or the six kinds noted by Willard Thorp in his 'Historical Note' to the Northwestern-Newberry edition, pp. 425–28.
14. Most critics now agree that Melville's 'pilfering' habits of composition in his early works are as important to the fictiveness of his books as his autobiographical bent.
15. Reynolds, p. 14.
16. John Seelye in *Melville: The Ironic Diagram* (Evanston: Northwestern University Press, 1970), pp. 46–7, believes that White-Jacket is initiated out of, not into, the purgatory that is his man-of-war world.

4

Moby-Dick as Anatomy

by A. ROBERT LEE

> Concerning my own forthcoming book—it is off my hands, but must cross the sea before publication here. Dont you buy it—dont you read it, when it does come out, because it is by no means the sort of book for you. It is not a peice of fine feminine Spitalsfields silk—but is of the horrible texture of a fabric that should be woven of ships' cables & hausers. A Polar wind blows through it, & birds of prey hover over it. Warn all gentle fastidious people from so much as peeping into the book—on risk of lumbago & sciatics.
> —Letter to Sarah Huyler Morewood, 12? September 1851[1]

1

So Melville, genially mock-apologetic and as haphazard as always with his spelling and punctuation, gave warning to a favourite Pittsfield, Massachusetts neighbour about the possible consequences for her health of tackling *Moby-Dick* (1851). In casting himself as some craggy Ancient Mariner likely to inflict 'lumbago & sciatics' with his 'polar' whale-narrative, he reveals great neighbourly charm and an instance of the playfulness which never lay far absent from his make-up. He also confirms how well from the outset he understood the darker subversive purposes behind his 'forthcoming book' (which did indeed 'cross the sea' before American publication to appear in England as *The Whale*). When, however, in one of the very first reviews, Evert Duyckinck, the influential Editor of the *Literary World* and an early and loyal Melville admirer, spoke admonishingly of the story's 'piratical running down of creeds and opinions', he but touched upon the restless and massive exploratory radicalism of spirit which had conceived *Moby-Dick*.[2]

For even as Melville played himself up as the incarnation of Yankee courtliness (in similar vein a year later he would describe the labyrinthine *Pierre* (1852) as 'a rural bowl of milk' to Sophia Hawthorne),[3] he was also signalling something of the deep underlying iconoclasm—the risk-laden curiosity as he saw it— of *Moby-Dick*. Such, at least, can be inferred from the imagery of his letter and its beguiling sea-talk of a tale 'worn of ships' cables & hausers', blown through with 'a Polar wind' and threateningly hovered over by 'birds of prey'. If, however, according to this account 'by no means the sort of book' for a Sarah Morewood or other and similar 'gentle fastidious people', exactly what sort of book *had* Melville written? The accounts and interpretations have multiplied dizzyingly, beyond anything Melville himself could possibly have foreseen. Yet even on his own view, looking back upon this sixth full-length narrative since he made his literary bow with *Typee* in 1846, he had good reason to believe that beneath *Moby-Dick*'s outward show of a tale of the Pacific whale fisheries he had written nothing less (as he told Hawthorne in his effervescent correspondence of 1851–52[4]) than a 'hell-fired' and 'wicked' book whose truest inclinations lay calculatedly hidden from immediate view.

Whatever the chequered reception of the book, however, one note has been recurrent: before anything else *Moby-Dick* yields sumptuous adventure, latterday Homeric epic dressed out in American legend and format. Sequences like Ishmael's arrival in New Bedford and Nantucket, or his serio-comic first meetings with Queequeg, or the *Pequod*'s New Year's Day departure, or subsequent major episodes like 'The First Lowering' (Ch. 48), the exhilarating three-day final chase (Chs. 133–35) and the whale's destruction of Ahab and of his eclectic, polymorphous crew, massively underscore *Moby-Dick*'s power as sheer eventful story-telling. This certainly rang true for the small minority of contemporaries, of whom Duyckinck was one, who initially read and praised the narrative; it rang even truer for the 1920s generation of editors and critics like Raymond Weaver, D. H. Lawrence (in his *Studies in Classic American Literature*), John Freeman and Lewis Mumford, all of whom played a most honourable part in Melville's rehabilitation.[5] It was essentially their efforts which paved the way for his recognition as a key contributing voice to the American Renaissance, the efflorescence of nineteenth-century American thought and expression called for in exhortation like Ralph Waldo Emerson's *Nature* (1836) and 'The American Scholar' (1837) and vindicated not only by Emerson himself and Melville but pre-eminently by Thoreau, Whitman, Hawthorne and Emily Dickinson. Subsequent readerships patently have reaffirmed *Moby-Dick*'s power as story-telling, the pursuit of the white whale by Ahab, Ishmael and their *Pequod* ship-of-all-nations as the irresistible stuff of epic.

Nonetheless, understandable as has been the appeal of *Moby-Dick* as 'voyage-out' (or 'drama done'[6] as the Epilogue puts matters), so from the start, too, it has always rightly been suspected of containing altogether cannier and less explicit 'lower layers' (143). These, time and again, Melville successfully camouflaged, sending even his keenest acolytes off on wrong, or at least confusing, trails. For once launched into the text via Melville's purposive three-part opening of 'Etymology', 'Extracts' and 'Loomings', the reader embarks with the *Pequod* upon at least two other intimately related journeys: the first into a historic, 'actual' whaling industry with its base in New England Yankee capitalism and documented from Melville's own experience in all its rituals and argot and danger; the second into a wholly more inward and mythopoeic 'wonder-world' (16), a journey which rests for its effect upon the appeal to the sympathetic visionary imagination. Both journeys blend and interweave brilliantly, seamed as they (and the surface tale of the *Pequod*'s hunt for the whale) are with speculative asides, digression, veiled runs of meaning and Melville's distinctive kind of jokiness. Further, both play into the wholly aware manner in which *Moby-Dick* points to itself as a kind of readerly journey, the text as encirculation beginning with its own end and ending with its own beginning as Ishmael 'escapes alone' (470) to tell his story.

All this compounded 'journeying' bears inescapably upon the ways in which for Melville the world's truths, actual and mythic, avail themselves to unremitting Seekers (as he believed himself and his co-Manichaean Nathaniel Hawthorne to be) after Absolute or Final Meanings. The terms in which he repeatedly spoke of attaining Truth—'striking through', 'diving', 'probing' and the like—he expressed with vivid and brilliantly arresting force in 'Hawthorne and his Mosses', his momentous *Literary World* review written as he undertook his labours with *Moby-Dick* and which led on to what on Melville's part became the effusive neophyte-and-master friendship following the discovery that they were both near neighbours at Pittsfield and Lenox. Melville's essay not only gave voice to his brimming admiration for Hawthorne but his astonished late personal discovery of Shakespeare, a 'shock of recognition' he could barely contain. For in Shakespeare, even more than in the Hawthorne he exalted as 'a great deep intellect, which drops down into the universe like a plummet', he saw nothing less than the apocalyptic ability to fix and anatomize Truth:

> But it is those deep far-off things in him; those occasional flashings-forth of the intuitive Truth in him; those short, quick probings at the very axis of reality:—these are the things that make Shakespeare, Shakespeare. Through the mouths of the dark characters of Hamlet, Timon, Lear, and Iago he craftily says, or sometimes insinuates the things, which we feel to be so terrifically true, that it were all but madness for any good man, in his own proper character, to utter, or even hint of them.[7]

Just as Melville himself increasingly came to believe that the 'true' reality of the world lay ensnared almost to the point of undecipherability behind a slippery surface of puzzlements—Truth as his 'Hawthorne and his Mosses' review calls it which reveals itself by 'cunning glimpses', 'covertly' and 'by snatches' —so, not only in *Moby-Dick* but subsequently in *Pierre*, key Piazza tales like 'Bartleby, the Scrivener' (1853) and 'Benito Cereno' (1855) and most strikingly *The Confidence-Man* (1857), he designed his fiction to match. *Billy Budd* (1888–91), also, his superb valedictory 'inside narrative' of innocence made stuttering and violent in a world regulated by the killingly dutiful 'forms, measured forms' of the Veres and the fevered love-hate of the Claggarts, reveals Melville in his old age no less abating in the wish to understand Truth's masquerade.

Melville never lost touch with the world about him, not at any rate the ex-mariner and one-time South Seas harpooner ('harpooneer' in his own nineteenth-century usage) who spoke out of keenest experience of having dipped his hand 'into the tar-pot' (14) and of a whaler as his 'Yale College and Harvard' (101). But he clearly always recognized the possible, and even likely, gap between words and things. Each instance of his lively, skilled sleights-of-hand and intended doubleness of meaning—'careful disorderliness' (304) is his general phrase for how *Moby-Dick* is constructed—particularizes his writer's acknowledgement of the general provisionality of all language and codes. Words he insists, and in *The Confidence-Man* triumphantly makes his credo, serve if not absolutely as Notes Towards a Supreme Fiction then almost so, and nowhere more than when an anatomy or globalized articulation of Truth is involved.

It is the nature of that discrepancy between words and things (Michel Foucault's recent *Les Mots et les Choses* reminds of a Cartesian point-of-departure) which finds expression in the white whale, Moby-Dick as living ocean mammal yet one whose word-like 'Egyptian' hieroglyphic markings, other-worldly whiteness and apparent ubiquity across time and space Melville offers as dramatic testimony to the way things and 'meanings' operate fictively—mythically—and so resist all final encapsulation. Whether in 'Etymology' or 'Extracts' (both of which I shall come back to), or symptomatic detail like the Spouter Inn painting which Melville hintingly terms 'a boggy, soggy, squitchy picture truly' (20), or the masthead Golden Doubloon (Ch. 99)—the whale's so-called 'talisman' (99) and interpreted mirror-fashion by each crew-member in turn—the point is again to show how definitions arise, things which can be perceived as absolute fact but which time and again double as wholly relative and provisional, that is as nothing less than fictions. This process Melville calls attention to throughout the narrative of *Moby-Dick* (it might in fact be said to constitute the narrative), typically in the ostensibly literal but in no small measure *pastiche* book-catalogue of whales (Ch. 32) or the astonishing *symboliste* discourse on colour-mythology in 'The Whiteness of the Whale' (Ch. 42), both in their different but complementary ways 'fictions' which have arisen in the understanding of the 'factual' whale which finally dives from view.

Melville the fallen American grandee obliged to make his way down into the Pacific could hardly have doubted the literal, awesome *fact* of whales—their power, beauty, bulk, ocean intelligence and guile—but Melville the literary writer-diver could also see that like the world itself, the whale lay intricately enshrouded in every manner of myth, the object of ancestral hunter and manhood cults, of religious superstition, and of folklore and popular tales and songs both past and present. As a deity, too, of sorts, for many cultures it provided a centre for the great erotic celebratory rituals of art. Accordingly, Moby-Dick the whale links back to its point of origin in Mocha Dick, the literal historical sea-creature, and functions doubly as a composite source for all the acts of definition, whether Ishmael's, Ahab's, the crew's, or by implication, the reader's own. As it takes that last dive, Ahab fatally entangled in the harpoon-lines like his prophet Fedallah before him and the *Pequod* sunk, so it takes down with it the possibility of all final definition. It leaves behind 'a closing vortex' (470), a 'button-like black bubble' (470), Truth once more sealed off from definitive human access and only Ishmael as 'orphan' (470) literally and symbolically left afloat inside Queequeg's coffin to bear witness and continue like 'the devious-cruising Rachel' (470) yet further circles of pursuit. In his own way, thus, Melville, too, 'says' his truths 'craftily', altogether as surreptitiously as the Hawthorne his *Literary World* piece pronounced with genuine magnanimity 'this Portuguese diamond in our Literature'.

In one sense he had done so right from the beginning. *Typee*, for instance, speaks disingenuously of telling 'the unvarnished facts' of his Polynesian *wanderjahr*, but neither it nor *Omoo* (1847) does any such thing.[8] *Mardi* (1849), two years later and Melville's flawed attempt at a more philosophical canvas, throughout (and wearingly) exhibits its self-awareness as a would-be map of Truth—in all of its sixteen-island odyssey and in the allusions to the *Koztanza*, the imaginary epic of Dantean proportion invented by Melville to illustrate his thoughts on creativity and self-expression. Even *Redburn* (1849) and *White-Jacket* (1850), for all that Melville referred to them dismissively as no more than 'two *jobs* which I have done for money',[9] in their allusions to the 'patching' and 'weaving' of different garments hint at the analogous process whereby literary texts are patched and woven into their author's version of Truth. By the time Melville wrote *Moby-Dick*, he had also ingested Carlyle's *Sartor Resartus* (1836) and though its influence did not work everywhere to his stylistic advantage, it assuredly confirmed his own instinct that Truth always 'clothes' itself in the deceiving garb of appearance. It was *Sartor Resartus*, too, which provided a source for phrasing of the kind used by Ahab when he speaks of 'striking through' the pasteboard-mask of reality (144). Thus despite the reputation he acquired largely on the basis of *Typee* and *Omoo* as the 'true-life' sailor-turned-romancer, nearly all of Melville's fiction embodies the belief that Truth rarely discloses itself whole or unknottedly and that as a consequence art has no alternative but to negotiate its relationship with reality obliquely, or as he deliberately understates it in *The Confidence-Man* with 'variability in expression'.[10]

Whatever else, then, may be said to be expressed in *Moby-Dick*'s quest-form and amplitude of detail—the pursuit of oil both for literal profit and as a source of different kinds of 'light', the revengeful Prometheanism of Ahab, the gladiatorial clash of Man against Other—it most signally also bids to explore the protean ways in which Truth undergoes definition. For some this has led to a fatal strain in the writing, Melville all too frequently prone to over-pitching his rhetoric and tone. But to a majority it has clearly installed him as one of the age's braver spirits, an exemplary American-Victorian voyager of the mind as well as the body. In saying devotedly of Hawthorne that the world was 'mistaken' to believe the New England author of *Mosses from an Old Manse* (1846) and *The Scarlet Letter* (1850), a 'sequestered, harmless man, from whom any deep and weighty thing could hardly be anticipated',[11] he might have said as much or more of himself, the Melville who struggled to finish *Moby-Dick* first land-locked in his Berkshire 'Arrowhead' home and then in the Summer humidity of Manhattan.

Accordingly, whether one believes the book best accounted for as simply the greatest of Western sea-stories, and/or (to borrow again from Melville's letters) 'ontological heroics'[12] carefully smuggled out in the guise of a purported whale-hunt narrative, it also, for his detractors to the point of disabling obsession, attempts nothing less than an anatomy of the world, in Viola Sach's recent formulation a *liber mundi* or would-be

Book of Revelation.[13] The *Pequod*'s seeming 'actual' journey so serves as the vehicle for the book's complex of other quests, and indeed none more important than that pledged to explore the competing overlap of classifications and codes (all in their way 'Etymologies' and 'Extracts') whereby mankind has sought to express reality. Quite as much as it seizes the attention through its ostensible story, *Moby-Dick* also bids for our attention as Melville's *omnium gatherum* of how Truth in all its linked parts and filaments goes on being endlessly mythified and how tauntingly it eludes any single comprehensive scheme of definition. Little wonder that Melville time and again spoke admiringly of those like Emerson who could 'dive' and 'plummet' after Truth, even though they might surface with 'bloodshot eyes'.[14] Dissent as he did from Emerson's Transcendentalist good cheer (to the point of pillory in the form of Mark Winsome in *The Confidence Man*), he saw himself utterly as a fellow writer-diver determined to strike uncompromisingly for the ultimate condition of things—for Truth itself and no less. It is with the manner in which Melville uses the 'story' in *Moby Dick* to anatomize the world that the present essay is concerned.

2

In the Preface to 'Extracts' as 'Supplied by a Sub-Sub-Librarian' (one of the many surrogate 'diver' figures in the text) Melville teases his reader with the notion that as much as *Moby-Dick* might overall be thought 'veritable gospel cetology', plain whaling narrative, it equally amounts to 'higgledy-piggledy whale statements' (2). This seeming frolicsome half-category nicely underlines the book's *sui generis* design. In the same spirit, I don't want to press that Anatomy be invoked as some inflexible genre, but more as a conveniently approximate description aimed at capturing the encyclopaedic impulse and the play of speculative intelligence at work in *Moby-Dick*. Which is not to suggest that *Moby-Dick* cannot claim something of its own tradition or different literary analogues, beginning not least with classical 'journey' antecedents like the *Iliad*, the *Odyssey* and the *Aeneid* and their great catalogue set-pieces of Quest and of Arms and the Man. With an eye to *Moby-Dick*'s more explicit sources, one can also relevantly invoke Old

75

Testament stories like that of Jonah, Dante's *The Divine Comedy*, Brant's *Narrenschiff*, and slightly later, Camoes's *The Luciads*, all in their respective ways 'anatomies', to which should be added Montaigne's *Essays* and Robert Burton's *The Anatomy of Melancholy*, two works whose energy of allusion Melville responded to enthusiastically and as important models. All of these share the urge to make definition itself—the necessary human process of seeking to name Truth—a major drama.

In this respect, too, modern prose narrative can be said to have established its 'anatomical' tradition. From Cervantes's *Don Quixote* and Samuel Richardson's *Clarissa* (or Fielding's *Tom Jones*) onwards, the way leads steadily towards essential modernist 'anatomies' like Proust's *A la Recherche du Temps Perdu*, Joyce's *Ulysses*, Mann's *The Magic Mountain* and even a minor post-war classic like Grass's *Der Butt*. For American literature in particular, whether prose or poetry, the drive to invent matching 'anatomical' imaginative forms for the nation's space and plenitude has been perennial, whether in a Puritan glossary like Cotton Mather's *Magnalia Christi Americana*, or nineteenth-century landmarks like Poe's *Eureka* and Whitman's *Leaves of Grass*, or in classic modern American Long Poems like Hart Crane's *The Bridge*, Ezra Pound's *The Cantos* and William Carlos Williams's *Paterson*. Of *Moby-Dick*'s fictional legacy—in size at least—the list would include among others Faulkner's Yoknapatawpha novel-cycle, John Dos Passos's *U.S.A.*, Norman Mailer's *The Naked and the Dead*, and latterly postmodernist ventures of the order of William Gaddis's *The Recognitions*, John Barth's *The Sot-Weed Factor* and most notably Thomas Pynchon's *Gravity's Rainbow*. Each narrative, to be sure, achieves its own accent, but shares also the characteristically American compulsion to articulate the world's (and especially the New World's) plenty. In this sense, too, *Moby-Dick* clearly shows its American cultural origins, while belonging to the wider listing given above.

It does no harm to acknowledge that on most first readings of the book, *Moby-Dick* can rather give the impression of having lost faith with its own 'story'. In actual fact, it never does, though one needs patience and a certain readerly trust to establish one's balance amid the proliferating detail and apparently endless fecundity of allusion and digression. For all the different 'Etymologies' and 'Extracts' (not just those which open the book) not only link each to the other in one contrapuntal chain, they also play against and into the unfolding 'story' of the hunt. Indeed it becomes a fascinatingly moot point which hunt in fact *is* the story, Ahab's and the *Pequod*'s for the whale or Melville's for the different' keys which will unlock the world's secrets and patterns of order.[15]

Even so, as we work our way through each element in *Moby-Dick*'s 'ballast' we are never allowed to put out of mind the coming final encounter, Ahab and his 'Anarcharsis Clootz deputation' (108) made up of 'meanest mariners, and renegades and castaways' (104) bound for their fatal come-uppance as the White Whale at last surfaces and turns to face its pursuers. The rhythm of that 'story' pushes and presses behind each and every apparent digression, whether signposted through the nine successive 'gams' (themselves patterned as three triads); prophetic paintings such as those in The Spouter Inn (Ch. 3) and behind Father Mapple's pulpit (Ch. 8); stories-within-stories like that of the *Town-Ho* (Ch. 54); the all-reflective, cabalistic Doubloon (Ch. 99); Fedallah's *Macbeth*-like prophecies (Ch. 117); the inversion of the *Pequod*'s needles (Ch. 125); and as earlier mentioned, the culminating three-day chase (Chs. 133–35). Melville also supplies a gallery of anticipatory warning voices, early on that of the dockside Elijah (Chs. 19 and 21), and in turn those of Captain Mayhew and his crazed Shaker prophet Gabriel of the *Jeroboam* (Ch. 71), the blacksmith Perth, Ahab's possible benigner *alter ego* (Chs. 112–13), the Holy Fool Pip (Chs. 99 and 129), the forlorn Captain Gardiner of the *Rachel* (Ch. 128) and the First Mate Starbuck (Chs. 110 and 132). All of these individual voices unmistakably underline and advance the forward momentum of the hunt and remind us as the *Pequod* makes its way down the line (the harpoons 'baptized' in the fire and in the harpooners' blood, and Ahab's pipe, hat and quadrant all thrown to the sea) of the inescapable pending rendez-vous with the whale.

And as equally, Melville persists in developing throughout what I am calling his story-anatomy: the world and its defining truths held up for intensest scrutiny, whether through the agency of Ahab's brute Prometheanism, each respective crew-member's understanding, or overall, Ishmael's encompassing and near-oneiric contemplations. One of the many possible measures of *Moby-Dick*'s achievement lies precisely in the balance of these two dynamics, a 'story' which by its width of impact now exists as part of the stock of Western narrative legend and a story-*anatomy* which invites all but the most unresponsive reader to interpret the book's 'queer proceedings', to quote Ishmael on Queequeg's religious observances (30), as nothing less than Melville's greatest, eye-bloodying 'dive' for Truth.

3

To speak of *Moby-Dick* as Anatomy requires the fullest consideration of how Melville establishes the whale—both Ahab's White Whale and the whale in its overall *genus*—as the book's essential lodestone and point of radius; for the whale it is and not Ahab nor Ishmael nor the *Pequod* and crew which acts as the centre to which all else is periphery. Unfortunately, a great deal of the criticism of *Moby-Dick* has moved off from that perception, whether in the study of Ishmael's rôle as narrator, or of Ahab as avenger and Gothicized and Byronic *persona*, or the more general issue of whether the book's imagined world exists only on its own self-referential terms and as such gains or loses. For from the outset, Melville emphatically calls attention to the composite manner in which the whale must carry all the book's essential meanings.

The whale is first encountered through 'Etymology', an ingenious piece of lexical and grammatical mimickry which lists Whale in different languages, beginning with the Ancient tongues like Hebrew, Greek and Latin, moving on to the major Western European vernaculars (including English, French and Spanish), and arriving in the Pacific with Fegee and the playful-sounding Erromangoån. The sheer differences of register dramatize the gaps between naming processes, the different tics and assumptions of ear, eye and voice behind each vernacular tradition. The whale itself, 'round', 'rolling' and 'wallowing', according to the etymologies for Swedish, Danish, Dutch and German (and cited by Melville from dictionary sources in Webster's and Richardson's), seems almost to have gone missing, or at least to have fallen into some distant obscurity within the plethora of words and classification. The 'LATE CONSUMPTIVE USHER' invoked by Melville as 'supplying' these etymological whale-words, 'pale', 'threadbare', loving to 'dust his old grammars', presumably has met with his bodily and metaphysical ill-health by constantly seeking to extract organizing sense from sound and from the related discovery that language endlessly and conflictingly 'delivers that which is not true', to adapt slightly Melville's next quotation from yet another explorer-diver, the great Elizabethan geographer Richard Hakluyt.

Then, in 'Extracts', as supposedly given by another 'mere painstaking burrower', the unthanked and under-esteemed Sub-Sub Librarian on Melville's tongue-in-cheek testimony, each successive quotation we are invited to think no more than 'a glancing bird's eye view' (2) of the whale—the implication clearly being the necessity of infinitely yet more 'diving' and 'plummeting' to get at the truths of Leviathan. Even in sum, thus, and when read crowdingly one upon the other, these 'Extracts' serve as no more than working classificatory morsels, passing indicators, for the whale; or in the Sub-Sub's own terms, 'higgledy-piggledy whale statements' (2) as against 'veritable gospel cetology' (2), precisely an analogy for how the components in *Moby-Dick* contribute to the narrative as an imaginative whole. The litany built up by the 'Extracts' extends across all time and space, from the Book of Genesis to ongoing whale-songs, and includes further whale-allusions from the Bible, from 'Histories', New England Primers (grammars again), Prefaces, Parliamentary Speeches, Lives, sea-ditties, selected authors both Ancient and Modern, and even from 'Something Unpublished', another low-key piece of Melvilleian whimsy. 'Extracts' indeed they are, just as for all its narrational energy and density, Melville acknowledges *Moby-Dick* to offer no more than 'extracts' of Truth, and just as by extension and if we choose to act on his tipping the wink, all language no more than 'extracts' parts from Truth's whole. Melville's interweaving imagery of Etymology and Extracts, and his clever *personae* of schoolteacher Ushers and 'consumed' Sub-Sub-Librarians, point utterly to *Moby-Dick* as an anatomy.

Anatomizing the world's truths—by 'Etymology', 'Extraction' or analysis of the whale's and world's 'languages'—clearly also implies for Melville in *Moby-Dick* a journeying towards, if not actually into, the transcendental, that 'wonder-world' (16) beyondness which he suggests lies to the far other side of all words and outward visible phenomena. In Chapter 68, 'The Blanket', for instance, he hints that his difficulties in decoding the whale, and reality at large, go well beyond problems of lexis and epistemology; he argues that the world's different languages, alphabets, hieroglyphs and vernaculars indicate sources which transcend all merely human co-ordinates. His 'text' in this he makes the great Sperm Whale whose skin he alleges carries the insignia of other, more 'mystic-marked' realities:

> In life, the visible surface of the Sperm Whale is not the least among the many marvels he presents. Almost invariably it is all over obliquely crossed and re-crossed with numberless straight marks in thick array, something like those in the finest Italian line engravings. But these marks do not seem to be impressed upon the isinglass substance above mentioned, but seem to be seen through it, as if they were engraved upon the body itself. Nor is this all. In some instances, to the quick, observant eye, those linear marks, as in a veritable engraving, but afford the ground for far other delineations. These are hieroglyphical: that is, if you call those mysterious cyphers on the walls of pyramids hieroglyphics, then that is the proper word to use in the present connexion. By my retentive memory of the hieroglyphics upon one Sperm Whale in particular, I was much struck with a plate representing the old Indian characters chiselled on the famous hieroglyphic palisades on the banks of the Upper Mississippi. Like those mystic rocks, too, the mystic-marked whale remains undecipherable. (260)

The Sperm Whale—and again the world—as 'obliquely crossed and re-crossed with numberless straight marks in thick array' indeed suggests undecipherability, reality as a vexed and vexing connundrum and subject only to provisional interpretation. However energetic man's will to anatomize the world, it eludes and mystifies him, always and everywhere suggesting 'far other delineations'. At best, we come up with Extracts, partial, multiple and largely conflicting, readings of Truth.

In Chapter 79, 'The Prairie', Melville takes the point still further, speaking of the Sperm Whale's Egyptian 'pyramidical silence' (292), and concentrating on the whale's face and brow. Here again, the notion is advanced that the wrinkles encode some strange elusive hieroglyph, a language, say, like Erromangoan (from 'Etymology') or 'Chaldee', which resist almost every effort at decipherment. He refers to two pioneer decipherers, Champollion and Sir William Jones, the one a landmark Egyptologist, the other the unraveller of Asiatic religions and languages:

> Champollion deciphered the wrinkled granite hieroglyphics. But there is no Champollion to decipher the Egypt of every man's and every being's face. Physiognomy, like every human science, is but a passing fable. If then, Sir William Jones, who read in thirty languages, could not read the simplest peasant's face in its profounder and more subtle meanings, how may unlettered Ishmael hope to read the awful Chaldee of the Sperm Whale's brow? I but put that brow before you. Read it if you can. (292–93)

Melville's text implies that, read the whale as we will—not just its brow but its whole anatomical being—it will rarely yield up its 'profounder and more subtle meanings', even (or especially) to the scholars. Our anatomies but touch surfaces, the outward appearance of things. And so the whale, so the world; yet the compulsion to probe and categorize remains irresistible both for Ishmael-as-narrator and behind him Melville-as-author. Furthermore, it is a compulsion drama-tized right from the start in 'Loomings':

> as for me, I am tormented with an everlasting itch for things remote. I love to sail forbidden seas, and land on barbarous coasts. (16)

The unquenchability of that voice (Ishmael's ostensibly) points up even further the book's overall ambition, its appetite precisely for taking on the whale-world's meanings. It pervades almost every aspect of the anatomizing in *Moby-Dick*, at once restless, inquisitive, and if one so permits, endlessly engaging.

4

Broadly, *Moby-Dick* develops its constituent anatomies in two ways, those of chapter-length or more and those which Melville builds out from some specific detail into paradigms of subtly larger implication and meaning. The longer anatomies especially take their cue from the 'Etymology', 'Extracts', 'Loomings' triangulation, each reflective of Melville's own decoding procedures, the world read for the reader according to the author's grammar. With the *Pequod* launched on a New Year's Day, and Ishmael and Queequeg ritually 'married' and put through their ceremonial 'signing-on' with the gargoyle 'fighting Quakers' (71), Bildad and Peleg, Melville offers the first of the longer anatomy sequences, 'Knights and Squires' (Chs. 26–7), a cast-list of sorts which he immediately deploys to suggest that the *Pequod* carries other and more emblematic travellers and seafarers—all by their own different lights bound upon a quest to 'name', 'dissect' and 'pursue' the whale.

The overt purpose of 'Knights and Squires' is to introduce the Mates Starbuck, Stubb and Flask, then the harpooners Queequeg, Tashtego and Daggoo, and in turn Pip and something of the rest of the crew. But Melville soon discloses that he wishes us to discern far more in this account of the literal ship's company. Just as in 'The Ship' (Ch. 16), Melville makes clear that the *Pequod* doubles as both a real New England whaler and also a more daedal craft, a kind of mythical sea-beast itself, so the crew are depicted as seasoned actual mariners and at the same time *personae* of a kind with the warrior-listings of the *Aeneid* or Shakespeare's soldiery in his History plays. Both officers and men Melville carefully transforms into a mythicized, heraldic 'deputation':

> They were nearly all Islanders in the Pequod, *Isolatoes* too. I call such, not acknowledging the common continent of men, but each *Isolato* living on a separate continent of his own. Yet now, federated along one keel, what a set these Isolatoes were! An Anacharsis Clootz deputation from all the isles of the sea, and all the ends of the earth, accompanying old Ahab in the Pequod to lay the world's grievances before that bar from which not many of them ever came back. (108)

A New England whaling-crew thus become the argonauts of legend each embarked upon a world-ship—which is also a Ship of Fools and a Death-Ship (the *Pequod* being named for an extinct Indian tribe)—'isolatoes' yet part of 'federated' humankind pledged under Ahab's aggrieved command to hunt down the ineffaceable and all-encompassing white whale. Melville's 'anatomy' here moves strikingly between the actual and the precisely marvellous, the real which is also fantastical, so that yet again we recognize ourselves at one level enrolled upon a perceptibly nineteenth-century whaler in search of oil and at another and in the mind's eye upon a journey for abundantly more transcendental fare. In 'Knights and Squires', 'story' and 'anatomy' so blend into each other, and so establish the pattern to follow.

That pattern invariably emerges as one in which ostensible whaling 'fact' is made to resonate with other implication and ballast. In 'Cetology' (Ch. 31), for instance, Melville's seeming book-categorization of whales comes over accurately enough; but in no way can it be thought simply a literal 'cetological System' (117). It offers no less than bibliographical *pastiche*, a sublime mock-catalogue, in which each whale, filed tongue-in-cheek under Folio, Octavo or Duodecimo, defies both its definer and its purported definition. Not for nothing does Melville confide at the beginning of the chapter: 'The classification of the constituents of a chaos, nothing less is here essayed' (117). He also avers that his object 'is simply to project the draught of a systemization of cetology' (118), as if 'cetology' were the world's plenitude and almost impossibly unamenable to any one system (even a literary whaling-narrative). All systems thus for Melville work partially and only out of their own governing languages and assumptions; his achievement in 'Cetology' is to make the point through so engaging a trope, texts as a library classification system for the larger Text of the whale itself.

In turn, each subsequent longer anatomy explores reality as harbouring other schema and other classificatory agendas. Each, too, builds on its predecessor, widening the book's allusive range and reaffirming Melville's 'anatomical' design overall. In 'Moby Dick' (Ch. 41), the whale's prowess as legend—as being thought ubiquitous in time and place (158)—is given minute attention, a perfectly visible, literal whale yet also an emissary life-form from other realms ('the gliding great demon of the seas of life' 162). It is this white whale which can sponsor 'unearthly conceits' (152), 'fabulous narrations' (158), the proliferating versions and counter-versions conceived by whalemen each

83

'wrapped by influences all tending to make his fancy pregnant with many a mighty birth' (156).[16] To account in any final way for such profusion and fictioneering would be, we are told, in Melville's by now familiar metaphor, 'to dive deeper than Ishmael can go' (162). In 'The Whiteness of the Whale' (Ch. 42), the whale is anatomized from another perspective, the massive 'colorless, all-color' (169) of whiteness itself, whiteness as one of the world's great mystic keys or languages which runs through Day and Night, Appearance and Void, Totem and Taboo. In mapping out 'the incantation of this whiteness' (169), a quite astounding anatomical paradigm, Melville constructs yet another detailed chain of analogies and links. Not only does 'The Whiteness of the Whale' read bracingly on its own terms, it utterly reaffirms the energy of mind behind Melville's curiosity, in Scott Fitzgerald's phrase for Gatsby, his own gift for wonder.

'The Honor and Glory of Whaling' (Ch. 82) continues in just the same manner, a further 'dive into this matter of whaling' (304) and a Melvilleian *tour-de-force* of how whaling's different heroes and avatars reflect the mythologizing processes endemic in the human imagination. And as legend is made of the whale and its pursuers and worshippers, so inferentially of the world and its definers. The book abounds in matching similar sequences like 'Of the Monstrous Pictures of Whales' (Ch. 55ff.), listings of how whales over time have been delineated in painting and sculpture yet at the same time an enquiry into the psychology of picturing itself; 'The Grand Armada' (Ch. 87), an account of a literal whale-school but equally a poetic tribute to Nature's massive generative reservoirs of life; 'Fast-Fish and Loose-Fish' (Ch. 89), at once a pseudo-legal tract on whaling rights and far headier discourse to do with Freedom and Necessity, the Self as sovereign yet inextricably tied into the greater social and historical whole; 'Heads or Tails' (Ch. 90), an 'anatomy' of male and female sexual principles which jocularly re-plays some of the phallic double-talk of 'The Cassock' (Ch. 95); and 'A Bower in the Arsacides' (Ch. 102), the depiction of a Tranque whale-skeleton which Melville ingeniously elaborates into a composite image of Life amid Death, a homage to the cyclical ebb and flow of energies he associates with the Weaver God. All of these 'anatomies' invite fuller consideration, but in sketching their intricately-skeined, fecund and double play of meaning and their overall linkage—the world as given in Melville's *Moby-Dick* stupendously and circlingly linked in a great chain of hieroglyph and symbol—I hope to have sufficiently confirmed how their 'stories' work alongside and as part of that of Ahab, the *Pequod* and the whale.

5

The smaller 'anatomies' in *Moby-Dick* by no means have wanted for critical attention, whether Ishmael's opening vista of 'thousands upon thousands of mortal men fixed in ocean reveries' (12), or the depiction of the *Pequod* as 'a ship of the old school' (67), 'a thing of trophies' (67) and 'a cannibal of a craft' (67), or the masthead cabalistic doubloon (358ff.) which Pip in an old American bit of bawdy calls 'the ship's navel' (365) and which causes Starbuck to observe—as he witnesses the different responses elicited by the Equadorian golden coin with its Andean and zodiac engravings—'There's another rendering now; but still one text' (363). All the other similarly 'anatomized' objects in *Moby-Dick* work to the same assumption (one which engaged equally the likes of Emerson, Thoreau, Whitman and Hawthorne) that the world's 'texts' sponsor one upon another 'rendering'. Hence, for instance, the Spouter Inn ante-room (Ch. 3) serves as a historic museum of past whaling trophies and bric-à-brac and (like Hawthorne's 'moon-lit' study in 'The Custom House' sketch of *The Scarlet Letter*) as an analogue of sorts for the House of Fiction ahead. Or, for his part, Queequeg under Western eyes appears outlandish enough to be credible paradoxically; yet also he embodies an instance of human 'text', as Melville's bookish metaphor has it 'in his own proper person a riddle to unfold' (399), 'a wondrous work in one volume' (399), 'living parchment' (399). Thus Queequeg personifies an anatomy in himself; and an anatomy of his world lies also bewilderingly engraved in the 'interminable Cretan labyrinth' (32) of his chessboard tattoo, a copy of which Ishmael watches him transferring to his coffin and surmises must be 'a mystical treatise on the art of attaining truth' (399).

Detail of this order abounds in *Moby-Dick*, link following link. Where Ahab's is the great Promethean would-be penetrative intelligence, Ishmael's is the more speculative, pondering each object, teasing other worlds of meanings from within the outward form. Two such details are the mat-weaving, which Melville artfully turns into a larger metaphor of the interaction of Free Will, Chance and Necessity in the shaping of human affairs (Ch. 47) and 'The Monkey-Rope' (Ch. 72), which refers at once to literal whaling procedure (the slicing off of the blubber) and to the 'Siamese ligature' (271) which 'metaphysically' (271) binds all men together. Ship, crew, or white whale itself, and be the organizing viewpoint Ahab's or Ishmael's, each world-object Melville thus daringly metamorphizes from fact into fiction, sign into signal.[17]

One representative shorter 'anatomy', however, must do service for the others, 'The Spirit Spout' (Ch. 51). It was, as we know from Melville's letters, a chapter which caught the fancy of Sophia Hawthorne and in which she sharp-sightedly discerned the larger design of *Moby-Dick*.[18] In 'The Spirit Spout' Melville ostensibly addresses himself to 'a silvery jet' (199) which seems to rise from the sea, as quickly disappear, and to linger in each sailor's mind as seen the once but never twice. The spout, indeed, as Melville says, gives the impression of being both an actual phenomenon and a 'flitting apparition' (201). For Ahab it betokens his quest and for the *Pequod*'s crew both the 'real' object of their vocation and each man's projection of his destiny. Thus real yet imagined, the spout usefully exemplifies most of the book's 'anatomies', an instance of the whale's (and the world's) literal particulars or body yet equally of a corresponding other, more immanent, signification. It also underlines once again that the *Pequod*'s 'whaling voyage' (16) at every turn equivocates between the literal whaling-world and the 'wonder-world' (16) first mentioned in 'Loomings'. Whether the focus, chapter upon chapter, is the whale's skin, brow, mouth, face, ambergris, spermaceti, genitalia *et al*, Melville renders each of this accumulating stock of 'anatomies' as purposefully double as the spirit-spout.

Given, then, the self-acknowledging 'mighty theme' (379) of *Moby-Dick* as a whole, we can extend no small sympathy to Ishmael when he confesses his inadequacy to the task of deciphering in entirety the whale. In Chapter 55, 'Of the Monstrous Pictures of Whales', he says warningly:

> there is no earthly way of finding out precisely what the whale really looks like. And the only mode in which you can derive even a tolerable idea of his living contour, is by going a whaling yourself; but by so doing, you run no small risk of being eternally stove and sunk by him. Wherefore, it seems to me you had best not be too fastidious in your curiosity touching this Leviathan. (228)

In 'The Tail' (Ch. 86), which dilates upon the *trompe d'oeil* of whether in fact the whale does have a tail, he expresses himself almost exasperatedly, asking sympathy (and company) in the risky, unending business of 'dissecting' or 'anatomizing' the whale/world's Leviathanic detail: 'Dissect him how I may . . . I go but skin deep; I know him not, and never will' (318). As Melville's 'simple sailor' (14) yet also his surrogate 'masthead' (Ch. 35) philosopher of Truth, Ishmael could hardly say otherwise; similarly Melville himself in his Letters and Journals just as repeatedly confesses himself defeated in uncoiling Truth from falsity, each centre from its circumference.[19] However custodially Ishmael acts in narrating *Moby-Dick*'s 'anatomies' and 'dissections', whether in the form of his own emotions presumably recollected in tranquillity, or Ahab's fatal solipsism that he alone can 'strike through' to total unmasked Truth, or the triple and mutually modulating perceptions of the *Pequod*'s Mates, or Queequeg's arcanely 'tattooed' (29) and 'corkscrew' (143) interpretings of the whale-world, or Fedallah's dark, cabalized Zoroastrianism, or the world as seen turned upside down in Pip's holy dementia (a vision in which 'looking' and 'seeing' have truly come unstuck), no one dissection does the book permit as remotely all-encompassing or final. Precisely that is acknowledged, too, in 'The Battering-Ram' (Ch. 76), in which the whale's forehead is likened to 'a dead, blind wall' (286), a wall to recall that which closes round Pierre Glendinning in The Tombs and around Melville's fellow scrivener Bartleby. Behind that wall—the whale's, the world's, reality's—hidden and only glimpsed through occasional cracks and apertures lies (perhaps) Truth. The chapter, among several other things, underscores Melville's own frustrations as an inscribed Truth-seeker in the following:

> For unless you own the whale, you are but a provincial and sentimentalist in Truth. But clear Truth is a thing for sala-mander giants to encounter; how small the chances for pro-vincials then? (285–86)

On this standard, Melville's own, his Truth-seeking (and finding) unsurprisingly falls short of success, even given *Moby-Dick*'s scale of canvas; but for his admiring reader success lies elsewhere—in the unflagging, heroic persistence of his anat-omizing—an achievement which wholly complements his 'polar' whale-book's other, and generally better-recognized, adventureliness.

NOTES

1. Merrell R. Davis and William H. Gilman (eds.), *The Letters of Herman Melville* (New Haven: Yale University Press, 1960), p. 138.
2. Evert Duyckinck, 'Melville's *Moby-Dick*; or The Whale', *The Literary World* (two notices), 15 November and 22 November 1851.
3. *Letters* (op. cit.), Melville to Sophia Hawthorne, 8 January 1852, p. 146.
4. *Letters* (op. cit.), Melville to Hawthorne, 29 June 1851, p. 133, and 17? November 1851, p. 142.
5. See, in turn: Raymond Weaver, *Herman Melville, Mariner and Mystic* (New York: George H. Doran Company, 1921); D. H. Lawrence, *Studies in Classic American Literature* (New York: T. Seltzer, 1923); John Freeman, *Herman Melville* (London: Macmillan and Co., English Men of Letters Series, 1926); and Lewis Mumford, *Herman Melville: A Study of his Life and Vision* (New York: Harcourt, Brace and Company, 1929).
6. These, and all subsequent quotations, are from the Norton Critical Edition of *Moby-Dick* (New York: W. W. Norton & Co., 1967), ed. Harrison Hayford and Hershel Parker, pending issue of the definitive Newberry-Northwestern edition. The 'drama done' is taken from the opening sentence of the Epilogue, p. 470. All other page references are to the Norton edition.
7. 'Hawthorne and his Mosses' first appeared in *The Literary World*, August 17 and 24 1850.
8. I have tried to establish this dimension of Melville's writing elsewhere. See '"Varnishing the Facts": *Typee* and the Art of Melville's Early Fiction', *Durham University Journal*, Vol. LXXII, June 1980, pp. 203–9.
9. *Letters* (op. cit.), Melville to Lemuel Shaw, 6 October 1849, p. 91.
10. *The Confidence-Man*, Chapter XIV.

11. 'Hawthorne and his Mosses', (op. cit.).
12. *Letters* (op. cit.), Melville to Hawthorne, 29 June 1851, p. 133.
13. Viola Sachs, *The Game of Creation* (Paris: Editions de la Maison des Sciences de l'homme, 1982), p. 1.
14. *Letters* (op. cit.), Melville to Evert Duyckinck, 3 March 1849, p. 79.
15. I do not wish to open up again here the scholarly issue of how Melville in fact went about the different draftings of *Moby-Dick*. That has been admirably dealt with by Harrison Hayford in his 'Unnecessary Duplicates: A Key to the Writing of *Moby-Dick*' in Faith Pullin (ed.) *New Perspectives on Melville* (Edinburgh University Press, 1978), pp. 128–61.
16. This observation parallels exactly Melville's slightly later definition of whaling itself: 'One way and another, it has begotten events so remarkable in themselves, and so continuously momentous in their sequential issues, that whaling may well be regarded as that Egyptian mother, who bore offspring themselves pregnant from her womb. It would be a hopeless, endless task to catalogue all these things' (99). The reference to the Nut-Isis-Osiris Egyptian fertility deities is well-enough known; but the point to be stressed in this context is that both whalermen and whaling are seen as complementary energies, the one defining the other, the other eluding definition.
17. These I have dealt with at length—and I apologize if there is some slight overlap—in '*Moby-Dick*: The Tale And The Telling', *New Perspectives on Melville* (op. cit.), pp. 86–127.
18. *Letters* (op. cit.), Melville to Sophia Hawthorne, 8 January 1852, p. 146.
19. Typically Melville ends the first part of his 'Hawthorne and his Mosses' (op. cit.), with a description of Hawthorne as 'a seeker, not a finder yet', a comment to match Hawthorne's own better-known account of Melville in his *Journal* for November 1856, as a man who 'can neither believe, nor be comfortable in his unbelief'.

5

'Grown in America': *Moby-Dick* and Melville's Sense of Control

by ERIC MOTTRAM

1

In his study of Freud, Bruno Bettelheim uses distinctions between *Naturwissenschaften*, natural sciences, and *Geisteswissenschaften*, sciences of the spirit or the soul, in both method and content, which might well have appealed to Melville. The former are situated in the requirements of general laws, made through experimental replication and mathematical analysis, and thereby permitting prediction. The latter 'seek to understand the objects of their study not as instances of universal laws but as singular events', events which, as in human history, 'never recur in the same form' and 'can be neither replicated nor predicted'.[1] The texts of the American Renaissance dramatize the imbalances and explorations set in motion when a culture self-consciously desires both to inherit laws and to project the individual on an open road. Melville's heroes launch themselves towards absolutes or find themselves encountering plurals and relatives—Pierre's 'ambiguities'—and struggle to recover. But these routes of law and non-recurring events, symbols in systems and objects in individuality, are never to be experienced abstractly: they control plots as they control policies in society. Richard Slotkin shows *Moby-Dick* inheriting the hunter myth, gathering its American forms from the previous two centuries, reported through the Ishmael figure as he encounters the exemplary extreme case. This sailor's self-release from and involuntary return to the Tahiti of 'peace and joy', a possible society on a variety of islands or near islands, is an escape from the hunt. His captain's urge is a grim route into total enclosure, a hunt for the singular and absolute, uncaring that it is a form of cannibalism, since both whales and hunters are events in an ecology they violate.[2] As James Thurber reports Harold Ross, the editor of the *New Yorker* magazine, asking his distinguished staff on one memorable occasion, 'Is Moby Dick the whale or the man?'[3]

But within these extensions and developments of controlling, mythical behaviour exist immediately socio-political issues: what should be done with the inheritance of law and of the dominance-submission organization of previous societies, in a culture which had to pride itself on being an official demonstration of egalitarian democracy. In William V. Spanos's terms, *Moby-Dick* is 'an interrogation of the traditional representational structure that the American artist, despite his insistent effort to break with the *Logos* of the Old World, re-inscribes into the uncanny formlessness of his re-newed occasion'.[4] Therefore, Ishmael is steadily rendered uncertain of his bearings in a world previously announced to be a system laid out as a total order, not so much for discovery or uncovering as for a walk in a legitimized artifice. Is the White Whale 'agent' or 'principle', asks Ishmael throughout the text of his narrative. In terms of a nearer and less metaphysical urgency, *Moby-Dick* constructs a plot for the transformations of labour and identity within a capitalist industrial democracy into old games which have returned to challenge nineteenth-century America will to progress away from obsessions with hierarchy associated with 'Our Old Home', Europe. These are games of victory through conquest, hunt and eliminatory triumph. Melville understood those representative men of power who haunted Carlyle and Emerson, and their inheritors, notably displayed as the embodiments of 'heroic vitalism' by Eric Bentley in 1944,[5] men existing through permission to dominate and command allegiance from some de-historicized charisma.

The scene is triple—the whaling industry which dominantly

supplied energy to America until the early 1870s, the American struggles between self-reliance and community, and the Protestant inheritance of a supposedly heretical, Manichean polarization of the Cosmos into equal power for Good and Evil. But Melville also plots in those governing nineteenth-century descriptions of the world which urged towards epic over-all accounts of total continuity, interrogated increasingly as the century wore on, to the point of pluralism and relativity. *Moby-Dick* barely resists the need to believe all is connected and to penetrate surface multiplicity to detect interior singularity— desires which continue to penetrate America both in the state's imperialism and in the fiction of ambivalent epic paranoia— Thomas Pynchon's *Gravity's Rainbow* as primary example of that mania Samuel R. Delany identifies in his *Dahlgren*: 'the over-determined human mind would rather have everything relevant, even if the relevance is simple-minded.'[6] To which his hero, Kid, responds:

> I used to have a friend who'd say: 'When you're paranoid, everything makes sense'. But that's not quite it. It's that all sorts of things you know *don't* relate suddenly have the air of things that *do*. Everything you look at seems just an inch away from its place in a perfectly clear pattern. . . . Only you *never* know *which* inch to move it.

Emerson put it this way: 'Nature will be reported. All things are engaged in writing their history. . . . The air is full of sounds; the sky, tokens; the ground is all memoranda and signatures; and every object covered with hints, which speak to the intelligent.'

In the chapter called 'The Tail', Ishmael discourses on the impossibility of knowing the whale's tail totally, beyond human perception. It has 'five great motions' but they have to be interpreted through perception, which includes chances of language, ability and mood. In 'The Mat-Maker', the enclosure of all the episodes in the fiction, and its extension into the universe, are given as a system of warp and woof related to necessity and free will, with Queequeg's Polynesian sword slapping the mat with chance. Ahab's desire is a discontent obsessed by a need to know and penetrate the tail, to be absolute in his attack on it as a sign of the absolute—

except that any object assumed to be such a sign would serve his purpose. His delusion is related in 'Hawthorne and his Mosses' (1850) to Shakespearian figures whose 'mystical blackness' penetrates to an interior of things—in turn related to Hawthorne's own 'black conceit': 'Through the mouths of the dark characters of Hamlet, Timon, Lear, and Iago, he craftily says, or sometimes insinuates, the things which we feel to be so terrifically true that it were all but madness for any good man, in his own proper character, to utter, or even hint of them. Tormented into desperation, Lear the frantic king tears off the mask, and speaks the sane madness of vital truth.'[7]

But such absolutist, mad desire is countered by writings— about the tail, for instance—which seek dis-covery in the sense of dis-closure of what can be perceived to be there. In his 1962 poem 'A Later Note on Maximus Letter No. 15', Charles Olson, one of the earliest and finest discoverers of Melville for America,[8] provides a skeleton key to open experience. He speaks of a concept of history according to Herodotus:

> a verb, to find out for yourself:
>
> 'istorin, which makes any one's acts a finding out for him or her self, in other words restores the traum: that we act somewhere
>
> at least by seizure, that the objective (example Thucidides, or the latest finest tape-recorder, or any form of record on the spot
>
> as against what we know went on, the dream: the dream being self-action with Whitehead's corollary: that no event
>
> is not penetrated, in interaction or collision with, an eternal event[9]

Truth is an investigative enaction—as *Moby-Dick* is—through document and discovering perception. Whitehead presents 'the actual entity, in virtue of being *what* it is, [being] also where it is. It is somewhere because it is some actual thing within its correlated actual world.'[10] Or, as Buckminster Fuller puts it: 'I live on Earth at present,/ and I don't know what I am./ I know that I am not a category./ I am not a thing—a noun./ I seem to be a verb,/ an evolutionary process—/ an integral function of the universe.'[11] Thinking of 'big patterns', he combines them with evolution, not absolute stasis, and resultant paranoia. Process is delivered through what Olson read in Melville—'poetic thinking', that perception of necessity, free will and chance operating as open-ended perception:

> The most poetical experiences of my life have been those moments of conceptual comprehension of a few of the extraordinary generalized principles and their complex interactions that are apparently employed in the governance of universal evolution.

An event is a living thing within process of nature and human nature. Total expression of the whale's tail is discovered to be impossible—language and perception are limited: 'I know him not and never will.' Even a limited account may depend on mood. Making a mat, 'with my own hand I ply my own shuttle and weave my own destiny into these unalterable threads', while Queequeg's 'impulsive, indifferent sword' strikes the woof in a variety of ways and finally 'shapes and fashions both warp and woof' as chance. The weave is the product of 'chance, free will, and necessity—no wise compatible—all interweavingly working together'. The tail itself is a triune structure of fibres in strata, and this is its source of power. Indeed, the whole bulk of the leviathan is knit over with a warp and woof of muscular fibres and filaments. The narrator may try to compare it with other objects but it resists being made into a symbol. It is itself, its own power in process. As Zukofsky writes of a creature as small as the whale is gigantic—the mantis: 'The ungainliness/ of the creature needs stating', but 'the facts are not a symbol.' The issue is: 'The actual twisting/ Of many and diverse thoughts/ What form does *that* take?'[12]

In 'The Grand Armada' the whale's breeding 'indifferently at all seasons' is a fact of non-symbolic independence. Ishmael can write of it through 'chance comparison' but never reach a 'completed fabric'. The tail's mobility may be observed, even tabulated as five motions, but it is not a tyrannized object in a coded world whose signs are conceived as readable from a known system—as if, Ishmael writes, all men were Free

Masons with their 'signs and symbols'. The whale remains 'full of strangeness, and unaccountable to his most experienced assailant. Dissect him how I may, then, I but go skin deep.' Something of how this knowledge saves Ishmael from Ahab's fate can be reinforced from a letter to Hawthorne in 1851:

> If any of those Powers choose to withhold certain secrets, let them; that does not impair my sovereignty in myself; that does not make me tributary. And perhaps, after all, there is *no* secret. We incline to think that the Problem of the Universe is like the Freemason's mighty secret, so terrible to all children. It turns out, at last, to consist in a triangle, a mallet, and an apron,— nothing more! We incline to think that God cannot explain His own secrets, and that He would like a little information upon certain points Himself. We mortals astonish Him as much as He us.[13]

The end of 'The Tail' in fact parodies God in Exodus xxxiii.23: 'I will take away mine hand, and thou shalt see my back parts; but my face shall not be seen.'[14] Melville, in writing, 'I cannot completely make out his back parts; and hint what he will about his face, I say again he has no face', undermines the totalitarianism of the Bible. This is why he wrote to Hawthorne, again in 1851, that he felt 'secure' and 'spotless as the lamb' in having written 'a wicked book'.[15]

Ishmael survives. Ahab drowns roped to his own illusion, a symbolic albino whale. But the *Pequod's* captain is not unique; his career is characteristic of the Christian exploitive West. He believes he knows what Nature is and that his duty is to conquer it. The colourless whale has to be covered in conceptual language, to be given a human name (in parody of Adam's alleged naming of his initial world), and then identified as the Problem. As Ishmael writes in 'Moby Dick': Ahab 'piled upon the whale's white hump the sum of all the general rage and hate felt by his whole race from Adam down; and then, as if his chest had been a mortar, he burst his hot heart's shell upon it.' A main cause of human violence against human and other species, according to Wilhelm Reich, is pent-up orgasmic energy, which needs to burst for relief. So Melville's image from weaponry may well have considerable depth of accuracy. An origin of warfare lies within the race of Adam itself, part of that 'wild vindictiveness', 'frantic morbidness' and identification of the whale with human 'bodily woes' and 'intellectual and spiritual exasperations'. Under illusion, the whale becomes 'the monomaniac incarnation of all those malicious agencies which some men feel eating in them, till they are left living on with half a heart and half a lung'. In addition, 'one half of the world' is malignant for 'modern Christians', and monomaniac aggression is a result—and certainly the *Pequod*'s crew, including Ishmael, follow their leader. Together they instance the Christian Western majority and its leaders: 'mongrel renegades, and castaways, and cannibals—morally enfeebled also, by the incompetence of mere unaided virtue or right-mindedness in Starbuck, the invulnerable jollity of indifference and recklessness in Stubb, and the pervading mediocrity in Flask'.

As Ishmael has no total expression of the tail, nor has he an explanation for Ahab and the crew's 'abandonment' to this 'evil magic [in] their souls'. The colourless beast has been coloured and symbolized—as 'The Whiteness of the Whale' makes explicit—by 'mystical cosmetic'. Everything must be a sign in a conquest system under human unease. Ahab's power is that he can persuade other men that he can direct their urge to read the sign and kill the threat of the non-human. He can rely on 'dread' in the human as it confronts whiteness and the nonhuman. 'I'd strike the sun if it insulted me', Ahab exclaims ('The Quarter-Deck')—assuming he could reach the sun as a later generation would reach the moon and elsewhere in 'Space' which used to be called Cosmos. The sign surface is to the *Pequod* mind a 'pasteboard mask' over a reality which must be conquered in assumed understanding. In fact, understanding the Enemy may well stand in the way of victory. In Ahab's cabin ('The Chart'), the charts, covered with 'lines and shadings [of] courses over spaces that before were blank'—as colourless as the whale—are one with the wrinkle lines on the leader's forehead, the tokens, memoranda and signatures Emerson thought he saw everywhere. To adapt Blake's damnation, he has become what he beholds.[16] Puzzling over chart signs parallels his confrontation, in 'The Sphinx', with the 'black and hooded head' of a sperm whale as if it were oracular for 'the secret thing that is in thee'. Melville's characteristic imagery of diving in the unfathomable, of endless stairs in Piranesian prisons, spirals, circles, bottomless foundations, reappears to reinforce Ahab's insane Prometheanism:

> Of all divers, thou hast dived the deepest. That head upon which the upper sun now gleams, has moved amid this world's foundations . . . Thou hast been where bell nor diver never went; hast slept by many a sailor's side, where sleepless mothers would give their lives to lay them down. . . . Would now St. Paul would come along that way, and to my breezeless-ness bring his breeze! O Nature, and O soul of man! how far beyond all utterance are your linked analogies! not the smallest atom stirs or lives in matter, but has its cunning duplicate in mind.

Ahab may admit that language can never express the system of analogies, but he recalls the wayside revelation of Paul that broke through the mask to interior meaning. Besides, cross-examining for the secret which will confer power is profoundly part of the Oedipal scene—as if there were always a fixed eternal parental figure who can be found to yield up its force. In this chapter, the Sphinx even replaces the mother by the sailor's side, the origin which will not release offspring into an open life. In 'The Castaway', the black cabin-boy Pip will be forced to dive into mad contact with 'wondrous depths', 'the unwarped primal world', 'the loom' where God weaves—and return with 'the sane madness of vital truth', or what is taken to be such by Ahab, who treats him partly as Lear treats his Fool, before his own madness gives him hallucinations of truth. This encounter is the turning-point of Ahab's career ('The Log and Line'), but it is possible that Olson and others after him connect it too closely to Shakespeare's play—Olson goes so far as to speak of 'Ahab speaking Lear's phrases'.[17]

Melville acknowledges his own fascination with the power of secrets and answers in an 1849 letter to Evert A. Duyckinck and proposes that wisdom itself is diving—a kind of obsessed prospecting in a universal archaeological site. Once gain it is clear that Ahab is representative, and therefore followed:

> Now, there is something about every man elevated above mediocrity, which is, for the most part, instinctuly (sic) per-ceptible. This I see in Mr. Emerson. And, frankly, for the sake of the argument, let us call him a fool;—then I had rather be a fool than a wise man.—I love all men who dive. Any fish can

swim near the surface, but it takes a great whale to go down stairs five miles or more; & if he don't attain the bottom, why, all the lead in Galena [an Illinois lead mine] can't fashion the plummet that will. I'm not talking of Mr. Emerson now—but of the whole corps of thought-divers, that have been diving & coming up again with bloodshot eyes since the world began.[18]

But manic divers need another kind of activity to thought. In common with many crazed leaders, in Shakespeare and in history, Ahab is lured into the false securities of superstition, masquerading as wisdom or pseudo-depth archaeology quite as much as any of the Confidence-Man's avatars. He keeps a pet priest like any cultist, although it is noticeable in 'The Whale Watch' that when the Parsee prophesies to him that 'neither hearse nor coffin can be thine', that before death he has to see one hearse 'not made by mortal hand' and one whose 'visible wood . . . must be grown in America', Ahab uses the cult system to boost his confidence: 'I am immortal then, on land and on sea.' Mansfield and Vincent rightly parallel superstitious instances in *Macbeth*, Rabelais and Scott. Ahab's kind of power depends precisely on a supportive weave of signs. Priests are mere security agents for rulers who reject principle and process for a structuralism of signatures. There can be no chance for Hitler or Aleister Crowley.

Ishmael, the ambivalent survivor of the *Pequod*, and composer of the ambiguous narrative, full of gaps, survives on one of those coffins, made by Queequeg, wielder of the sword of chance—and buoyed up on a black bubble generated by the sinking whale-ship. What we read, then, is in part how Melville found it impossible entirely to relinquish his Calvinist training to biblical vision of the universe as symbolic agency, even if he names his survivor, his outsider, from Genesis as 'a wild man; and every man's hand against him'. He knew that the diabolism of *Moby-Dick* included its implicit refusal of closed totality, that chance profoundly involved the wild, the non-Christian, a possible cannibal, a black man with whom Ishmael sleeps in at least the positions of erotic love ('The Counterpane'): 'you had almost thought I had been his wife', clasped in 'his bridegroom grasp'. The Polynesian is tattooed with 'an interminable Cretan labyrinth of a figure, no two

parts of which were of one precise shade'. The patchwork quilt
so blends with his body that 'it was only by the sense of weight
and pressure that [Ishmael] could tell that Queequeg was
hugging him.' If the harpooner is a minotaur, he is friendly
and needs no sacrifice of maidens and youths. He has a home
on an island, but it is a Tahiti and no tyrannical Crete.

But such is the form of brotherhood required for Ishmael's
release from the Ahab magic evil, and it recurs in a less
sensual, more sensuous form in the counter-power of 'A
Squeeze of the Hand', which immediately follows, and counters,
Stubbs' abandonment of Pip to the loom of madness in mid-
Pacific. It is through the sperm of the whale, 'so dearly purchased', that Ishmael squeezes his 'co-labourers' hands' in
'abounding, affectionate, friendly, loving feeling'. In his later
family life, he dreams of paradise as angels with the hands in
jars of spermacetti. The 'dark pelt' of the whale's penis
becomes an erotic mockery of the church hierarchy's 'full
canonicals' (Mansfield and Vincent tell us that 'archbishoprick'
was Melville's deliberate 'apparently archaic spelling' to
reinforce his phallic pun).[19] Ahab, too, has a wife and small
boy, which he briefly remembers but whom he will never see
again. Such leaders need no family and no heirs.

Ishmael actively sustains the power enclosure—as Olson
observes, 'like the Catskill eagle, Ishmael is able to dive down
into the blackest gorges and soar out to the light again' (he is
referring to the end of 'The Try-Works').[20] He is not a 'passive
and detached observer' with a 'chorus' function, a fiction by
which Melville can create Ahab's 'privative' world of 'blasphemies and black magic', and yet emerge from 'the struggle
and catharsis', like Melville from his book, 'spotless as the
lamb'.[21] On the contrary, he is participant from the first page
of 'Loomings', making decisions as well as responding to
situations and discovering them. One kind of possible Ishmael-
Melville identification in escape from dominance appears in
the *Journal of a Voyage from New York to London*, where, with his
fellow passengers sea-sick in the state-rooms, Melville writes
'& I alone am left to tell the tale of their misery'—a mild joke
which, however, draws in, for us, both the Book of Job and the
Epilogue to *Moby-Dick*.[23] But Ishmael's function is far more
significant than mere survivalism. It is he who hears Father

Mapple out, who sees and understands Bulkington, and who learns something of Ahab's privacies from Elijah ('The Prophet')—his 'deadly skirmish with the Spaniard before the altar in Santa. . . . the silver calabash he spat in . . . losing his leg last voyage, according to the prophecy'. (It is best to recall that Elijah worshipped Jehovah and Ahab's wife worshipped Baal.) Ishmael reports Pip's solitary insights, experiences the spermy squeezings, and lives a various life, with a richly combinative mind, which can take up Ahab inside its own processes of discovery. It is he who states Ahab's 'fatal' pride and who falls asleep gazing into the try-works while on duty at the helm, a highly active resource in the circumstances! Unfitted even for a steering control, he loses sight of the compass as he gazes into the fire, and hallucinates that the tiller is inverted and he steers with his back to the prow ('The Try-Works'). The 'artificial fire' of the whale industry exposes the ship in the image of another artifice of totality, the Christians' Hell:

> . . . the rushing Pequod, freighted with savages, and laden with fire, and burning a corpse, and plunging into that blackness of darkness, seemed the material counterpart of the monomaniac commander's soul. . . .

So Ishmael observes how the Carlylean captain of industry controls the latent diabolism of a nineteenth-century hunt for sources of energy—not only whale oil but the whale as any part of nature which has to be used to keep man elevated. Ishmael relies on the morning sun to dispel artificial fire with its 'only true lamp', but knows that it cannot conceal the fact of swamps and barrens, 'all the millions of miles of deserts and of griefs beneath the moon . . . [nor] the ocean, which is the dark side of this earth, and which is two thirds of this earth'. When Ecclesiastes says 'all is vanity', he means 'ALL'— Melville's capitalization. Such is Melville's own fictional context for his sense of Hawthorne's fictions (and it is certainly well distributed throughout 'The Encantadas'). He recalls the artificial, allegorical fire of 'Earth's Holocaust' which consumes 'all vanities and empty theories and forms', but also 'the hither side of Hawthorne's soul, the other side—like the half of the physical sphere . . . shrouded in a blackness, ten times black'.

Ishmael suspects the man 'who hath more of joy than sorrow in him'; Melville writes of Hawthorne's 'ever-moving dawn that forever advances through [his darkness], and circumnavigates his world', but never dispels the vestiges of Innate Depravity and Original Sin which, in his writings, take the form of a 'black conceit', 'the blackness of darkness' beyond his 'bright gildings'.

In *Moby-Dick* the manic human embodiment of blackness is a white Quaker, a scion of America's major energy industry. He demands and commands obedience. As the Romantics' nineteenth-century heroic Great Man, he exudes natural dominance. In 'The Specksynder', he exacts homage of 'instantaneous obedience' but uses rule or 'private ends'. The sea-captain's legitimate rights of command within ship's hierarchy yield to 'that certain sultanism of his brain . . . incarnate in an irresistible dictatorship'. Ishmael's criticism of this representative man is unequivocal:

> For be a man's intellectual superiority what it will, it can never assume the practical, available supremacy over other men, without the aid of some sort of external arts, and entrenchments, always in themselves, more or less paltry and base.

Ishmael contrasts an alternative leadership—Melville being no egalitarian anarchist. 'True princes' need no such 'external arts' through which the false princes achieve power 'through their infinite inferiority to the choice hidden handful of the Divine Inert'. Both kinds are, nevertheless, superior to 'the dead level of the mass'. Mansfield and Vincent show Melville mediating these beliefs through a passage from Goethe's *Dichtung und Wahrheit* (1811–31) which Emerson had used in his lecture on 'Human Life' in 1839–40:

> . . . the most fearful manifestation of the Demoniacal, is when it is seen predominating in some individual character. . . . it is seldom that they recommend themselves to our affections by goodness of heart; a tremendous energy seems to be seated in them, and they exercise a wonderful power over all creatures, and even over the elements. All the moral powers combined are of no avail against them; in vain does the more enlightened portion of mankind attempt to throw suspicion upon them as deceived if not deceivers—the mass is still drawn on by them.

101

Seldom if ever do the great men of an age find their equal among their contemporaries, and they are to be overcome by nothing but the universe itself.[25]

If by 'universe' we may read unfathomable process, including the whale, it is the more understandable why Melville checked a passage in the 1673 works of Sir William Davenant[26] which reads like a summary of *Moby-Dick*: '. . . for God ordain'd not huge Empire as proportionable to the Bodies, but to the Mindes of Men; and the Mindes of Men are more monstrous, and require more space for agitation and the hunting of others, than the Bodies of Whales.' From *Moby-Dick* may be construed a nineteenth-century text which speculates on how the modern dictator emerges from the eighteenth century's benevolent dictator and the élitist members of the Founding Fathers of 1776, as the West, and in particular the United States, moved towards high finance industrial capitalism under centralized controls. The new leader, proposed as a 'true prince', like the harpooner in the whale-boat, or the creative sensibility, in a state of calm at the moment of action, faces the dictator's will—in Olson's terms: 'the whale itself's swiftness, Ahab's inordinate will, and the harpooneer's ability to strike from calm only. *The inertial structure of the world is a real thing which not only exerts effects upon matter but in turn suffers such effects.*'[27]

2

When Ishmael describes Ahab as 'of greatly superior force', the text takes up the American Renaissance obsession with the imbalances of democratic control. Control moves towards vortex—the sinking of the *Pequod*, the secessional war of 1860, the emergence of Carnegie, Rockefeller and Pierpont Morgan, for example—instances of the visibility manifested by 'the subterranean river of untapped, ferocious, lonely and romantic desires, that concentration of ecstasy and violence which is the dream life of the nation'.[28] When the image of the leader first appears in Freud's writings, in *Totem and Taboo* (1913), his 'first qualification . . . is that he remain uninvolved with those he leads, and at the same time destroy his followers' wills to remain separate.' In his study of Freud, Philip Rieff continues:

102

'It is possible that the liberal interregnum has ended and another age has begun: the age of the hypnotic persecuting father', in which

> 'I love Big Brother' is the perfected slogan of erotic submission. . . . If Freud seems to discern in all politics a certain quality of madness, it is appropriate to recall that he considered the state of being in love not only like being hypnotized but as 'the normal prototype of the psychoses'. . . . 'The credulity of love' becomes, in Freud's extreme and hostile view, 'the most fundamental source of authority'.[29]

Moby-Dick is explicit: nothing can break the absolute manic enclosure under human hierarchy except a counter-control from the involuntary or inert in nature—Goethe's 'universe itself', without manipulative symbolism under false allegiance. The magic ceremony of loyalty enforcement in 'The Quarter-Deck' seals in that allegiance with a potion—as strong as Brangäne's—an intersection of industrial weapons into an axis which the leader vibrates, and a hypnotic eye contact between leader and followers which takes in superstitions of eye control, mesmerism and gaze management from the history of power. The liquid 'spiralizes' into the men. The circle of crew around Ahab's hand on the harpoon axis extends to the circles around Pip's descending head and the circles radiating from the vortical sinking of the *Pequod*, a vessel which sets sail on Christmas Day and is named after the first Indian people to be exterminated by white colonialists. These circles cover 'the dark side of this earth', radiate from the whale in its vortex, descending with the head man, 'overcome by nothing but the universe itself', who believed Moby Dick to be singular malevolence within and embodying that universe. In that context, democracy is not a counter-system of electoral controls but an emotional solidarity of heart and sex, extended to an angelic paradise of bottled sperm. It is hardly hopeful. The rest is anarchic heart individualism against the head, Innate Depravity and the 'heroic vitalist' re-write of history as the lives of Great Men.

Ahab's legitimate control under law shifts to authoritarian demand, and then confronts another mythical force in the plots of power—the triangulation of Prometheus, Zeus and the vulture or eagle, a triune which attracted nineteenth-century writers as if it were their own invention (Marx, Shelley and Mary Shelley notably). The theft of force or fire or sperm must seal confidence in the leader's fallibility. Ahab's confidence—and he is a prior avatar of the Confidence-Man whose multiple career undermines the *Fidèle* in 1857—extends to becoming a transmitter of cosmic electricity between sky and ocean ('The Candles'). But the theft proves a sterile gesture, almost a joke in its parody of the promethean fire-stealer. The monomaniac is not an artist. He puts his linguistic skills into the art of persuasion and his religiosity into elaborate ritual and the fire-cult of Zoroaster. When man aspires to godhead in the West, he is damned whether he has chosen that course or not. 'Growing up to Godhead' (*Paradise Lost*, Book 9) is, since Eden, a passage towards a villainy which continually edges into the melodramatic and therefore the ludicrous, as well as the lethal. Total depravity within the destructiveness of Claggart and other masters-at-arms, the sea lawyers, in Melville's texts moves towards that comic villainy Lawrence Olivier detected in Richard III. That the occasion is in fact still deadly can be sharpened through the image of the Covering Cherub which, in Blake's *Milton*, 'advances from the East'—as the 'man in cream-colours' does at the outset of *The Confidence-Man*—a self-seeking, manic selfhood, which takes form as an urge to total control. The Covering Cherub is Control, and as Shakespeare allows his exponent of *Realpolitik*, Claudius, to aver: 'Madness in great ones must not unwatched go.' Ishmael's report on Ahab is accurate: 'all my means are sane, my motive and my object mad' ('Moby Dick').

Freud recognizes, as Thomas Mann does in 'Mario the Magician' and Orwell in *Nineteen Eighty-Four*, that extreme allegiance has a distinct erotic element. Starbuck, first mate, recognizes its force:

> My soul is more than matched; she's overmanned; and by a madman! . . . he drilled deep down, and blasted all my reason out of me! I think I see his impious end; but I feel that I must help him to it. Will I, nill I, the ineffable thing has tied me to him; tows me with a cable I have no knife to cut. ('Dusk')

Such a relationship cannot be resolved through a classic dialectic between charisma and reason, between nature and law. Nor can Jack Chase's leadership in *White-Jacket*, or even less, the control exerted by Mad Jack. The latter, a lieutenant on the *Neversink*, gives obeyed orders which countermand those of Captain Claret, and saves the ship. He is skilled, 'loved all round', and exhibits 'natural heroism, talent, judgement, and integrity, that is denied to mediocrity' (Ch. 27). Claret and Cuticle Cadwallader are grotesques of naval law, not of false charisma—parodies of Carlyle's notion in Lecture Six in *On Heroes and Hero-Worship and the Heroic in History* (1841): 'in all human Authorities, and relations that men god-created can form among each other, there is verily either a Divine Right or a Diabolical Wrong.' The final serious form appears in *Billy Budd, Sailor*, plotted through a triangulation of human law, innate depravity and god-like innocence, within which captain and master-at-arms encounter an allegiance in the charismatic lower-deck leader whose innocence precipitates a treason charge. Budd instances Carlyle's 'child-man' whose 'child-like greatness [is] simple, open as a child, yet with the depth and strength of a man'—'a sort of upright barbarian'. Budd's inarticulateness, his lack of Ahab's linguistic persuasiveness, kills him. As Carlyle writes: 'There is no act more moral between men than that of rule and obedience. Woe to him that claims obedience when it is not due; woe to him that refuses it when it is.' After examining a collection of parameters of this field in *The Naked and the Dead* (1948), Norman Mailer, the American writer who so closely inherits both Carlyle's and Melville's need to interrogate hero and leader practices, perceives, in *The Deer Park* (1955), a further apposite myth within the grim series:

> For beyond, in the far beyond, was the heresy that God was the Devil and the One they called the Devil was God-in-banishment like a noble prince deprived of true Heaven, and God who was the Devil had conquered except for the few who saw the cheat that God was not God at all.[30]

Within Melville's studies in control, there lies, as in those of Brockden Brown, Poe and Hawthorne, such profound trans-actional ambivalences: Hawthorne's 'Young Goodman Brown' is the most salutary case in point. In all four writers, human superiority operates the Manichean polarity. Melville understands a further extension in exhibiting Ahab's control as a form of that engineering of nature which preoccupied the century, the railroad. The whale becomes 'the modern railway', and in 'Sunset' Ahab says:

> The path of my fixed purpose is laid with iron rails, whereupon my soul is grooved to run. Over unsounded gorges, through the rifled hearts of mountains, under torrents' beds, unerringly I rush! Naught's an obstacle, naught's an angle to the iron way![31]

The straight and horizontal iron way, the verticals of ocean and space, and the circles and vortex—these terms construct the imaginative armature which supports *Moby-Dick*, as if dramatizing Carlyle's 'Force, Force, everywhere Force; we ourselves a mysterious Force in the centre of that.'

If a great man is indeed 'the lightning' that 'kindles' other men, 'The Candles' dramatizes with what force. The fire-tipped tri-pointed masts are presented as 'gigantic wax tapers before an altar', before which, in turn, 'the enchanted crew' stand silent. The priest of fire bows before the gold doubloon's 'three peaks as proud as Lucifer' ('The Doubloon'), and Ahab cries out that 'the white flame but lights the way to the White Whale' (the dire human need to mythicize and conquer whiteness is detailed in 'The Whiteness of the Whale' as one primary motive for 'the fiery hunt'). He even feminizes himself as a queen who needs fertilizing by 'the clear spirit of clear fire', and lets the lightning flash through his skull: 'Light thou be, thou leapest out of darkness; but I am darkness leaping out of light, leaping out of thee.'

His harpoon, forged in Perth's fire ('The Forge'), under the surveillance of Fedallah, the Parsee, and baptized 'in nomine diaboli', now burns with 'a serpent's tongue' of flame as Ahab reminds the crew of their enchantment by oath of allegiance— 'the great man, with his free force directs out of God's own hand, is the lightning', are Carlyle's words. But 'in nomine diaboli' appeared from the first as a core of the book, on the flyleaf of that volume of Shakespeare which included *King Lear*, *Othello* and *Hamlet*, where Melville made his rough notes for *Moby-Dick*.[32] 'An aristocracy of the brain'[33] thus yields to

maniac paranoia. But superstition inhers throughout the
dramatis personae of the book. Ahab is initially mythicized
by Peleg in 'The Ship' as 'a grand, ungodly, god-like man'.
That he is named after 'a crowned king' Ishmael attempts to
scorn: 'And a vile one. When that wicked king was slain, the
dogs, did they not lick his blood?'[34] Peleg replies that Ahab
'has his humanities', in particular his family. But when Ahab
actually recalls wife and boy in 'The Symphony', immediately
preceeding the final catastrophe, it is within one of the few
moments of self-criticism in the text. He has become, he says, a
mad fool, 'cannibal old me', his own judge of his own 'doom',
the fatal totalizer confronted with the riddle of himself: 'Is it I,
God, or who, that lifts this arm? . . . turned round and round
in this world, like yonder windlass.'

Ahab's riddle, and the riddle of compulsive allegiance in
'Moby Dick', may be compared with the riddle of Jackson's
power in *Redburn*, and that sense of the unknowable nature of
control even in such precise criticism of the authoritarian as
White-Jacket. The penultimate chapter of 'The World in a
Man-of-War' is a list of refusals to extend the narrative and its
probings, while providing considerable potentialities for further
enquiry. The narrator's ecstatic love for noble Jack Chase will
be sealed in 'a carrick-bend' and a hand kiss for 'my liege lord
and captain of my top, my sea-tutor and sire'. The *Neversink*
will be stripped, but the democracy of the main-top remains to
counter a hierarchical society of authoritarian legalism:

> . . . a brother-band, hand in hand, all spliced together . . . We
> have seen our last man scourged at the gangway; our last man
> gasp out the ghost in the stifling sick-bay; our last man tossed to
> the sharks. Our last death-denouncing Article of War has been
> read. . . .

'Ever-noble Jack Chase' leads, Melville believes, on 'a never-
sinking world frigate' made and commanded by God the Lord
High Admiral. History is a long cruise under 'sealed orders'.
But inside what might appear to be a closed package lies the
unknown as incomplete to men as the tail: 'we ourselves are
the repositories of the secret packet, whose mysterious con-
tents we long to learn. There are no mysteries out of ourselves.'
Therefore, 'the smallest cabin-boy is as wise as the captain'—

and we are back with Pip and Ahab crazily conferring in 'The Cabin'. The 'domineering code of Law', the Articles of War, are necessity; the 'brother-band' is free-will; chance lies with secret 'repositories'. Timonism, the haunting depression in Melville's texts, a melancholic despair against any free potentiality in existence, is resistible, but only just.

The condition of local democracy and local noble leaders, 'true princes', is over-all hierarchy, therefore. Somewhere in the *Pequod* lives Bulkington, in whose eyes 'floated some reminiscences that did not seem to give him much joy' ('The Spouter-Inn'), who embodies the sea-desire to be away from the social, the port, the hearthstone, the island Tahiti—a figure akin to the wary and armed, and pathetic, Pitch in *The Confidence-Man*—the figure of Ishmael's belief that 'in land-lessness alone resides the highest truth, shoreless, indefinite as God' ('The Lee Shore'). Images of restlessness and indefinition rest here in open process, the eternally radiating and plunging of the potential prince. For, as a parody of 'finally', energy is a word with no denotation in conclusive form—in philosophic terms, neither *arche* nor *telos* encloses process; in Olson's terms:

> To Melville it was not the will to be free but the will to over-whelm nature that lies at the bottom of us as individuals and a people. Ahab is no democrat. Moby-Dick, antagonist, is only king of natural force, resource. . . . (Melville) had a pull to the origin of things . . . He sought prime. . . . the (whaling) industry is the scale of the total society . . . a sweated industry. . . . the Pacific is a sweatshop. Man, led, against the biggest damndest creature nature uncorks. The whale-ship as factory, the whale-boat as precision instrument. . . . It is the friendship of men which is love. . . . In that play (*Coriolanus*) the only place Melville heavily marks is the long passage in which Coriolanus and Aufidius meet and embrace. They are captains with the soldier's sense of comrade. Melville's is the seaman's, of a shipmate. . . . In the Ahab-world there is no place for 'converse with the Intelligence, Power, the Angel' [Melville's notes for Moby-Dick in the Shakespeare volume]. Ahab cannot seek it, for understood between him and Fedallah is a compact as binding as Faust's with Mephistopheles. . . . a league with evil closes the door to truth. . . . (Ahab) does not seek true converse.[35]

But the sixteenth-century Faustian contract, as Goethe well understood, especially in part two of his *Faust*, is central to the West's urge to control nature, from the Renaissance onwards. Ahab is caught up in a larger control than his own and his prometheanism, and which he only partly perceives, in his lack of converse. His industry, on whose securities his per- missions are born, is the type of that issue which Lynn White dates to the year of *Moby-Dick*'s composition:

> The emergence in widespread practice of the Baconian creed that scientific knowledge means technological power over nature can scarcely be dated before 1850, save in the chemical industries, where it is anticipated in the eighteenth century. Its acceptance as a normal pattern of action may mark the greatest event in human history since the invention of agriculture, and perhaps in nonhuman terrestrial history as well.[36]

Since, for the Christian West, man 'is not simply part of nature: he is made in God's image', and has been given Nature to control and exploit, 'the decoding of the physical symbols of God's communication with man' lead to the discovery of 'how his creative spirit operates':

> . . . modern Western science was cast in the matrix of Christian theology. The dynamism of religious devotion, shaped by the Judeo-Christian dogma of creation, gave it impetus. . . . viewed historically, modern science is an extrapolation of natural theology and . . . at least partly to be explained as an Occi- dental, voluntarist realization of the Christian dogma of man's transcendence of, and rightful mastery over, nature.

Ahab, the Quaker, inherits that Christian desire to exert violent control from cosmic permission, particularly against any object which appears uncoloured by classification, undis- coverable, unexploited, albino (Melville had witnessed the result of missionary work in the Pacific and recorded some of it in *Typee* in 1846). Moby Dick is unique and like the 'virgin' peak Everest has to be conquered 'because it is there', slaugh- terable on the altar of heroic vitalism. As Lawrence writes in the course of investigating Poe, 'to know a living thing is to kill it. . . . the desirous consciousness, the SPIRIT, is a vampire.'[37] Mad heroes of 'intuitive truth' who yield to total control desire, 'the very axis of reality' in 'Hawthorne and his Mosses', cease 'to serve the State', or the *socius*, the ship, precisely at the point the Ahab figure dramatizes. A contrasted disobedience is offered in Thoreau's 'Civil Disobedience' (1849), but the sheer ambivalence of submission and subversion is the core of that duplicity Lawrence recognized in nineteenth-century American texts—and Lawrence himself inherited Carlyle's leadership needs. In 'The Spirit of Place' he writes:

> . . . men either live in glad obedience to the master they believe in, or they live in a frictional opposition to the master they wish to undermine. In America this frictional opposition has been the vital factor. . . . pull the democratic and idealistic clothes off American utterance, and see what you can of the dusky body of IT underneath.[38]

IT is 'the spell of the old mastery . . . the deepest *whole* self of man, the self in its wholeness, not idealistic halfness'. Thoreau advised 'let your life be a counter-friction to stop the machine'[39] since 'a very few—as heroes, patriots, martyrs, reformers in the great sense, and *men*—serve the state with their consciences also, and so necessarily resist it for the most part; and they are commonly treated as enemies by it.' Melville substitutes wariness for civil disobedience. Even Jack Chase is 'a little bit of a dictator' in his 'essential superiority', in his passion for the Rights of Man and his 'partisan blade in the civil commotions of Peru' (Ch. 5). But Chase has 'a clear open eye' in contrast to the mesmeric gaze of Ahab or the 'snaky black eye' of Bland.

Further, between confidence in Chase and non-confidence in Bland, Cuticle and Claret stand the blandly confident gentlemanly authorities of Benito Cereno and Amasa Delano, the one reduced to 'ghost authority' by a slave revolt, the other blindly secure in his *Bachelor's Delight*—to which we may add the lawyer-narrator of 'Bartleby', a once secure authority in Wall Street, reduced to bewildered 'ghost authority' by a suicidal nay-saying copyist. The captains of 'Benito Cereno' are 'incapable of sounding such wickedness as they have thrust upon them'. The motto, 'Follow Your Leader', in white chalk on the Spanish slave ship's prow will of necessity be parodied by the skeleton of a white aristocrat, brother of the captain in whom 'was lodged a dictatorship beyond which, while at sea, there was no earthly appeal'.

To the yea-sayers who offer their lives to whatever fiery hunt, and yea-sayers who have too much baggage to cross frontiers freely, Melville presents nay-sayers like Hawthorne.[40] Ahab apparently says 'NO! in thunder' but in fact is deeply obedient to his own created obsession: 'a vulture feeds upon that heart for ever; that vulture the very creature he creates' ('The Chart'). He is never independent—as the potential artist Ishmael is; even in sleep, 'common vitality' leaves him. His dreams become singular, he awakes in terror, 'a vacated thing, a formless somnambulistic being, a ray of living light to be sure, but without an object to colour, and therefore a blackness in itself.' Awake, the leader colours the 'indefiniteness' of whiteness with the colour of hunt. He is therefore typical: 'Wonder ye then at the fiery hunt?' ('The Whiteness of the Whale'). The 'inscrutability' of any existence, suggesting independence, without defined tail and without fixed *arche* and *telos*, beginning and end, must be forced to yield, be disclosed. How does any man escape such imprisonment?

> I, Ishmael, was one of the crew; my shouts had gone up with the rest; my oath had been welded with theirs, and stronger I shouted, and more I did hammer and clinch by oath, because of the dread in my soul. A wild, mystical, sympathetical feeling was in me; Ahab's quenchless feud seemed mine. With greedy ears I learned the history of that murderous monster against whom I and all the others had taken our oaths of violence and revenge.

Two Ishmaels exist in *Moby-Dick*—the sailor for whom signing on is his avoidance of possible murder or suicide—'my substitute for pistol and ball' or Cato throwing himself upon his sword ('Loomings')—and the writer composing a text in the later security of married domesticity. Certainly the latter does not eliminate the former, as he creates a text of the commonplaces of power. No man can exclude himself confidently from the majority urge to obey. No singular truth can be evinced to explain the interactions of dominance and subordination.

Heidegger defines the essence of truth as freedom; it is 'does not originally reside in the proposition', but through 'the openness of comportment': 'all working and achieving, all

111

action and calculation, keep within an open region within which beings, with regard to what they are and how they are, can properly take their stand and become capable of being said.'[41] The Ishmaels' freedom is the unknowable incompleteness of the triune weave of necessity, free will and chance—'all this to explain, would be to dive deeper than Ishmael can go.' As to what possible law could control a *socius* based democracy *and* hierarchy, *and* include the triune weave, Melville was still investigating in *Billy Budd, Sailor*.[42] Captain 'Starry' Vere is one last leader whose 'diligent tracings-out [do] not belie the obvious deduction' ('Ahab's Leg'):

> To trail the genealogies of these high mortal miseries, carries at last among the sourceless primogenitures of the gods; so that, in the face of all the glad, hay-making suns, and soft-cymballing, round harvest moons, we must needs give in to this: that the gods themselves are not for ever glad. The ineffable, sad birth-mark in the brow of man, is but the stamp of sorrow in the signers.

Father Mapple's agonized Oedipal nostalgia for enclosure in God the Father is no answer, and even an old-style benevolent despot like Vere has to knuckle under to the laws of treason, since he serves the Monarch. *Moby-Dick*'s narrator's reticences operate as gaps in the kind of continuity that one kind of reader may demand. Given his enthusiasm for system, Melville resists to an extraordinary degree the filling in of his interstices with religious or ideological controls. If the initial motive for Ishmael's embarcation is to avoid murder and suicide, his narrative ends in the murder and suicide of other men, which cause a gap—a black air bubble and a wild man's coffin. The federated keel of all nations ('Knights and Squires', Ch. 27) sinks under its own fatal hunt for absolutes to kill to eliminate dread. The White Whale only just survives the oil industry and the promethean conqueror and his followers. To write on this text may only mean a laying out of strategies of entry and probe. 'The circumnavigating *Pequod*', 'the world-wandering whale-ship' is discovered in 'The Grand Armada' carrying 'no cargo but herself and crew, their weapons and their wants', plus 'clear old prime Nantucket water', three years' water—an ark of self-sufficiency, the dream of an independent state. Then the Malays move out from Java Head: Ahab 'was now both chasing and being chased to his deadly end'. Ishmael's language for the sperm whales being hunted here is military—'detached companies', 'marching armies', 'close ranks and battalions', their spouts 'like flashing lines of stacked bayonets' against human 'weapons'. The panic distraction of the 'gallied' whales is identical with human behaviour under pressure of claustrophobia: 'Best, therefore, withhold any amazement at the strangely gallied whales before us, for there is no folly of the beasts of the earth which is not infinitely outdone by the madness of men.' As the harpooned whale heads into the herd, Ishmael invites any reader to identify with mass-hysteria: 'For as the swift monster drags you deeper and deeper into the frantic shoal, you bid adieu to circumspect life and only exist in a delirious throb.'

The throb includes the action of wounding and killing, and killing 'at leisure'. Men 'dash each other to death' and so do whales; Ishmael probes to the point where conscious decision is relinquished, where men lose history and give themselves up to the dictates of the body, to desire and 'delirium'. The earlier pattern of whales in 'their semicircle . . . swimming on, in one solid but still crescent circle' gives way to the circles of the assaulted herd. The text then takes up the 'circus-running sun . . . within his fiery ring' and the 'circumnavigating' ship to develop their bases into a characteristic vortex which draws in information until the scene becomes exemplary, a metonymic example. The whale-boat enters 'that smooth satin-like surface, called a sleek, produced by the subtle moisture thrown off by the whale in his more quiet moods'. But beyond 'this central expanse [of] enchanted calm which they say lurks at the heart of every commotion' lie those circles which fundamentally challenge Emerson's comfortable version of serendipitous enclosure in his essay 'Circles'[43]:

> And still in the distracted distance we beheld the tumults of the outer concentric circles. . . . We must watch for a breach in the living wall that hemmed us in; the wall that had only admitted us in order to shut us up.

NOTES

1. Bruno Bettelheim, *Freud and Man's Soul* (London: Chatto and Windus/ Hogarth Press, 1983), p. 41.
2. Richard Slotkin, *Regeneration Through Violence* (Connecticut: Wesleyan University Press, 1973), pp. 538–54.
3. James Thurber, *The Years with Ross* (1957; Harmondsworth: Penguin Books, 1963), p. 72.
4. William V. Spanos, 'The "Nameless Horror": The Errant Art of Herman Melville and Charles Hewitt', *Boundary 2*, Vol. IX, No. 1, Fall 1980 (State University of New York at Binghampton), 127–39.
5. Eric Bentley, *A Century of Hero-Worship: A Study of Heroism in Carlyle and Nietzsche, with Notes on Wagner, Spengler, Stefan George, and D. H. Lawrence* (Boston: Beacon Press, 1957).
6. Samuel R. Delany, *Dahlgren* (New York: Bantam Books, 1975), p. 846.
7. Jay Leyda (ed.), *The Portable Melville* (New York: Viking Press, 1952), p. 407.
8. Charles Olson, *Call Me Ishmael* (1947; New York: Grove Press, 1958). Olson's graduate thesis, 'The Growth of Herman Melville, Prose Writer and Poetic Thinker', dates from 1932.
9. Charles Olson, *Maximus Poems IV, V, VI* (London: Cape Goliard Press, 1968), no page numbers.
10. A. N. Whitehead, *Process and Reality: An Essay on Cosmology* (1929; New York, The Free Press, 1969), p. 75.
11. Buckminster Fuller, *I Seem to Be a Verb* (New York: Bantam Books, 1970).
12. Louis Zukofsky, *All, The Collected Shorter Poems 1923–1958* (New York: W. W. Norton, 1965), pp. 75–6.
13. M. R. Davis and W. H. Gilman (eds.), *The Letters of Herman Melville* (New Haven: Yale University Press, 1960), p. 125.
14. Herman Melville, *Moby-Dick*, ed. L. S. Mansfield and H. P. Vincent (New York: Hendricks House, 1952), p. 786.
15. *Letters*, op. cit., p. 142.
16. William Blake, *Jerusalem*, Chapter 2, line 15 in D. V. Erdman (ed.), *The Poetry and Prose of William Blake* (New York: Doubleday, 1970), p. 176.
17. Charles Olson, 'Lear and Moby-Dick', *Twice a Year No. 1* (New York: Fall-Winter 1938); *Call Me Ishmael*, op. cit., p. 60.
18. *Letters*, op. cit., pp. 78–80.
19. *Moby-Dick*, op. cit., p. 797.
20. *Call Me Ishmael*, op. cit., p. 57.
21. Ibid., p. 58.
22. Leyda, op. cit., p. 388.
23. *Moby-Dick*, op. cit., p. 831.
24. Leyda, op. cit., p. 406.
25. *Moby-Dick*, op. cit., pp. 678–79.
26. Ibid., p. 679.
27. Charles Olson, 'Equal, That Is, To the Real Itself', *Human Universe and Other Essays* (1965; New York, Grove Press, 1967), p. 122. The italicized passage is from Hermann Weyl, *Philosophy of Mathematical and*

Natural Sciences (New Jersey: Princeton University Press, 1949), p. 105.
28. Norman Mailer, *The Presidential Papers* (London: André Deutsch, 1964), p. 38.
29. Philip Rieff, *Freud: The Mind of the Moralist* (London: Methuen, 1965), pp. 236–37.
30. Norman Mailer, *The Deer Park* (New York: Putnam's Sons, 1955), pp. 330–31.
31. Bruce Mazlish (ed.), *The Railroad and the Space Program* (Cambridge and London: MIT Press, 1965).
32. *Call Me Ishmael*, op. cit., p. 52.
33. *Letters*, op. cit., p. 126.
34. *Moby-Dick*, op. cit., 637–52.
35. *Call Me Ishmael*, op. cit., pp. 12–56.
36. Lynn White, 'The Historical Roots of Our Ecologic Crisis' (1967), *Dynamo and Virgin Revisited* (Cambridge and London: MIT Press, 1968), pp. 75–94.
37. D. H. Lawrence, *Studies in Classic American Literature* (1915–22; New York: Doubleday, 1953), p. 79.
38. Lawrence, ibid., pp. 17–18.
39. H. S. Canby (ed.), *The Works of Thoreau* (Boston: Houghton Mifflin, 1937), pp. 791, 796–97.
40. *Letters*, op. cit., p. 125.
41. D. F. Krell (ed.), *Martin Heidegger: Basic Writings* (London: Routledge and Kegan Paul, 1978), pp. 124–25.
42. Eric Mottram, 'Orpheus and Measured Forms: Law, Madness and Reticence in Melville', Faith Pullin (ed.), *New Perspectives on Melville* (Edinburgh: Edinburgh University Press, 1980), pp. 229–54.
43. Herman Melville, *The Confidence-Man*, ed. Elizabeth S. Foster (New York: Hendricks House, 1954), p. lxxvii.

6

'All's o'er, and ye know him not': A Reading of *Pierre*

by RICHARD GRAY

Herman Melville completed his sixth and greatest novel, *Moby-Dick*, in the summer of 1851. The book must have cost him an enormous amount in terms of imaginative energy, moral effort, and sheer physical strain: and yet, within a few weeks of completing it, he was already at work again preparing his seventh novel, which was eventually to be called *Pierre: Or, The Ambiguities*. In many ways, *Pierre* represented something of a new departure for Melville. For, in the first place, it was set on land rather than at sea; and, in the second, with its aristocratic hero, its dark and fair ladies, its concern with the issues of love and money, and its use of secret letters and hidden portraits to propel or complicate the plot, it seemed to belong in a tradition of domestic romance that was immensely popular at the time. Melville, whose five books prior to *Moby-Dick* had produced an annual income of less than $1,600, clearly felt himself under some pressure to produce something that would, as he put it, pay 'the bill of the baker',[1] and in the early stages at least he appears to have been convinced that his new novel would do exactly that. At the beginning of 1852, for example, he wrote to Sophia Hawthorne to assure her that his next book would be, not 'a bowl of salt water' like his whaling

116

story but 'a rural bowl of milk'—more suited, the implication was, not only to the delicate sensibilities of Sophia herself but to a larger, novel-reading public that was predominantly female. While only a few weeks later, in a letter to his English publisher, he was even more openly confident. *Pierre*, he insisted, was 'very much more calculated for popularity . . . being a regular romance, with a mysterious plot to it, stirring passions at work, and withall, representing a new and elevated aspect of American life'.[2]

Such declarations of confidence can hardly be read without a sense of irony now. For, far from improving Melville's standing as a professional writer, *Pierre* served to worsen it radically. Reviewers received his new, domestic romance with greater and more concerted hostility than any of his previous efforts: 'a gigantic blunder', declared one, 'an objectionable tale, clumsily told', insisted another, while a third simply dismissed it as 'the craziest fiction extant'.[3] And any hopes Melville might have had concerning its appeal with a wider reading public were soon to be disappointed: only 283 copies were sold within the first eight months of publication and over the next few years it proved considerably less popular than even *Moby-Dick* or *Mardi*. The sense of irony does not spring entirely from this, however. It stems also from the fact that any reader of the book is likely to be struck by the discrepancy, the sheer size of the gap, between what Melville apparently intended to do and what in fact he did. *Pierre* is most emphatically not 'a rural bowl of milk': on the contrary, it is one of the darkest, bleakest, and bitterest of Melville's narratives, a story that follows 'the endless, winding way' of its hero's life and its narrator's thoughts to a conclusion that is little short of nihilistic. Melville may have set out to write something that would appeal to the contemporary taste for domestic melodrama and genteel sentiment. What he ended up with, however, was something quite different: a book so thoroughgoing in its scepticism that it examines its own *raison d'être*, its own claims and assumptions and, in this respect as well as in the subversive nature of its techniques, the self-reflexive character of its idiom, seems to anticipate the post-modernist novel.

The self-reflexive, self-referential nature of *Pierre* is perhaps

117

less surprising when one remembers the autobiographical basis of much of the book. One critic has suggested that *Pierre* represents an act of psychic withdrawal after the great, creative venture of *Moby-Dick*, another has described it as 'a Freudian exercise in psychic recovery'[5]; and, however much one may quarrel with the further implications of these remarks— the way they tend to confuse the psychological origins of the story with the story itself—they do point to certain things that are worth emphasizing and examining. First, and most obviously, they point to the fact that just as Pierre we are told, 'dropped his angle into the well of childhood, to find what fish might be there',[6] so Melville, his creator, has done exactly the same: as Henry Murray has shown, there are 'highly probable originals'[7] in Melville's life for most of the incidents, places, and people that appear in Pierre's story. The biographical detail is transposed in some cases and embellished in others; nevertheless, while writing about Pierre, Melville must have had the sense of looking at himself as if through a glass darkly—or rather, to use an image that recurs throughout the book, as though in a slightly distorting mirror. Beyond that, they also point to, or to be more accurate hint at, the centripetal structure, the inwardness of the story. Melville makes his hero a writer, writing a book that sounds very much like—and sometimes even echoes—the one in which he appears; a writer, moreover, who sets out to write something popular, using as his vehicle a thinly fictionalized version of his life, and then discovers that he cannot or will not do so. 'Who shall tell all the thoughts and feelings of Pierre', Melville asks,

> when at last the idea obtruded, that the wiser and profounder he should grow, the more and the more he lessened his chances for bread. . . .[8]

The question occurs towards the end of the narrative, by which time Melville must have recognized that his own chances for bread had radically diminished. And in reading it the reader is likely to feel, not for the first time, that he has been caught in a Chinese box of fictions, a book in which everything comments on its own origins, making, and development.

118

This Chinese box aspect, this sense of an artifice that calls attention to its own artificiality is perhaps most obvious at the beginning of *Pierre*. It can hardly escape the notice of even the most inattentive reader that, when we first encounter the protagonist, he is living in a world of fiction. The opening paragraph, for example, offers us what is effectively a parody of the language of conventional, pastoral romance.

> There are some strange summer mornings in the country, when he who is but a sojourner from the city shall early walk forth into the fields, and be wonder-smitten with the trance-like aspect of the green and golden world. Not a flower stirs; the trees forget to wave; and all Nature, as if suddenly become conscious of her own profound mystery, and feeling no refuge from it but silence, sinks into this wonderful and indescribable repose.[9]

That 'indescribable' might just be a touch of Melvillean irony, and the reference to silence may perhaps anticipate the narrator's later claim that Silence is the only Voice of our God: but, on the whole, this passage, with its references to the 'sojourner from the city', its clichés of thought and expression ('wonder-smitten', 'green and golden world'), its histrionic rhythms ('Not a flower stirs; the trees forget to wave . . .'), and its utter self-consciousness (a self-consciousness which is then, interestingly enough, projected on to the subject)—in all this, the passage seems to be insisting on its status as a conventional pattern, an invented object. This, we infer, is a world of appearances, masks and mirrors: an inference justified not only by the frequent references to masquerades and reflections in subsequent pages but, more simply, by the narrator's preference for the word 'seems'.

The sense that we are being introduced to a sort of pseudo-reality, a counterfeit realm, is nurtured in a variety of ways, and not least by the characters' taste for theatricality. It is not just that Pierre and his mother, and Pierre and his beloved Lucy Tartan, address each other in heightened terms, although they certainly do this—terms borrowed from *Romeo and Juliet*, say, or some other familiar text. Nor is it just that Pierre tends to see 'the illuminated scroll of his life' through the spectacles of the books he has read. It is that both the protagonist and those around him actually call attention to the artificial nature of their conversations (Pierre, for instance, concludes one flight of wit with his beloved by declaring, 'Very prettily conceited, Lucy') and seem intent on turning most of their actions and relationships into a kind of sport, a game: 'playful', for instance, is another word that recurs throughout those opening pages, most notably in the sections dealing with Pierre and his mother—who in *their* 'playfulness', we are told, introduced 'a certain fictitiousness' into 'one of the closest domestic relations of life' by referring to each other as 'brother' and 'sister'. Nor is the narrator himself immune from this tendency. For not only does he, like the characters, use an elaborately foregrounded, 'high profile' language, full of awkward neologisms ('amaranthiness', 'tinglingness', and 'preambilically' are just three random examples) and elaborate conceits ('the striped tigers of his chestnut eyes leaped in their lashed cages'); he is also inclined to remind us, in case we have forgotten, that he *is* the narrator, bound to go backward and forward in time 'as occasion calls' and compelled 'by immemorial usage' to do such things as provide a scrupulously conventional 'inventory' of Lucy's charms when she first appears. 'Is human life in its most human dimension a work of fiction?' asks Ortega y Gasset in *History as a System*; 'Is man a sort of novelist of himself who conceives the fanciful figure of a personage with its unreal occupations and then, for the sake of converting it into a reality, does all the things he does . . .?'[10] A similar question seems to be asked by Melville at the beginning of the novel, via both the characters and the narrator; and the answer, for the moment at least, appears to be 'yes'.

Then into this dream kingdom comes another apparition: the 'mysterious, haunting face' of Isabel. To some extent, Isabel is like a figure out of Poe: associated with another realm of ghosts and the sea, endowed with 'a death-like beauty' principally focussed in her large eyes, her musical voice, and the 'flowing glossiness of her long and unimprisoned hair', she is a mixture of the Madonna and La Belle Dame Sans Merci. More relevant to the present context, however, is the opportunity she clearly offers Pierre of moral and imaginative liberation: for she is, as one critic has put it, 'the eternally baffling object of human speculation, and . . . also speculation itself"[11]—or, to put it another way, she suggests at once Otherness, the world beyond the mask and the mirror, and the Muse, that creative force that might just make a glimpse of Otherness possible. Certainly, it is in these large terms that Pierre sees her. After receiving her letter, for example, he believes that now at last he will be able to 'tear all veils', 'strike through' masks, 'see . . . hidden things', and leave his father's house (which is, surely, at once a fictive house and the house of fiction) for 'boundless expansion' and the 'infinite air'. And shortly after this—in a passage which curiously anticipates Camus's description of the moment when 'the stage sets collapse' and the feeling of the absurd rushes in on an individual—Pierre, we are told, felt 'on all sides, the physical world of solid objects now slidingly displaced . . . from around him, and . . . floated into an ether of visions'.[12]

But, and it is a large but, there are things that Pierre does not see or, if he does see, chooses not to acknowledge. Isabel, in so far as she appears to open the door to another realm of experience and indeed to suggest that realm, does not belong to the world of words, articulate speech and intelligible action. The first thing we hear from her is a primal scream, a shriek to 'split its way clear through [Pierre's] heart, and leave a yawning gap there'; and most of her life, we discover later, has apparently been spent in mysterious, anonymous places that she either cannot or will not name, places where she felt 'all visible sights and audible sounds growing stranger and stranger' to her. Of course, she has been drawn into contact of a kind with people—compelled, she reveals, by the desire to understand what words like 'father' and 'dead' signify; of course, too, she learns to read and communicate—specifically, so as to decipher 'the talismanic word' inscribed on a handkerchief that once belonged to her (and Pierre's) father; and, of course, finally she tells her story, her 'vague tale of terribleness'—or, as she puts it, enables her brother to read 'in the one poor book of Isabel'. To say all this, however, is to leave certain quite crucial things out of account. Isabel tells her story, admittedly, but sensing that it is full of 'wonders that are unimaginable and unspeakable', she relies for much of the telling on 'the utter unintelligibleness, but the infinite significancies of the sounds of the guitar' that is her constant companion. She lives in the world now, certainly, but she longs for nothing so much as to leave it, to withdraw into non-being: 'I pray for peace', she declares,

> for motionlessness—for the feeling of myself as of some plant, absorbing life without seeking it, and existing without individual sensation. I feel that there can be no perfect peace in individualness . . . I feel I am in exile here.[13]

And Pierre responds to her, it may be, but what he responds to is her *image*: at first, 'the vague impression that somewhere he had seen traits of the likeness of [her] face before' and then, later, the conviction that in her he can discern a reflection of his father as depicted in the chair portrait. The cruel paradox is that Isabel's value lies precisely in her qualities of motionlessness and wordlessness, those aspects of her that lie beyond conceptualization and verbalization, and that she cannot explain herself, or indeed be explained by others, in anything other than a fiction—or, to use the stronger terms favoured by Melville, without jugglery or imposture. At one point in the novel, when he is trying to decide what to do about Lucy now that he has committed himself to Isabel, Pierre is compared by the narrator to 'an algebraist': 'for the real Lucy', we are told.

> he, in his scheming thoughts, had substituted but a sign—some empty x—and in the ultimate solution of the problem, that empty x still figures; not the real Lucy.[14]

In a bitterly ironic way this, as it turns out, sums up what happens to Isabel as she tries to describe herself, to Pierre as he charts the rest of his course, and to Melville himself as— becoming more and more convinced that 'this world is a lie' and that even 'the truest book in the world is a lie'—he attempts to tell their tale.

'I am a nothing. It is all a dream—we dream that we dreamed we dream.'[15] Pierre makes this declaration of unbelief, couched in what are for him characteristically Romantic terms, towards the end of the novel. Long before this, however, it is clear that in committing himself to Isabel Pierre is not, as he purports to believe, committing himself to Truth but to a further if different level of illusion. Quite apart from his tendency to respond to Isabel's image, the shadowy reflections that he catches from her, there is the fact that he continues to judge people and make decisions in the most obviously fictive terms. It was not, after all, a critic or even the narrator of the book who first directed attention to the parallel between Pierre and Hamlet; Pierre himself invites this comparison and then, spurred on by what he sees as the negative example of Hamlet's indecision, decides to act at once. The sense of artifice continues, fed by references not only to Shakespeare but to Dante, and perhaps most effectively underlined by Pierre's unwillingness to acknowledge the true nature or at least the full scope of his motives, and by his continued reliance on false—which is to say, at once deceiving and self-deceiving—names. Isabel is his sister; and yet the fact that they have only known each other as adults makes her seem something other than a sister. She is also mysterious and powerfully attractive, prompting feelings that are rather more than simply fraternal. 'Now Pierre', we are told,

> began to see mysteries interpierced with mysteries and mysteries eluding mysteries; and began to seem to see the mere imaginariness of the so supposed solidest principle of human association.[16]

The brother-sister relationship has been rendered purely fictive, a matter of names and shadows; and Pierre responds to this, not by asserting a truth, but by elaborating an alternative fiction, the pretence that he and Isabel have been secretly married. Perhaps, the narrative suggests, Pierre is prompted to adopt this course, 'the nominal conversion of a sister into a wife', by his 'previous conversational conversion of a mother into a sister'. The point is well taken: here as before, the implication is, Pierre is playing with words, constructing an artifice that enables him both to conceal and to express incestuous feelings. He has devised a new set of signs, another opaque vocabulary, with which to misinterpret things.

It is worth stressing the fact that at the very moment when Pierre, inspired by his devotion to Isabel, commits himself openly and wholeheartedly to what he calls 'the inflexible rule of holy right', the narrator does the same. 'I shall follow the endless, winding way', the narrator tells us, 'the flowing river in the cave of man'[17]: this, only two paragraphs after Pierre has declared that he will pursue the 'path' of Truth. The parallel is

useful, I believe, in the sense that it highlights at least two
things. In the first place, it helps to emphasize the fact that
Pierre—unlike, say, Ishmael in *Moby-Dick*—is not the narrator of his own story. He writes a book eventually, but the
book he writes is not the one we read: on the contrary, it is
the book we read *about*—*within* the book that an anonymous,
third-person narrator writes. The distinction is significant; for
it means that whereas Ishmael (along with all Melville's
other, earlier, first-person narrators) can be said in the end to
stand outside his experience, discover some at least of its
objective truth, and be liberated by that discovery, Pierre
remains trapped like a fly in amber within the fiction that
bears his name. And, in the second place, it anticipates the
discovery, made eventually by author, narrator, and reader
alike that the quest for Truth that *Pierre* the book embodies is
just as abortive as the one upon which Pierre the character
embarks. In this respect, something that Mary McCarthy
said once about Vladimir Nabokov's *Pale Fire* seems relevant:
when we read *Pale Fire*, she explained,

> a novel on several levels is revealed, and those 'levels' are not
> the customary 'levels of meaning' of modernist criticism but
> planes in fictive space. . . . Each plane or level in its shadow
> box proves to be a false bottom; there is an infinite regression,
> for the book is a book of mirrors.[18]

Part of this sense that *Pierre* is, to use McCarthy's phrase, 'a
book of mirrors' is due to something I have mentioned in
passing already: which is the sheer obtrusiveness of the
narrator, the feeling that he is always there mediating, shaping,
and in the process distorting experience. Sometimes, as in the
example quoted earlier, he insists on reminding us of the rules
he feels compelled to obey, the conventional forms through
which he and other storytellers have habitually filtered experience. At others, he emphasizes the opposite: the sheer arbi-
trariness of the structures he has adopted, the random nature
of his fictional devices. Book XVII, for example, begins in this
fashion:

> Among the various conflicting modes of writing history, there
> would seem to be two grand practical distinctions, under which
> all the rest must subordinately range. By the one mode, all

124

contemporaneous circumstances, facts, and events must be set down contemporaneously; by the other, they are only to be set down as the general stream of the narrative shall dictate; for matters which are kindred in time, may be very irrelative in themselves. I elect neither of these; I am careless of either; both are well enough in their way; I write precisely as I please.[19]

Elsewhere, in the same vein, the reader is advised that he can 'skip' certain chapters if he prefers to, and that he must not expect a consistent portrait of Pierre but catch 'his phases as he revolves'. Whether the emphasis is on the conventional or the arbitrary, however, the effect remains the same: to focus attention on the making of the text and, by extension, on the conversion of objective experience into (to adopt Borges's useful phrase) 'a mere labyrinth of letters'.[20]

But it is not just that the narrator is conspicuously there, reminding us of his presence; he is reminding us too, and continually, of the sheer hopelessness of his task. It is idle, he admits to us, to attempt to penetrate into the heart and 'inmost life' of Pierre or indeed anyone since 'in their precise tracings-out and subtle causations, the strongest and fiercest emotions of life defy all analytical insight.' Equally, it is pointless to try to tell anyone anything,

for—absurd as it may seem—men are only made to compre-hend things which they comprehended before (though but in embryo, as it were). Things new it is impossible to make them comprehend, by merely talking to them about it.[21]

In effect, the lines of communication between author and subject and those between author and reader are all irremedi-ably blocked: things remain resistant to explanation and there is a 'universal lurking insincerity' in 'even the greatest and purest written thoughts'. And because of this one measure of a book's authenticity, or rather its relative lack of inauthenticity, becomes the extent to which it does not even attempt to explain, does not try to contain, does not pretend that it has rendered a coherent and conclusive vision of life. As the narrator puts it:

while the countless tribes of common novels laboriously spin veils of mystery, only to complacently clear them up at last . . . yet the profounder emanations of the human mind . . . never

125

unravel their own intricacies, and have no proper endings: but in imperfect, unanticipated, and disappointing sequels (as mutilated stumps), hurry to abrupt intermergings with the eternal tides of time and fate.[22]

The implication of what Melville was getting his narrator to say, in passages like the one I have just quoted, were (as Melville was well aware) at once dispiriting and slightly terrifying. There is, it gradually emerges from the story of Pierre, a vacuum at the heart of things, a central emptiness, a hollowness, a silence—and 'how can a man get a Voice out of Silence?' Self-evidently, he cannot. There are, in fact, only two responsible courses of action open to him. Either he can pursue a state of non-being: that condition of quietness, apartness, and passivity that Isabel sometimes desires—and that, as Pierre observes him, the inscrutable 'mystic-mild' Plotinus Plinlimmon seems to have achieved.[23] Or, alternatively, he can *choose* to join the 'guild of self-imposters', comforting himself with the knowledge that, while his forgeries and impostures do little real good, they will, if performed in the right spirit—which is to say, a self-reflexive, self-conscious one—do little significant harm either. 'There is infinite nonsense in the world on all . . . matters', proclaims the narrator,

> hence blame me not if I contribute my mite. It is impossible to talk or to write without throwing oneself hopelessly open; the Invulnerable Knight wears his visor down. Still, it is pleasant to chat ere we go our beds; and speech is further incited, when like strolling improvisatores of Italy, we are paid for our breath.[24]

The casual, jokily resigned attitude that the narrator adopts here is by no means sustained throughout the book: as any reader of *Pierre* will verify, the tone fluctuates violently between irony and anger ('Oh what a vile cheat and juggler man is!'), exhausted acceptance and pure, blind rage (God is referred to at one point as 'the eminent Juggularius'), absurd humour and apocalyptic nihilism. Throughout the changes of tone, however, the essential thrust remains the same: what we are reading, the narrator reminds us, is a 'knavish pack of cards',[25] a game, a fabrication. Nor does he depend simply on telling us this; the form of the narrative, which is parodic and discontinuous,

126

serves to remind us of it on almost every page. The literary allusions and references, for example, are quite startling in their number, breadth, and complexity, including in the opening pages not only the Shakespeare mentioned earlier but Sir Thomas Browne, De Quincey, Disraeli, Milton, and the English Romantic poets. There are deeper, more sustained parallels not only with the novel of romantic sensibility but also with Gothic romance and Jacobean drama; the style offers pastiches of a number of writers—Carlyleian twists of syntax, for instance, mingle with Biblical rhythms, while passages that recall Emerson collide with others reminiscent of Shelley; and the characters issue as much out of literature as life—with, at one end of the spectrum, Pierre reminding us of the traditional Byronic hero and, at the other, numerous minor characters recalling the porters, tinkers, and constables of Shakespeare. Given the sheer abundance and consistency of such allusiveness, and setting aside the obvious point that Melville was hardly a crowd-follower, it is difficult to see how all this can be dismissed (as it has been by some critics[26]) as an example of an author being lamely derivative. Melville knew what he was doing. Pastiche, as he was neither the first nor the last to realize, can be a useful tool in the hands of someone bent on creating a realm of surfaces, an insistently figurative, self-evidently artificial world in which books, whether by choice (as in earlier examples of this genre) or by necessity (as in *Pierre* and later examples) refer to nothing except themselves.

So, even after swearing themselves to the cause of Truth, both Pierre and his narrator remain trapped in a spider's web of words. As the narrative edges forward—one, brief section rapidly replacing another, reaching nervously in various directions and towards different points in time—the sense of inwardness, of being imprisoned in a labyrinth, grows stronger and ever more inescapable. Pierre begins writing a book in which, the narrator tells us, 'he seems to have directly plagiarized from his own experiences, to fill out the mood of his apparent author-hero'.[27] The parallel with Melville, borrowing from his own experiences to fill out the mood of *his* author-hero, is so obvious as to be hardly worth mentioning; and perhaps more interesting here is the fact that the use of the word 'plagiarized' alerts us to the fictional nature of Pierre's raw material. Pierre's life is fictive, not just because Melville has invented it, but also to the extent that (as we have seen) there is 'a certain fictitiousness' in all Pierre's relationships—and, in addition, in the sense that his entire story, from its sentimental beginnings to its Gothic conclusion, offers us a series of parodic masks; the book that he writes could consequently be described as a fiction of a fiction compounded of fictions. Not content with such dizzying involutions, our storyteller at this point takes *us* within the story he tells too. 'Let us peep over the shoulder of Pierre, he suggests, and see what he is writing there . . . Here . . . is the last sheet from his hand, the frenzied ink not yet entirely dry.'[28] At such moments, narrator and reader exist within the interior of the narrative as minor, choric characters; as a corollary of this, they, or rather we, share in the prevalent mood of narcissism—as we watch ourselves watching Melville/Pierre watching himself.

In this connection, it is worth mentioning the shadowy references to incest and incestuous feelings that run through the book and that reach their climax in the story of Pierre's 'marriage' to Isabel. It is not enough, I think, to explain these in terms of the book's parodic framework. Certainly, the tradition of the sentimental novel permitted veiled hints at such deliciously shocking matters, and the motif of incest fits in well with Melville's tendency, towards the end of the book, to present Pierre as a reflection of the Promethean Christ figure of Romantic myth. The fact that this is so, however, does not exclude the further possibility that, in playing upon the idea of incest, Melville was hoping to remind the reader of his young author-hero's narcissism and the solipsistic thrust of the narrative. Like many a young American hero, Pierre discovers that his father has failed him, that the 'niched pillar . . . which supported the entire . . . temple of his moral life'[29] has been broken; he therefore sets out to rebuild the temple by accepting the moral responsibilities which, he feels, his father has abrogated—to assume the place vacated by Mr. Glendinning and so, in effect, become his own father. All he ends by doing, however, is embracing his own image, a projection of infantile obsessions. As far as the later course of his life goes, in fact, the young American hero he most resembles—or, to be more accurate, anticipates—is Quentin Compson in William Faulkner's *The Sound and the Fury*. For both Pierre and Quentin end by retreating from the sound and the fury of things into a preoccupation with a 'lost sister' that at once encapsulates and exacerbates their narcissism. In both cases, it hardly matters whether or not the physical act of incest occurs since the main point is the simple fact of the attraction and its sources[30]; and in both cases, of course, a further retreat is made into suicide— self-absorption and self-enclosure leading inevitably, it seems, to self-destruction. Even this particular parallel should not be pushed too far, however. For whatever the darkness of the first three sections of *The Sound and the Fury*, Faulkner does try to locate an alternative vision in the fourth; Quentin's way is not, apparently, the only one. By contrast, as I have tried to suggest, Pierre's psychological and sexual inversion is a mocking reflection of Melville's own sense (by turns bitter, ironic, and desperate) that he has been caught in a hall of mirrors: in this respect, the book is as much of a prison for the author as it is for the hero.

By the end of the book, of course, Pierre is (if one can use the phrase in this context) quite literally in prison, in 'a low dungeon' where 'the long tiers of massive cell-galleries above [seem] partly piled on him'. The sense of being trapped in a fiction continues: 'Here then, is the untimely, timely end', Pierre declares to himself,

> —Life's last chapter well stitched into the middle; Nor book, nor author of the book, hath any sequel, though each hath its last lettering![31]

More important for our present purposes, however, Pierre feels oppressed at this juncture, not so much by laws or by people, as by 'the stone cheeks of the walls' in his 'granite hell'. As several critics have observed, references to rocks, stones, and stony structures run throughout *Pierre*.[32] The book is, after all, dedicated to 'Greylock's Most Excellent Majesty', the highest mountain in Massachusetts, which Melville could see from his writing desk; the Mount of Titans (based on Mount Greylock) and the Memnon Stone (modelled on Balance Rock, near Pittsfield) perform important functions within the narrative; and both the rural and the urban environments the characters inhabit are described principally in terms of their stoniness. It is not difficult, I think, to see the purpose of all this: rock, in this novel, becomes the central image of the material, it replaces the whale as an emblem of being—all that Wallace Stevens would later term 'things as they are'. Nor is it difficult to see what the crucial property of rock in *Pierre* (the pun on 'pierre', the French word for 'stone', may or may not be intentional) is; rock, Melville insists, is utterly impenetrable and uninterpretable, offering nothing more than a series of blank surfaces. Admittedly, attempts may be made from time to time to name an especially noticeable configuration of rocks; we are told, for instance, that 'a singular height' not far from Pierre's ancestral home has been variously (and somewhat confusingly) termed The Delectable Mountain and the Mount of the Titans—and that the Memnon Stone was thus 'fancifully christened' by Pierre himself (although very few people, the narrator adds, would either know it by this name or indeed consider it worth naming). Admittedly, too, something, some hieroglyphic or message may be inscribed on a particular rock: like the 'half-obliterate initials—"S. ye W"' that Pierre finds 'rudely hammered' on the Memnon Stone and never satisfactorily deciphers. Such things, however, remain no more than surface scratchings, doomed efforts to name the unnameable and know the unknowable. For,

> Say what some poets will, Nature is not so much her own ever-sweet interpreter, as the mere supplier of that cunning alphabet, whereby selecting and combining as he pleases, each man reads his own peculiar lesson according to his own peculiar mind and mood.[33]

Which brings us back to Pierre, in his 'granite hell'. By the end of the novel, Pierre's attempts to name and to know the world have ceased—just as, indeed, those of Melville are about to—and he finds himself at once overpowered and mocked by the brute materiality of the world. The rocks and mountains which he christened and on which he tried to scratch some messages have now narrowed to a set of prison walls; and while he may feel like Ahab, that he would like to thrust through those walls he clearly believes that he cannot.

The final paragraph, describing the tableau of Pierre and Isabel dead in one another's arms, is worth quoting here:

> 'All's o'er, and ye know him not!' came gasping from the wall; and from the fingers of Isabel dropped an empty vial—as it had been a run-out sand-glass—and shivered upon the floor; and her whole form sloped sideways, and she fell upon Pierre's heart, and her long hair ran over him, and arbored him in ebon vines.[34]

The ambiguity of those first words is surely intentional. For while most readers will assume, quite reasonably, that it is Isabel who speaks here, addressing her words to Frederic Tartan and Charlie Millthorpe, the very strangeness of the phrase 'came gasping from the wall' (combined, perhaps, with the feeling that it was never incumbent on Tartan or even Millthorpe really to know Pierre) suggests other, admittedly tentative possibilities. It could be Pierre himself, talking to the other characters, or indeed to the narrator and the reader; it would not, after all, be the first time he had referred to himself in the third person. Or, for that matter, bearing in mind the references to rocks, stones, and walls that run through the novel, it could be the visible objects of the world, addressing themselves mockingly to Melville, reminding him that for all his attempts at naming them they remain unidentified and anonymous.

' "All's o'er, and ye know him not!" ': by the time Melville finished *Pierre*, there was really only one major distinction to be made between him and his young author-hero. Locked in a fictional jailhouse just as Pierre was, mocked in just the same way by the blankness of its walls, Melville at least knew, to his own profound dissatisfaction, what the alternatives were: either silence or artifice, stillness or imposture. One could either sit staring at those walls and, in a gesture of total passivity, try to assume something of their blankness and impenetrability. Or one could attempt to break through them, in the certain knowledge that all one would find beneath their immediate surface would be another surface—and then, after that, another.[35] 'Far as any geologist has yet gone down in the world', declares Melville in Book XXI of *Pierre*,

> it is found to consist of nothing but surface stratified on surface. To its axis, the world being nothing but superinduced superficies.

By vast pains we mine into the pyramid; by horrible gropings we come to the central room; with joy we espy the sarcophagus; but we lift the lid—and no body is there!—appallingly vacant as vast is the soul of a man![36]

To anyone familiar with postmodernist literature, this description of superinduced superficies will probably recall not only the writers I mentioned earlier—that is, Vladimir Nabokov and Jorge Luis Borges—but also such things as, say, Roland Barthes's claim that texts can be seen

as constructions of layers (or levels, or systems) whose body contains finally no heart, no kernel, no secret, no irreducible principle, nothing except the infinity of their own envelopes— which envelop nothing other than the unity of their own surfaces.[37]

The parallel is there, certainly: but there *is* a difference, and it is a crucial one. For there is no escaping the intense bitterness, the sheer rage and sense of betrayal, that runs through the passage from *Pierre* that I have just quoted (and, indeed, through the entire book): feelings which, it need hardly be said, are conspicuous only by their absence from Barthes's remarks and from most of the fiction of Nabokov and Borges. Part of Melville, it is clear (and a significant part of him at that), wanted to utter a thunderous 'no' to the idea of 'surface stratified on surface'; to that extent, at least, he was rather more than just a progenitor of postmodernist writing, and *Pierre* itself is something other than just a distant anticipation of books like *Ficciones* and *Pale Fire*. In his seventh novel, as in so much of his work, Melville's heart tried desperately to reject what his head told him. Which accounts not only for the book's anger, occasional awkwardness, and acidity, but also for its power as an expression of that impulse most of us feel at one time or another: the impulse to believe, that is, even if only in the possibility of belief, however perversely and despite all the evidence.

NOTES

1. *Pierre; Or, The Ambiguities* (1852), p. 294. All references are to the New American Library, New York, 1964 edition.
2. *The Letters of Herman Melville* edited by Merrell R. Davis and William H. Gilman (New Haven, 1960), pp. 146, 150.
3. *Melville: The Critical Heritage* edited by Watson G. Branch (London, 1974), pp. 294, 298, 303.
4. *Pierre*, p. 135.
5. Edward H. Rosenberry, *Melville* (London, 1979), p. 90. See also, Richard Chase, *Herman Melville: A Critical Study* (New York, 1949), p. 103.
6. P. 322.
7. 'Introduction' to *Pierre*, New York, 1949 edition, p. xxi. See also, Ronald Mason, *The Spirit Above the Dust: A Study of Herman Melville* (London, 1951), pp. 169–71.
8. P. 344.
9. P. 23. The other quotation in this paragraph is from p. 237.
10. New York, 1962. Quotations from *Pierre* in this paragraph are from pp. 25, 27, 44, 47, 58, 59, 79, 208, 297.
11. William Ellery Sedgwick, *Herman Melville: The Tragedy of the Mind* (New York, 1962), p. 153. See also, Murray, 'Introduction', pp. l–lxv.
12. P. 111. Cf. Albert Camus, *The Myth of Sisyphus* translated by Justin O'Brien (New York, 1959), p. 10. Other quotations from *Pierre* in this paragraph are from pp. 60, 91, 139.
13. P. 146. Other quotations from pp. 69, 144, 149, 152, 154, 176, 186.
14. Pp. 212–13. Other quotations from pp. 74, 241, 298.
15. P. 311.
16. P. 121. Other quotations from p. 208.
17. P. 135. Other quotations from p. 134.
18. Cited in Tony Tanner, *City of Words: American Fiction 1950–1970* (London, 1971), p. 34.
19. P. 280. Other quotations from pp. 243, 378.
20. Cited in Tanner, *City of Words*, p. 41.
21. Pp. 242–43. Other quotations from p. 92.
22. P. 170. Other quotations from p. 380.
23. There is 'something passive' about Plinlimmon, we are told; his face has 'a repose separate and apart—a repose of a face by itself'; and his features appear to express the belief that 'to respond is a suspension of isolation'. Pp. 328, 330.
24. P. 295. Other quotations from pp. 241, 242.
25. P. 380. Other quotations from pp. 298, 309.
26. See, e.g., Newton Arvin, *Herman Melville* (London, 1950), p. 227.
27. P. 342.
28. Pp. 341–42.
29. P. 94.
30. In *Pierre* the implication is that an act of incest has occurred; in *The Sound and the Fury* the implication is that it has not. A further ambiguity is

133

introduced into *Pierre* by the fact that we never knew for certain whether or not Pierre and Isabel do have the same father.

31. P. 402. Other quotations from pp. 402, 404.
32. See, e.g., H. Bruce Franklin, *The Wake of the Gods: Melville's Mythology* (Stanford, 1963), pp. 101ff. Edgar A. Dryden, *Melville's Thematics of Form: The Great Art of Telling the Truth* (Baltimore, 1968), pp. 118ff.
33. Pp. 383–84. Other quotations from pp. 160, 161, 383.
34. P. 405.
35. See 'Bartleby' and *The Confidence-Man: His Masquerade* for later explorations of these two alternatives.
36. P. 323.
37. 'Style and its Image', in *Literary Style: A Symposium* (London, 1971). I am indebted to Harold Beaver for drawing attention to the parallel noted here.

7

Melville the Mannerist: Form in the Short Fiction

by WILLIAM WASSERSTROM

1

On renewing the study of Melville's tales and sketches (most of which were written for American magazines between 1853 and 1856 and five of which became *Piazza Tales*, 1856), I have been startled to realize how truly acerbic they are when taken in bulk. It is not simply a power of blackness, not the mere echo of the 'No! In Thunder' that Melville attributed to Hawthorne in his 'Hawthorne and his Mosses' that is shocking. Rather there is an astringency—an acidity—that verges on the overpowering. It is this power and sting that somehow has been lost on recent generations of critics. Those who travel down Derridean ways, John Carlos Rowe, for example, or Barbara Johnson, have achieved some very adroit manipulations of glyph and image, certain brilliant uses of the deconstructionist notion of *différence* as applied both to *Billy Budd* and by implication to the *oeuvre* at large. But their method is by design exclusionary, an ideology of linguistics focused on the linguistics of ideology.

Even when we turn to the opposite reach of system, however, to Q. D. Leavis, we find her choosing to treat mordancy as an occasional thing, the mere tang of the tale. Indeed her very title, 'Melville: The 1853–1856 Phase' (in Faith Pullin (ed.), *New Perspectives on Melville*, 1978), all but promises to

135

muffle shock. No-nonsense brisk, commonsensical keen, enlivened by a Freudian touch here and there, Mrs. Leavis concedes that Melville's spirit during these three years was perhaps haunted now and then, more than a little vexed. But, she concludes, in none of these stories 'can I find any justification for Hawthorne's opinion [that] Melville's writings, for a long while past, have indicated a morbid state of mind'. On the contrary, she says citing 'I and My Chimney', Melville's 'reassuring good-humour [is] surely also good proof of its author's mental health'—as if Melville's uncertain state of mind, daily confronting the hazards of disaster, did not deliberately screen black comedy behind a skrim of good humour.

Without any intention to quarrel, therefore, I confess myself to be put off by Mrs. Leavis's reconstructionist style of commentary—Melville seen as a great master in a great tradition of Anglo-American letters—and the deconstructionist as well. Forgoing what Murray Krieger calls a fascination with 'Words about Words about Words'—that is, with the ply and play of post-modern theories which encompass criticism itself, reading in general and the genres of literature in full—I intend to concentrate on two principles of Melville's art.

One is well known, the custom of concealment, but the other, a habit of disarrangement, is to my mind not thoroughly enough appreciated. For nothing is more overt than Melville's compulsion to twist things awry, to work off-centre, even as a drive toward balance and proportion engenders plots and characters in pairs, symmetrically. He is in fact distinctive among American writers for inventing twin stories in which yea and nay are one—which is to say, Melville composes double tales in which contrasts coalesce and meaning dissolve in a discourse of oxymoron. Quite as symmetry and asymmetry are invariably aligned so too do harmony and dissonance, deformation and conformation fuse in fictions which intricately and unrelentingly display the fact of disorder within the most ordered structures imaginable. Derangement held in the tightest possible grip of composition, instability experienced as equilibrium, concealment paraded as revelation—with all the bonhomie of Satan himself Melville presides over the form, diptych, and the language, double-talk, governing his tales and sketches.

It is not just ambiguity I have in mind. Although Melville does not of course yield pride of place to other American writers who consistently resort to the language of irony, I propose to set aside that long and glamorous American love affair with irony, with paradox. For it is not this passion that fuels his energies, his opulence of invention, his ferocities, his force. In stressing a wilfulness that disarms itself; in evoking his assent to and dissent from the 'endlessness, yes, the intolerableness of all earthly effort'; in observing Melville confound the power of reason by insinuating discord into every nook and cranny of a work, big or small, it is incontrovertibly a species of mannerism I refer to. Flouting classic rules of fiction, Melville resorts to 'puzzles which cannot be solved', as the art historian E. H. Gombrich says of mannerism in painting, 'save by those who know what the scholars of the time believed to be the true meaning of Egyptian hieroglyphs' and other sorts of arcane learning. Add mannerist self-celebration and self-mockery to arcana of peculiarly American origin and we discover that what is perhaps truly stunning about Melville's accomplishment is the pervasiveness of *contrapposto*, an Italianate style of antithesis which contorts the figure by twisting a part of the body in a direction opposite to that of other main parts. Adapted for use in American prose narrative, *contrapposto* in Melville's hands is manifest in the motion of a figure and the movement of a fiction along two opposing axes simultaneously.

As this remarkable man's career confirms, therefore, the abiding centre of interest in our literature doesn't involve ambiguity merely but does implicate outright contradiction. Critics from the 1920s until now, however, from the Great Melville Revival at mid-decade down to the present day—on both sides of the Atlantic critics have neglected to sort out crucial reasons why the main elements in his best stories fail to cohere but manage triumphantly to adhere. Despite splendid work done in the sixty years following Raymond Weaver's pioneering labour, criticism—*pace* Richard Chase—has stopped short of addressing this peremptory subject in favour of studies sustained by one or another philosophical system or school of theory. If in the 1980s we are plagued by signs and symptoms, so it was that in the 1950s we were presented with musings on alienation, on the sway of nothingness over the life of the spirit, on the Absurd as an ultimate condition of things both in the life of the mind and at the heart of Melville's books. What seemed plausible then appears to be relatively inconsequential now. As a result no longer do we acquiesce in the kind of Existentialist creed Alfred Kazin so handily applied to *Moby-Dick*, where the role of an 'isolato', Queequeg or Ishmael among others, is said to 'put man's distinctly modern feeling of "exile" [and] abandonment', in our direct line of sight, at dead-centre stage.

For all the allure of Derridean or Freudian or Existentialist poetics, each school commits a heresy of history by finding Melville to be so extraordinary as to deserve a niche all his own. Zealous to plumb untold riches of language and myth and mind, Kazin along with many others overlook a mainstream of American writings whose hallmark is a roughness of grain in the texture and shape of a text. That it expresses an American grain, indeed, is apparent by way of analogy to the historic fact of irregularity in the very fabric of national culture. For it is not due to a failure of skill that the fluencies of form characteristic of British novels are absent from exemplary American books. And in Melville's instance, the more articulate and the more authentic his voice, the more authoritatively his imagination found ways to organize a certain presumed or suspected black hole in the nature of things within complex operations of plot which drive readers to a wit's end of credulity and incomprehension.

Unlike Poe or Hawthorne, men given not only to the construction of riddles but also compelled to riddle out solutions to the deepest dilemmas of being, Melville had no faith in the power of intelligence, no matter how resolute, over mystery, no matter how matter of fact. It is therefore a distinctive kind of eminence he acquires, a particular kind of honour which must be paid to a man of letters who refused to assign sensible cause to the least as well as most consequential events. Forgoing both ordinary good sense and transcendent wisdom, therefore, he found himself—indeed he made it the very seal and sign of his genius—animated by the strain of contriving mannerist ways to skew a tale, to work off-balance yet maintain

138

poise. Nineteenth-century Anglo-American gentlemen, above all else hearty, were accustomed to adopt a brave front of manliness in the very teeth of a gale; without doughty good humour all was lost. And Melville, who customarily hid within the deepest innards of a story his belief in one truism above all, in the unspeakable force of destructive power, enables us to follow him into innermost realm of Dis without loss of bearing. That he accomplishes this feat without often succumbing to the easy charm of irony is a triumph of grace. 'Never could abide irony; something Satanic about irony', go the bitter words of *The Confidence-Man*: 'God defend me from Irony, and Satire, his bosom friend.'

In disdaining Satan's device and soliciting God's defence Melville spoke double-edged words which neither fail to say what they mean nor quite fail to mean what they seem to say. Managing most of the time to leave open ultimate questions of meaning, to formulate and repudiate views offered and positions taken on events that run from grim to grisly, he has dazzled and perplexed nearly five generations of readers. What is not at all open to question, however, is horror at the universal experience of Betrayal, and Chaos his bosom friend. Until now the best effort to resolve questions of this kind, to assign a locale and a cause and ascribe a method circumscribing these aspects of Melville's attainment is Richard Chase's insistence on Romance as the American writer's true métier. Referring to stories in which Melville and others suspend in thin air motives, actions, persons—every last one purposefully not quite accounted for—Chase took up Henry James's ideas on Romance and applied these to the study of fictions which 'achieve their very being, their energy and their form, from the perception and acceptance not of unities but of radical disunities'.

Unfortunately Chase placed Melville within, then abandoned him to, a literary tradition alone—as if the vocation of letters elicits literature in isolation from other main activities of society. Beyond the briefest mention of 'doctrines of Puritanism' reinforced by 'frontier conditions' and the 'institutions of democracy as these evolved in the eighteenth and nineteenth centuries', Chase inserts the merest trace of historical fact. Romance may indeed help to account for Melville, but what on earth accounts for Romance? By no means does it express an American desire to discredit the ordering faculties of reason, even though it may well be seen as expressing an American impulse to deny the capacity of human intelligence to discover reasonable explanations for the principle of contradiction the whole world round. Whether or not *Moby-Dick* is, as R. W. B. Lewis believes, the 'supreme instance of a dialectical novel—a novel of tension without resolution', surely Melville's best books, *Moby-Dick* and *Billy Budd*, draw on *contrapposto* to portray the fact of discontinuity between the exercise of human will and the achievement of human welfare. Surely, too, both books portray treachery as the ruling form of contradiction above and below. Without in the least overstating the case it is fair to say that the best epigraph to Melville's career is found in Henry Adams's remark: 'Chaos is the law of nature, order is the dream of man.' Anticipating Adams's distasteful words, Melville invented a sub-genre of fiction which would unflinchingly proclaim and unfailingly disavow the sovereignty of chaos over the lives of men, the fate of nations and the laws of nature.

Although more remains to be said about disunity and irresolution and discontinuity, we are now in a position to add a useful item or two to the stock of ideas on contradiction in America. In order to understand what it is that obsesses Melville's mind and fouls his temper, let us try to correlate a leading tendency in classic American literature with a central motif in the life of society, a ruling idea of nation in the United States. Consider in this connection both the style and substance of a key question, put by James Madison in *The Federalist Papers*, touching the subject of political experiment as defined in the new Constitution, not yet adopted when Madison wrote. Who, Madison asked, would refuse to quit a 'shattered and tottering habitation' merely because the new house, though far more commodious than the old, 'had not a porch to it or because some of the rooms might be a little longer or smaller, or the ceiling a little higher than his fancy would have planned them'? Replace the phrase 'shattered habitation' with Articles of Confederation. And in addition to those Articles affix certain principal tenets of social and literary history stemming from the Federalist period and continuing in our own day. And you discover that it is this homely image, the trope of a habitable but unconventional building, which brings discernible traits of American sensibility into play, their instant of origin more or less coinciding with an end of enthusiasm for the recreation on these shores of a society which would simply perfect the English model of government.

Although the Constitution went against the grain of governance in Europe, Madison conceded, nevertheless this fabulous document in its asymmetry matched the mould of human character evolved under novel conditions of development in this not quite discovered country. Indeed, precisely because it was composed in an American grain, it dismissed any nostalgia of impulse, any afterglow of will to devise a flawlessly articulated mechanics of system, patterned on Newton's science, which simply ran itself. Neither consummately federal nor unambiguously national in design, as Madison's conceit confirmed, it refused to disguise the fact of contradiction at the heart of this unprecedented affair, the very scheme of things on this continent. Contradiction of course implied instability. And staunch and venturesome as the Founders were, none thrilled to the prospect of embracing a post-Newtonian heresy of government which called into serious question the nature of order itself, the rule of natural law on earth and in heaven.

What most unsettled them of course was the fear that new energies, released by these unexampled dynamics of the body politic, would be destabilizing in the extreme. Proposing to erect a 'habitation' without reference to any known plan of construction anywhere, American eighteenth-century statesmen uneasily girded themselves to risk the danger of gambling against very long odds. Today the impression of risk remains. But the sense of danger is diminished by that familiar axiom of social thought which asserts that living systems must tolerate a 'small asymmetry' in order to function at all. Because complete symmetry, though stable, is static, we are told in an essay on 'Symmetry in Physics and Information Theory' (1970), a 'little instability must be allowed'—as indeed Madison never ceased to contend in debate with Hamilton during long years of dissent on exactly this subject. 'There is in fact a split personality in the *Federalist* papers', Adrienne Koch says in

Madison's 'Advice to my Country' (1966). And the split is most
vividly revealed, the subject of disorder is itself most openly
addressed, by way of Hamilton's rejection of and Madison's
insistence on a transfer of power from a single sovereign to a
whole people whose will, uncontrolled in itself, was entrusted
to manage everything. The prospect was fearful. Still, facing
the danger of disaster, Madison and his colleagues anxiously,
bravely, adventurously abandoned the British doctrine of
equipoise. And in its place they inaugurated a system grounded
in conflict, in meliorable but irremediable tension between
self-interest and the public interest. Balancing risks and risking imbalance, renouncing an English belief in the science of
government, Federalists framed the subject of style in American
society according to doctrines which were before long to
infiltrate styles of structure in literature and general culture.

Insofar as a split personality rules the life of politics and
letters in the United States, it is entirely apt that the divided
and contorted self should represent the American type par
excellence, the national holotype in literature, and that
oxymoron should acquire a privileged status of discourse.
Which is to say that the sequence of images and ideas underlying both the Articles of Confederation and the Constitution
accords with principles of construction scaffolding the structure of major American books. Beginning with *The Federalist
Papers*, in which Madison bids his countrymen to enter and
inhabit a house that contained the idea of experiment, that
domesticated risk and accommodated peril and disarmed
distrust of the American Idea, danger—the spectre of chaos—
has lurked in every stick and stone, every sail and longboat,
every funnel and engine. From the late eighteenth century
until the present day, from Thoreau and Harriet Beecher
Stowe, through Whitman and James down to Fitzgerald and
Mailer and an entire host of post-modernists in art, archi-
tecture and letters, a defining feature of civilization on this
continent has been what Madison first and Poe thereafter,
following Bacon, called a certain strangeness in proportion.
For two hundred years literature in its turn has unveiled the
inner lives of people doomed to live in this permanently exotic

and unsettled state. Given the nation torn between the fervour of self-justification and the guilt of self-condemnation in all spheres of personal conduct and public policy, what awaits appraisal at last is the pressure of this moral drama on exemplary works. For it is nothing less than the convulsion of a whole people—or as Mark Twain and Melville often thought, a misfeasance common to the whole human race—that is disclosed by fictions in which mystification of plot somehow substantiates, justifies a text. No matter how fruitful in this connection the study of 'signifiers' may be, the galaxy of signs that preoccupy semioticians today, in Melville's instance it is 'signification' to which his work is riveted, the world itself toward which all signs tend. Granted that contradiction is displayed by words that obey rules of their own, the remarkable thing is Melville's constancy of attention to national scenes and historical settings, to the tyranny of function and the power of place over individual persons in a possibly predetermined world. And it is this concentration of interest, compacted by an iron grip of mind, out of which his linguistic energy, an art of oxymoron, undeniably stems.

2

This then is the drift of argument. But before applying its gist to specific tales, typically those in which Melville tangles with mystery and flirts with catastrophe, I must confess that there is an irremediable loss in my neglect of certain marvels of the canon. What is mainly lost is an accretion of detail. For the two fictions I have selected, 'The Town-Ho's Story' and *Billy Budd*—a paired pair of pairings on the theme of betrayal—constitute a sort of alpha and omega of Melville's imagination and can in consequence stand surrogate for the rest, short fiction and long. Inevitably, however, a penalty is paid for an absence of detail, for a failure to address particular stories, such as 'Benito Cereno', which do not yield easily to general ideas, however apt. Cost high or low, recalcitrant or no, each of the stories nonetheless unfolds, develops and completes its action by enclosing an arabesque of cross-purposes. Each possesses a counterpart even if it lacks a twin, even if it cannot make a proper diptych. Contemplating the stories that do not

143

congenially pair off—'The Apple Tree Table' and 'I and My Chimney'; 'Cock-A-Doodle-Doo' and 'The Happy Failure'; 'Bartleby' and 'Jimmy Rose'; 'The Piazza' and 'The Fiddler'; 'The Encantadas' and 'The Lightning-Rod Man'; 'The Bell-Tower' and 'The Story of Daniel Orme'—as well as those that congenitally do—'The Two Temples', 'Poor Man's Pudding and Rich Man's Crumbs', 'The Paradise of Bachelors and the Tartarus of Maids', 'The Jack Gentian Sketches' and so on—we find that the entire lot exploits contortion, irregularity, disproportion and is therefore perhaps illuminated by my gloss.

Allowing just a moment for a glance or two at 'Benito Cereno', however, we take an extra instant to observe Melville engaged in the risky business of suborning the idea of Truth itself in a story whose very substance is based on the power to distinguish between probity and perfidy, between the feigned and the bona fide, between mendacities of white and black. Melville so arranges and deranges the shape of things, however, that by the time last words are said in the closing talk between Don Benito and Amasa Delano, the story itself has belied its ostensible intent: to reaffirm the blessings of enlightened mind. For all its show of candour and comprehensiveness, therefore, despite a presumed symmetry in correlating the invented 'fiction' with a 'factual' Deposition, 'Benito Cereno' cozens a reader to think that the truth about Babo's mutiny is open and shut. Melville's queer disproportion of form fortunately comes to our aid, else we would be forced to take as given a tale that works its mystifying way through Delano's 'fictive' innocence of mind toward the demystifications of Don Benito's 'non-fictional' sworn testimony disclosing the 'true history of the *San Dominick's* voyage' down to the time of her arrival in harbour with the *Bachelor's Delight*.

Were this indeed all that Melville supplied, it would not be difficult to agree with Warner Berthoff that 'Benito Cereno' is 'essentially a *riddle*' and thus a 'twice-told tale, once for trial and once for confirmation'. Twice-told it surely is, but unconfirmed it remains too. Had it been a tale thrice-told, its key would still remain in Melville's safekeeping. Observing the Spaniards consistently fail in their attempts to undeceive

144

Delano but succeed in unsettling his mind, we are not in the
least amazed to discover Don Benito's Deposition also failing
and succeeding: it fails to answer certain questions but it
succeeds in inviting us to question certain answers. What
Melville recounts of deceptions practised by Benito Cereno on
the mutineers, by the mutineers on Delano—that 'invented
story' of slavish service and subservience with which Babo
turns the screw of deceit on the entire white company of
men—this is unimpeachable. But as the story ends he derives
no solace from Delano's benignity of temper, sweetness of
spirit:

> 'You are saved: what has cast such a shadow upon you?'
> 'The Negro.'

It is in view of this exchange, then, that we turn to
Melville's construction in the sentence following Don Benito's
formal statement to the court: 'If the Deposition have served
as the key to fit the lock of the complications that precede it,
then, as a vault whose door has been flung back, the *San
Dominick's* hull lies open to-day.' 'To-day' is the word properly
read? Or are not we misled by a hyphen that turns 'today'
away from *light of day*? What in consequence is one to make of
a Deposition which, under conditions imposed by Melville's
scruple and austerity of words, may not have served as a
means of enlightenment after all—despite the open hull? No
question that 'the nature of this narrative, besides rendering
the intricacies in the beginning unavoidable, has more or less
required that many things, instead of being set down in the
order of occurrence' should be 'irregularly given'. But the most
irregular and intricate of its aspects is a climax that concludes
not in a feast of light, of salvation and revelation, but in
darkness and silence.

Dying in the wake and shadow of 'the Negro', following his
leader, as Melville remarks at the last, Don Benito is haunted
not by the person of Babo in his rôle as chief mutineer, the
very 'helm and keel' of revolt, but by Babo's ingenuities of
deceit directed toward disreputable ends. Melville's obsessive
theme, it surfaces here by way of the Don's terror on contemplating Babo's near-miss. For it is not the memory of
Babo's actual mutiny that darkens his mind, in spite of 'blue

145

sea and blue sky' and 'bright sun' and gentle wind. It is rather a residue of rebellion that torments him and leads him to prefer death to life in a world where 'malign machinations and deceptions' could subvert the plain good sense of an American ship's captain, the most decent and pious man on earth.

The point of Benito's despair, incidentally, would not have been lost on Marlow as he reflects on Kurtz in *Heart of Darkness*, a seafaring tale on similar themes. Though technically unlike 'Benito Cereno', Conrad's novella also turns on the subject of hypocrisies, deceptions, lies—which in Marlow's nostrils reek with the stink of death, the unmistakable fetor of those decadent, colonial, imperial nations among which the enslavement of blacks was mitigated, presumably, by the lie of a white Christian burden. Coincidentally or not, deceit is the quintessential matter of both stories. It is therefore the power of duplicity Melville presents as a clear and present danger to the life of species. Having 'stood with me, sat with me, talked with me, looked at me', eaten and drunk with me, nevertheless you utterly misconstrued my nature, Benito Cereno sadly reminds Amasa Delano. Not only did you fail to see in me 'an innocent man', he continues this litany of causes explaining his silence, his hopelessness, fail to recognize in me the 'most pitiable of men', but in fact you mistook me 'for a monster' pure and simple. That 'you were in time undeceived' provides no comfort at all, others being far likelier than you to confuse subversion of mind with penetration of intelligence. And though Delano may well move 'through all ambuscades' protected by the 'Prince of Heaven's safe-conduct', Providence is a very choosy caretaker, not attentive or perhaps enterprising enough to preserve Delano from an ultimate misprision of judgement or concerned enough to preserve Don Benito from doom. Melancholy imposed by a cause so grave, Melville says at the last, 'ended in muteness upon topics like the above'.

With nothing to be said, best to say nothing, Benito Cereno concludes. And with nothing to be done, 'seeing all was over', Babo 'uttered no sound and could not be forced to'. Reversing and modulating the form of Satanism afflicting Billy Budd, Babo's aspect seems to say, 'since I cannot do deeds, I will not speak words.' Who then is the worse deceiver and betrayer and destroyer of men, the slave trader who in guilt renounces

146

the 'symbol of despotic command', his silver mounted sword, and prefers to appear at the trial with an empty scabbard 'artificially stiffened'? Or Babo who remains unabashed even as he 'met his voiceless end'?

3

In contrast to 'Benito Cereno', which exhibits Melville's short fiction at its mannerist best, at its most irregular—an art of fiction fluorescent with cross-purposes, kept afloat by cross-currents—'The Town-Ho's Story' is relatively regular in concept and composition. A self-contained episode of *Moby-Dick*, remarkable for its reliance not on a metaphysics of motive but on bizarre ties linking geography and character, it cannot be treated offhand, in Berthoff's fashion, as a service-able way to bring the white whale 'dramatically on stage soon after the revelation of Ahab's scheme of vengeance'. Insofar as Steelkilt's series of inexplicable and inexpiable crimes (his brutalization by the mate Radney, his secret power over Captain and crew, his mutiny and revenge) supposedly stem from the scene of Steelkilt's previous service on the Erie Canal and Great Lakes, we are notified that the American wilderness is not the less wicked for being picturesque. In a rollicking style familiar only to citizens of his new-found land, this 'Canaller' possesses hard-earned credentials for savagery acquired along 'three hundred and sixty miles, gentlemen, through the entire breadth of the state of New York; through numerous populous cities and thriving villages; through long, dismal uninhabited swamps and affluent, cultivated fields, unrivaled for fertility': Melville's rhetoric fattens as it follows the flow of one continual stream of 'Venetianly corrupt and often lawless life' on the westward passage of Clinton's ditch. For even if Steelkilt is to the naked eye cast in the mould of Billy Budd—a 'tall and noble animal with a head like a Roman and a flowing golden beard'—at bottom he is more a pagan of the Bowie knife, more Ashanti 'beast of prey' than Handsome Sailor.

Inexorably, then, a frontiersman who is imbued with free-booting wilderness ways finds himself cursed for his sins by having as a counterpart the mate Radney whom Melville outfits with two biographies that deliberately or inadvertently send mixed signals. A man as 'hardy, as stubborn, as malicious' and 'ugly as a mule', Radney is first said to be a 'Vineyarder', a native of Martha's Vineyard. But because no child of that velvety island, no one 'nursed at [this] maternal sea' could be expected to be as 'vengeful and full of social quarrel as the backwoods seaman' Steelkilt, Melville suddenly, either in a fit of distraction or vituperation, shifts Radney's birthplace to an island far less velvety of nurture, Captain Ahab's island. The point is, I think, to portray in Radney the dark side of Ahab's moon, the sour, the ignoble, the anarchic origins of Ahab's rage. I cannot in truth imagine surer justification to explain a test of will between Radney the superior officer, predictably vicious, and Steelkilt, an ordinary sailor said to be sometimes savage but usually civil unless provoked by a caprice of discipline, of law unjustly applied. What 'cozening fiend' tempts the chief mate? What suicidal turn of mind possesses Radney to 'meddle with such a man'? Exhausted from working the pumps on their leaky ship, Steelkilt is commanded to 'get a broom and sweep down the plank, and also a shovel, and remove some offensive matters consequent upon allowing a pig to run at large'. By no means incidental, this ticklish touch and tangle of plot offers augury of the most ominous possible kind. Because 'Steelkilt should have been freed from any trivial business not connected with true nautical duties', Radney's order is an insult that implicates the profoundest matter of *Moby-Dick* in its entirety. On demanding that Steelkilt shovel pig shit, the chief mate sets in motion a chain of events that culminates with the arrival, from remotest depths, of the white whale himself. As if to proclaim an alliance between primordial beast and pagan man, Moby-Dick is as it were summoned to visit his wrath on the fool who dared to dally with the energies of unspeakable force.

Thus does Melville's fantastical imagination correlate the guts of a ship with the offal of a pig and the bowels of the deep. And in a minor drama implicating two premonitory figures, peripheral to but inextricable from the main action, Melville associates a tempest of individual wills with an appetite for tempest inherent in a society destined by Providence to embody the tempestuousness of nature. This is not to say that the

Town-Ho affair is somehow verified by the author's careful compilation of social and geographical fact. But it is to notice Melville's habit of introducing enough history or psychology or biography to justify the burden his characters must assume in helping to determine the course and outcome of things. It is this habit of motivation, then, that recalls us to Radney, pure puzzlement of a man and mate. Is it as an islander that he's both 'domineering and outrageous' as well as 'foolish and infatuated'? Envying the Canaller's superiority in 'general pride of manhood', exhibiting behaviour not unlike Claggart's, is he like Claggart a man unhinged because he is a man unmoored?

For Melville, either in lapse or cunning of intention, on presenting two biographies back to back, informs us that the mate is not a Vineyarder at all but is possibly one of those 'naked Nantucketers' who, 'issuing from their anthill in the sea', seem to fancy themselves as owning the ocean quite as 'Europeans own empires; other seamen having but a right of way through it'. Set down on that Nantucket landscape of 'sea hermits' there is a breed of man like Ahab, patriarchal and grand. And though others are not, both orders of men take to the sea as to a calling. Because two-thirds of this 'terraqueous globe' serve as home and business and 'special plantation' for the Nantucketer, he alone 'in Biblical language, goes down to it in ships', conquering and parcelling out 'the watery world' like an 'Alexander of the oceans'. Not so Radney, an islander of totally ambiguous origins. Oscillating between the sociable place, Martha's Vineyard, and the stormy one, Nantucket (which as Melville remarks is 'no Illinois'), Radney is thus 'doubly doomed and made mad'. Aggrandized by rank, an ill-favoured and lost soul who 'rests and riots on the sea', Radney is totally incompetent to understand the 'mysterious fatality' which Steelkilt, 'wild-ocean born and wild-ocean nurtured', shares with Moby-Dick. Nothing less than this 'strange fatality', Melville says in wonder, pervading 'the whole career of these events, as if verily mapped out before the world was charted'—nothing other than some principle of predestination prompts the wild-ocean whale and wild-ocean man to collaborate in an action that prefigures the final catastrophe of the novel at its end. Rowing the longboat and chasing the whale, our 'mutineer' Steelkilt finds himself cast in the rôle of

149

'bowsman to the harpooneer' Radney. In this fateful rôle Steelkilt is totally miscast. For a state of true colleagueship does not unite bowsman and harpooneer but instead links bowsman and whale in a preordained tie. In that fearful moment of misadventure when their boat hits a ledge and spills Radney into the very maw of Leviathan, the 'inlander', purged of a passion to murder the islander, watches Moby-Dick consume Radney whole.

It is this certitude of a strange and mysterious and pre-ordained fatality governing the nature of things—this certitude of its power fused to a despair of certainty about its purpose—which in the main dictates the forms of Melville's art. Composing a 'fiction of shifting forms', as Larzer Ziff says in *Literary Democracy* (1981), Melville invented a literature of 'abrupt intermergings' in which fictive form slides in and out, back and forth from a 'formless void'. Or, returning to the frame of my argument, what shapes his fiction is less a certitude of void than incertitude itself, manifest in the mystery and strangeness and ominousness of fatality as a force in Creation. And because fatality though undisguised is never recognized until its end is done, its victims undone, Melville's rage at its ravages underlies stories whose forms encapsulate Creation itself, portrayed as scrupulously lawful and imperturbably criminal.

How else can one explain why as a race we are unremittingly drawn to or seduced by or transformed into agents of destruction despite the power of reason and in outright denial of the glory of love? Posing this question every way he could imagine, Melville allowed mystery to shape the surface of his thought even as fatality permeates the tone of his voice. So it is, finally, that in 'The Town-Ho's Story' he crystallized the fact of mystery in the form of utterance he especially cherished, the form he found truly expressive because it cannot be rendered by speech. Whatever it is that human language can convey and art can command Melville pronounces in the sound Steelkilt makes to the Captain who is about to flog him for insubordination. Shrouded in those sounds, in that untranslatable, undifferentiated hiss transmitted from the 'Lakeman' to the whaleman, is a sibilance of words whose literal sense is unknowable. What we do know is that the Captain's failure to flog Steelkilt is not due to fear of the man but to a communion between two persons who comprehend the unearthly terror of terror itself. It is therefore a riddle that centres this story, a puzzle of language whose solution is to be found somewhere deep inside a discourse of dread.

4

In like vein, by way of comparable means directed toward similar ends, Melville many years later strained to find a form to suit the subject of *Billy Budd*. Selecting an American literary prototype to perform a double historical rôle, that of an eighteenth-century archetype and a Christian holotype, he plunged his old-fashioned hero, his immortal child, into a Bunyanesque struggle against mysterious forces which must rout him, embodied in adversaries who must ruin him. Selecting a homeless Englishman whose true homeland is America not Great Britain, whose real name no one but 'God knows Sir', Melville supplies his anonymous waif with a set of aptitudes that cannot fail to undo him. Antithetically, too, he equips this sacrificial lamb with the energy to civilize the life of society, to incarnate by way of inchoate speech, the irreversible forward movement of a retrograde world.

Flaunting his flair for contradiction, therefore, Melville invented an oddity of literary form exactly synchronized with his theme. Because 'truth uncompromisingly told', the method and object of narrative in *Billy Budd*, is unavoidably discordant and ragged, 'the symmetry of form attainable in pure fiction' (the classic English novel) is inappropriate to the shape of a story which cannot conform to any known standard or style of narrative. Neither a 'romance' (that is, a traditional kind of American story in which there are no constraints on fancy because the aim is revelation) nor a pure fiction (that is, a story whose parts must gell so as to make realistic sense), *Billy Budd* is more concerned to represent the 'inner life of one particular ship' than to portray the 'career of an individual sailor'.

Instead of ship we are of course expected to read ship of state. Bared by Melville's 'inside narrative', the inner life of Captain Vere's H.M.S. *Bellipotent* is indeed deranged by the mystery of iniquity, fatality incarnate in the master-of-arms. No other explanation accounts for official trust in John Claggart, distrust and betrayal of Billy Budd. Melville, a writer who admired the doctrine of 'linked analogies' between nature and the human mind, believed too, as F. O. Matthiessen noted, in the symbolical significance of every natural fact. Relying on nomenclature, the names of ships and persons, Melville surveyed lines of intersection at which the purposes of society contradict the interests of the self, the points at which Divine Will and supernatural forces touch coherent but conflicting principles of social justice and scientific law. But the real reasons why this mean and murderous age must bedevil and discredit that noble and pacific man are lodged as usual in language, in the sequence of names which log Billy Budd's course from the instant of impressment to the moment of execution. And though all these intricate and ominous themes are by no means pulled tight by the string of names and titles Melville confers on his hero, nonetheless the name which summons up the natural genius of this unprecedented man does in fact also designate which forms of fatality are stirred by his presence. He cannot of course be known by the fairy tale title used in bad faith by Claggart: Handsome Sailor. Nor does Melville expect us to adopt the one given in 'The News from the Mediterranean', house organ of the British Fleet, which calls him William Budd. Plausible but misleading because recorded only in the falsified bureaucratic account of a phony uprising, William Budd is an official lie.

The one name which personified his nature is the name bestowed by that fatherly old man of the sea, his shipmate, the Dansker who recognizes him, in Wallace Steven's phrase, as 'A Child Asleep in Its Own Life'. Christened Baby Budd he acquires the eponym which identifies both his own inner life and that of the people he obliges. And 'whatever course American literature might follow tomorrow, we will always remember with gratitude that, thanks to spokesmen like Melville', according to Albert Guerard, our writing has made 'a contribution that only adolescence, fresh to life, can make: a concern for moral and spiritual integrity, enthusiasm, a total revulsion in the face of evil and corruption'. Reflecting conventional wisdom more than twenty years ago, Guerard's essay today must be qualified, amended, just enough to sort out other signals given by Melville's news. When the minor young assume major rôles in our key books the subject is scarcely ever highmindedness alone, fresh or frail, staunch or limp. And in presenting us with an amniotic and epic hero of a people that preferred to elevate the rights and sovereignty of the human person above and over the powers of state—hero of a people begot not in secret mutiny but in open though illegal and illegitimate dissent—on composing *Billy Budd* Melville was less drawn to his sailor's capacity for revulsion than he was fascinated by the problem of analysing all possible and improbable reasons why fatality, malignity, iniquity *also* advance the cause of good. How is it that the British model of civilization despite itself, despite a derision of trust and a flirtation with tyranny, mysteriously managed to improve the lives of those under its dominion?

Represented by a taut man of war in time of war, its equipoise tended by a vigilant and virtuous but as it turns out self-serving Master, Burkean in his taste for the arts and politics of decorum, himself the ensign and guardian of that conservative habit of European mind which Henry Adams said and Melville concedes is 'fortified behind power'—pitching and rolling in the heavy seas of canard and deceit, Captain Vere's ship is hard put to stay afloat. Panoplied to impose its species of order on a topsy-turvical world this vessel, this fleet, this police state, Great Britain itself, may well capsize in its own turbulence unless it shifts ballast. Which is to say that it must straightaway alter its conduct of affairs if it is to succeed in stabilizing power at home and abroad. In a piece of priceless luck, out of nowhere the agent of remedy arrives. Already noted for service in the cause of restraint on anarchy, on American democracy, and before long to acquire undying fame as a martyr in the cause of restraint on aristocracy, Billy Budd dampens the rage of revolution, defuses its wrath into a loftier and mellower and more sophisticated politics of equipoise than anyone has ever known. He represents, in a word, a heaven-sent instigator to progress in its pre-industrial form, a form which Melville presents as a clash between Providential theology and Enlightenment statecraft, between Calvinist dogma and Newtonian physics.

In tracing Billy Budd's birthmark, his stutter, to Satan's

cunning hand, in joining blockage of tongue in implosion of energy, Melville forcibly weds a theology of predestination to the First Law of Thermodynamics, the law of the conservation of energy. Formulated in the 1840s and until recently quite unassailable, the First Law (which says that energy may be transferred from one place to another, can be transformed into this shape and that—light from a candle heats the air—but cannot be created or destroyed) does indeed help to demystify Melville's transformation of moral energy into that lightning shot quick as a flame from a discharged cannon at night with which Billy Budd dispatches his accuser. 'I had to say something and I could only say it with a blow.' And because energy too must obey a law which encompasses both organic and inorganic matter, Melville in the final instant of Billy Budd's life, near the end of his own life, transmutes speechlessness into a mannerist style of eloquence. 'God Bless Captain Vere' Billy says, uttering words which are repeated 'without volition' by his shipmates. Echoing him as if charged with 'some vocal current-electric', officers and crew bless the man they had been tempted to curse, Billy Budd's executioner, and thus reaffirm the principle of contradiction as the sole means of palliation, of amendment, of modification and improvement in politics and morals.

Precisely the same principle, adhering the mystery of metaphysics to a science of fatality, supports Melville's decision to yoke his Handsome Sailor to the Master at Arms, to shackle this submissive rebel to that criminal cop. Whether or not the heavens open for Baby Budd, whether or not hell gapes for Jemmy Legs, neither man passes into oblivion but instead each accompanies the other offstage as if in obedience to the one law which, according to nineteenth-century theology and science, ruled the behaviour of matter and spirit in both visible and invisible spheres of being. Sealing an eternal alliance between two people doomed to destroy each other, natural law required that Melville caused both men to expire in barely distinguishable ways. Alive one moment and dead the next, one up and one down, both die without twitch or sound. Given the phenomenal absence of death throes in two bodies that just go slack, inert— Billy Budd's spasmlessness, despite hanging, is said to be 'no more attributable to will-power' than to 'horse-power'—in these mordant clues we are told to discern reasons why vice and virtue, iniquity and righteousness, good and evil obey a law of antithesis which is not limited to religion or government. For even if universal law stems from God and determines states of grace and reprobation, still its operation in the material world must disclose a polarity of force analogous to the force of polarity in a magnetic field. And it is the operation of this mysterious puzzle, polarity, which Melville's *raisonneur* the ship's doctor suggests that only 'scientific theologians' can profitably explore and possibly solve.

Unusual but by no means unimaginable, it is precisely this collection and collation of themes which divulge the inside story of persecution (the career of an individual sailor) and of suppression (the internal life of a particular ship). What is 'inside' this story is the fertility of fatality. And Melville, suddenly confronting the age of progress, struggled to define and locate the principle of contradiction in science and govern- ment and theology and psychology. For it was this principle, none other, that supported those 'most important reforms in the British navy' which led to historic 'political advance along nearly the whole line' of society as a whole. In setting his story in 1797, therefore, Melville joined historic time to modern times so as to subject the entire perverse process of human development to a dynamics of motion derived from a single cosmic principle. Referring to the distant past, to an era at once monstrous and marvellous because marked by a spirit both demonic and saintly, by 'the Revolutionary Spirit'—associating the 'Spirit of that Age' of a 'time before steamships, or then more frequently than now', with the spirit of modern times, Melville drew on a single mechanical law, Newton's, which dictated the behaviour of matter in all its manifold forms, organic and temporal no less than inorganic and spatial. Informed opinion, so Whitehead observes about the period contained by Melville's fiction and encircled by Melville's life, tended to veer from assuming the 'unique pre-eminence' of the 'notion of mass' as the 'final permanent quantity' in favour of the notion of mass as 'the name for a quantity of energy'. In 1797 and 1891, whether named mass and energy or energy and mass, matter itself was controlled by a 'single spring of action': gravitation.

In *Billy Budd*, then, absolute truth could be uncompromisingly told only if Melville included this mechanical law as a certain scaffold of metaphysics. Even as 'change of motion is produced by force', Jacob Bronowski observes, so too 'motion between masses, whether apple, moon and earth, planet and sun'—or as Melville incontrovertibly knew, between Billy Budd and Claggart—'is produced by gravitational forces which attract them to one another'. Gravitation in the here and now, theodicy here and hereafter, Newton and Calvin in tandem— these are the personages and polarities that define and control behaviour in a pre-modernist allegory which presents mass and energy and force in linked analogy with the morality and theology and politics of change, of motion, of progress.

There is where we situate the crowning mystery of this fiction, the final confoundment of my essay: can it be that things must get better, Melville wondered during his last days on earth, even as things inevitably get worse? For it is the perversity of order in an eternally disordered world he leaves us with, the legacy of a writer who held that a careful dis-orderliness is the fittest form for a truly American book. If he left unsaid anything else that really matters, it is Babo and Steelkilt and Baby Budd we must turn to, mannerists, elocu-tionists of silence.

8

Voices Off, On and Without: Ventriloquy in *The Confidence-Man*

by A. ROBERT LEE

'What sort of bamboozling story is this that you are telling me?'
  —Ishmael to the landlord of the Spouter Inn. *Moby-Dick*

'For who will meddle with a book professing to inculcate philosophical truths through the medium of nonsensical people talking nonsense—the best definition of its scope and character that a somewhat prolonged consideration has enabled us to suggest. A novel it is not, unless a novel means forty-five conversations held on board a steamer, conducted by personages who might pass for the errata of creation, and so far resembling the Dialogue of Plato as to be undoubted Greek to ordinary men. Looking at the substance of these colloquies, they cannot be pronounced altogether valueless; looking only at the form, they might well be esteemed the compositions of a March hare with a literary turn of mind. It is not till a lengthening perusal—a perusal more lengthened than many readers are willing to accord—has familiarized us with the quaintness of the style, and until long domestication with the incomprehensible interlocutors has infected us with something of their own eccentricity, that our faculties, like the eyes of prisoners accustomed to the dark, become sufficiently acute to discern the golden grains which the author has made it his business to hide away from us.
—*The Literary Gazette, and Journal of Archaeology, Science and Art*,
London, 11 April 1857

'There speaks the ventriloquist again . . .'
— *The Confidence-Man*

1

'QUITE AN ORIGINAL': it hardly surprises that Melville capitalized his phrase for the Cosmopolitan, the chief among the astonishing gallery of voices which make up *The Confidence-Man* (1857).[1] It applies with equal aptness to the book itself, a fictional world as singularly conceived and executed as any in his previous repertoire, beginning from the Lost Valley Polynesian half-paradise of Nukuhiva in *Typee* (1846) and extending through to the camouflaged scenarios of his *Putnam's* and *Harper's* shorter pieces of the mid-1850s which immediately precede and from which (together with his additionally written 'The Piazza') he made his selection for *Piazza Tales* (1856).[2] As Melville directs each feint and counterfeint in *The Confidence-Man*, it becomes virtually impossible not to acknowledge our ensnarement in a most rare and protean double-Masquerade (286): that witnessed as the ostensible sunrise-to-midnight journey of the Mississippi steamship the *Fidèle* bound down-river from St. Louis for New Orleans on All Fools Day; and that taking place actually within, or as an analogue of, our own brilliantly put upon and in every likelihood traduced, reading-experience. There can be few works of fiction, certainly of those written in the nineteenth century as well as landmark modernist narratives, in which author, text and reader are more precariously brought into conscious relationship, or in which they more adroitly are made to challenge and even undermine each other in the very process of seeking mutual recognition.

Original, then, *The Confidence-Man* was, and is, and for admirers, wholly as consequential as anything Melville wrote. It demonstrates an originality which asserts itself everywhere and at each unflagging turn and staging of the book. Whether one settles upon the opening (and seemingly magical) metamorphosis of the Christly 'man in cream-colors' (1) into the diabolized 'grotesque black cripple' (9), or Black Guinea's subsequent testificatory list of six or so 'ge'mmen' (12) through whom the narrative draws out all the other successive

Voices Off, On and Without: Ventriloquy in 'The Confidence-Man'

'passenger' voices, or upon the five mock-parabular stories-within-stories (in turn those of Goneril, the Cripple, John Moredock, Charlemont and China Aster), or upon the pseudo-authorial voice of Chapters XIV, XXXIII and XLIV which chimes in about the necessary artfulness of Fiction in matchingly artful apologies, or indeed upon almost any page of Melville's duplicitous prose with its recurring *mots clefs* of 'confidence', 'charity', 'trust', 'charming', 'shaving' and the like, the effect comes over as wholly of a piece. *The Confidence-Man*, wilfully (or knowingly at least) eschews plot, character in any conventional sense, even action; it offers instead talk, irrepressible, necessary human talk, as plausible yet as inconsistent and equivocal as humankind at large, and all of it worked into a superb dissonance of voices, a colloquium at once literal-seeming and fantastical and enacted with startling verve against the Twainian American backdrop of steamboat and frontier. For in this last of the full-length prose narratives published in his lifetime, Melville projects a view of History as utterly particular—American Life on the Mississippi at mid-nineteenth century, yet also, and well beyond any mere allegory, a surrealized, waking-dream Masquerade of recurrent human types and illusions. In serving these ends *The Confidence-Man* calls on nothing short of the most purposive, masterly ventriloquism.

Furthermore, underpinning the 'History' and the surface maze of sign and countersign and the supposed 'self-erasing' prose of *The Confidence-Man*,[3] Melville posits a complex 'solar' (272) metaphysics, a Cosmos glimpsed dimly from the *Fidèle*'s 'gentleman's cabin' (272), one of 'barren planets' (272), lights either in process of being extinguished (272) or actually out. This is a Cosmos whose riddles, transformational energies and sheer unknowable otherness, indeed appear as through a glass darkly, evidence of a strange overall directionlessness to motion. The whole bent of *The Confidence-Man* is to suggest dark not only during but before and after life, bookends as it were closing off yet also casting shadows across the animated human ado in between. And just as no sure and certain meaning attaches to so undeterminable a metaphysic (with its Heideggerian *Sein und Zeit* implications of an eschatology in which man's condition is inescapably one of anxiety), no more

159

does it to humankind and its unbidden arrival, existence and expiration as consciousness. Melville shows himself not a little the classic Victorian-American Man of Doubts (in Hawthorne's deft and perceptive phrase able neither to 'believe,' nor be comfortable in his unbelief')[4] when he sites the closing scenes of the book within the midnight darkness and 'waning light' (286) of the *Fidèle*'s world-cabin, having had his Cosmopolitan disingenuously tell the barber 'You can conclude nothing absolute from the human form' (254).

Nor, the narrative everywhere implies, can anything absolute be concluded from human discourse. The very medium of language, however brilliantly deployed (or precisely by being brilliantly deployed), comes back to a Chinese-box wayward-ness, words as ever inescapably self-referential and parasitic upon their own being. Thus the greater the confidence in all and every language-system the more reality goes on being fictional-ized and mankind yet further detached from that overarching Melvilleian desideratum, Truth. Melville's narrative, too, takes immense pains to show how each ruling illusion—and *The Confidence-Man* illustrates them in plenty—brings into play its own self-serving voicings and words; and how each of these in turn become fictions for others to believe or not; and how each of these believings (or unbelievings to reiterate Hawthorne's language) in their turn beget subsequent fictions.

In embodying this narrational echo-chamber of metaphysics and language, *The Confidence-Man* could with justice claim to operate as the exemplary postmodern text, subversive of and at all times deconstructing, its own idiom and imagined world. But whether that, or something rather (and blessedly?) less heady, it can hardly go on being regarded as merely some arcane satire of Christianity, or the cash-nexus, or even American optimism in all its uplift and traditional benignity. In as much as it does offer this satire, it does so only as the explicit outward guise of far more fundamental and ontological probing.

For the most part, however, and despite Melville's built-in warnings about the dangers of one-for-one interpretation, the main accounts have too often tended just that way, one or another (perfectly well intended) 'thematic' reading. Most of the stopping-off places since Elizabeth S. Foster brought out her indispensable Hendricks House Edition of *The Confidence-*

Man in 1954 are by now familiar: it allegedly represents Melville's corrosive vision of how the Devil in the guise of different confidence-men hoists Christianity by its own rhetorical petard and ethics; it indicts the 'spirit of the west' as no more than a bogus rationale for the American acquisitive appetite; it sees mankind as endlessly whistling in the philosophic dark and the dupe of false panaceas, beliefs and millenial credos, none more for Melville's own age than Emersonian Transcendentalism; it casts its net even wider to embrace the trickster-gods not only of American but world folklore and of religions as disjunct from Judaeo-Christianity as Hinduism and Bhuddism; and it signals Melville's leavetaking after the comparative failure of his previous books, the embittered literary Last Testament of an author unable to win the intelligent understanding of his nineteenth-century readership.[5] All of these, to be sure, deserve their hearing, and cast varying degrees of light on the text; yet, even taken together, they fail to meet the full controlling energy and contrapuntal play of meaning in operation throughout *The Confidence-Man*.

For by the very nature of its compositional tactics—its vortex (to use a term from the Epilogue of *Moby-Dick*) of different voices, the criss-cross of equivocation and mutually subversive viewpoints—it insistently seeks to slip free from any one mastering interpretation. Its entire imaginative inclination is to work more fugitively, a carefully staged open dialectic of voices and disputation each ostensibly authoritative and offered in good faith but so calculated as to persuade the reader that such is not so and to force him (or her) increasingly back on his own correspondingly uncertain mettle. For some this undoubtedly has the effect of diminishing, even of nullifying, the book. Melville intended no clear final meanings at all, runs the argument; the narrative stops and starts at random, interrupting the attention and at the risk of inertness; and the multiple equivocations begin to cloy as they follow in ever accelerating succession. A suspicion even arises that the voices prise free of their author's overall control, virtuosity for its own sake and at the price of the design as a whole.

Yet to others, myself among them, Melville's 'voices' and the ventriloquism which activates them, triumph exhilaratingly. Melville rarely falters in his Ship of Fools Cosmic and frontier high comedy, its vitality underwritten by a perhaps unexpected seriousness, especially as it has often been linked to the mood described in Chapter 49 of *Moby-Dick*, 'The Hyena', in which 'a man takes this whole universe for a practical joke'. In some measure, Melville's success indeed has to do with the implicit reference to the narrative's bustling, predatory and theatrically historic nineteenth-century Life on the Mississippi world; but even more it has to do with the razor-sharp juxtapositions and compound ironies of each verbal encounter. For as lifelike as Melville makes his busy river Masquerade—its passing use of actual geography, the movement about the decks and berths and cabins—so he also distances the narrative from its immediate material, a world truly as Chapter XXXIII says 'to which we feel a tie' (207), yet also, as in a discontinuous dream hallucination, 'another world' (207). Far from yielding some random 'forty-five conversations' (the number of chapters in the book), as the understandably perplexed though anything but unintelligent *Literary Gazette* reviewer surmised, however, *The Confidence-Man* invites us, in a perfectly calculated manner, to hear echoed our talking selves at work—voices within those ostensibly in action which pile contradiction upon contradiction and which underscore the fact that we are rarely either wholly the masters or the servants of the words we use and display a betraying willingness to dupe and in turn be duped whether by intention or (as in the case of Pitch) against and despite our every best avowed intention.

In this sense, it could be said that *The Confidence-Man* performs a dark but valuably therapeutic function, a narrative which irrigates (or seen another way which absorbs into itself) a whole rhetoric of confusion about absolute and relative Truth, that which unequivocally should be so and that which most equivocally is so. It also demonstrates the circuitry of offence and defence in most human communication, the intricate lattice-work of improvisational ends and means, argument licit and illicit. Melville's personal mood after the failure of *Pierre* (1852) and the falling sales of his earlier work may justifiably have propelled him to near-despair, none of it helped by his patrician self-guilt at falling short on the family obligations he believed due his wife Elizabeth, his young children, and his mother and sisters. But if despair and as the evidence suggests nervous desperation to the point of threatened violence did press close, it emphatically did not damage the acuity of his art. Given these personal strains and pressures, where are there to be found cannier, more honed or concentrated examples of his story-telling than in the best of his 1850s tales ('I and My Chimney', arguably, even makes his emotional difficulties over into a story in its own right) or in *Israel Potter* (1855), whose episodicity is reflected in the fact that it was first issued in Harper's *New Monthly Magazine* (1854–55) in nine instalments? Even *Billy Budd* (1888–91), though left in draft at his death three decades later, could well be thought by its striking compression and 'inside narrative' a belated carry-over from this earlier period.

In this, too, *The Confidence-Man* shows the benefits which accrued to Melville from writing to a shorter compass: the tough, elliptical phrasing, the concentration of aim in his satiric targeting, and the narrative's forward-propulsive rhythm and bite despite each rapid 'fade' and transposition of voice. Far from issuing out of a simply melancholic eve-of-career blackness on Melville's part, furthermore, *The Confidence-Man* positively thrives on its parodic appetite and inclinations. In imagining his American version of *As You Like It* (whose 'All the world's a stage' the Cosmopolitan allegedly calls to mind in his dexterous game of double- and triple-bluff with the Practical Disciple Egbert), appropriately played against the great iconic, arterial waterway of the American South-West, Melville assuredly wrote with his powers inspired and fully intact.

2

Voices, then: and the first of them, paradoxically, belongs to the Deaf Mute who comes aboard 'at sunrise on a first day of April' (1) and who 'speaks' only through New Testament quotation, a deific, whited, Jesus-like figure who may (or may not) be the first of the Confidence-Man incarnations. Immediately, he is also likened to the miraculous founding Godhead of the Incas, appearing 'suddenly as Manco Capac at the lake Titicaca' (1). But if Godhead he is, he also is 'in the extremest sense of the word, a stranger' (1), fair-cheeked and flaxen-haired and like the attenuated Bartleby barely *in* life by appearance; yet to another angle of vision he could well be the perfect contrary and utterly in life, the adept New York city slicker or American Artful Dodger, 'recently arrived from the East' (1) and thereby the incarnation of 'down-East' Yankee slipperiness, 'an original genius in his vocation' (1) in a manner which deviously secularizes the word 'vocation'. Is the Mute, then, a Messiah whose Christianity and message the world neither wants nor any longer believes? Or some cosmic, Proteus-like figure who by his every gesture and word confirms the impossibility of Absolute Faith (or Absolute Anything) in a world of fluid, kaleidoscopic appearance, transcendental, human or otherwise? Or the 'decoy' (13) who is Black Guinea and his 'gemm'en' successors turned inside out and who can reptilianly shift out of one shape and voice into another, a nineteenth-century Jeremy Diddler (to whom *The Confidence-Man* makes several references), at all times on the make and the personification of sharp-eyed frontier Ben Franklinism? In part, to be sure, he amounts to all of these. By his passivity and half-ghostly white blankness and 'lamb-like figure' (5), he offers in his very own person a live matching 'slate' to the one he holds up and which affords its beholders the dubious occasion of revealing themselves by how they interpret the Corinthian Scripture; hence he could be any number of identities and interconnecting kinds of double but principally Christ and Devil, Saviour and Tempter, Cosmic Godhead and Mississippi river con-man.

Either way, what perhaps more matters is his slate of quotations from Corinthians 1, 13, the discomforting, chalked up propositions that Charity thinketh no Evil, Suffereth long, and is kind, Endureth all things, Believeth all things, and never faileth (2–3). Seemingly thus *The Confidence-Man* offers one working absolute; but straightaway Melville sets it against its seeming opposite working absolute, the sternly forbidding 'NO TRUST', the barber's motto written up on a 'gaudy sort of illuminated pasteboard sign' (4) and to which the narrative returns at the closing midnight hour. And just as the Mute's 'Charity' refers both to high Christian-Utopian ethics and to the parodic and painfully countermanding less elevated 'game of charity' (11) which follows when Black Guinea catches coins thrown by the passengers in his mouth, so 'NO TRUST' inscribes both a Nay-Saying to the Cosmos at large and a far worldier message of no financial credit, an act of local prudence in a Mississippi frontier arena in which the hype, the con, the rip-off and the quick deal take place almost by rote. Both these two-fold inscriptions, Absolute in one way, Relative and open to competing 'textual readings' in another, Melville then situates within a whole further treacherous minefield of language—'fleecing' (the Mute has 'a long fleecy nap', Guinea a 'knotted black fleece'), 'shaving', 'credit', 'faith' (the *Fidèle* could easily be re-styled the *Infidèle*) and, above all, like a great linguistic beacon bedazzling and misleading the reader, the word 'confidence' itself.

And between 'Charity' and 'NO TRUST' *The Confidence-Man* offers a labyrinth of still other contrary utterance in which both the Confidence-Man voices and their passenger collocutors jostle for ascendance. To a post-Melvilleian readership schooled on the recent writing, say, of Jorge Luis Borges, Samuel Beckett or William Burroughs, the response to all this equivocating din of speech (and the metaphysics it assumes) may well be some Poundian vow of silence or a use of language pared down to its functional minimum. For Melville in *The Confidence-Man* the direction lies elsewhere, in talking through, at every speed and exhaustively, the Masquerade of human illusion to the point where the Word itself becomes chastened and drained of its capacity to mislead and obfuscate.

For to talk, however ensnaring, indeed is human, and given the book's silent opening charade, its preludial dumbshow of sorts, almost welcomely human, especially when, in response to the Mute, the following cataract of voices breaks out:

> 'Odd fish!'
> 'Poor fellow!'
> 'Who can he be?'
> 'Casper Hauser.'
> 'Bless my soul!'
> 'Uncommon countenance.'
> 'Green prophet from Utah.'
> 'Humbug!'
> 'Singular Innocence.'
> 'Means something.'
> 'Spirit-rapper.'

'Moon-calf.'
'Piteous.'
'Trying to enlist interest.'
'Beware of him.'
'Fast asleep here, and, doubtless, pick-pockets on board.'
'Kind of daylight Endymion.'
'Escaped convict, worn out with dodging.'
'Jacob dreaming at Luz.' (6)

To the one side of *The Confidence-Man* Melville sets up the avatar Confidence-Man voices, aided and abetted by a *faux-ami* authorial voice (that, for instance, which speaks in Chapters XIV, XXXIII and XLIV and in the several palindromic chapter-headings). Behind these, too, he implies his own actual authorial voice, the Author as a further species of tricksterly Con-Man, directing the entire cacophony of argument and exchange. And to the other side, as amply evident in these 'epitaphic comments' (6), we have the *Fidèle*'s passenger's voices, angled so as to echo with embarrassing closeness those of the book's readership. For do not the passengers' bafflements and guesswork blend slyly into the reader's, a mosaic of voices rendered as vivid telegraphese (the Mute is said to engage in 'pathetic telegraphing') which surely mimics our own uneasy and understandably guarded responses to the Mute and his message, a changing mix of disbelief, wonder, shame and sheer confusion?

These passenger voices, the forward column of many to follow, thus take on generic status: they belong to nineteenth-century American steamboat travellers who stand in for a yet larger Vanity Fair humankind; they give their testimony and contradictions across a 24-hour river journey which marks travel as emblematically double and transcendentalized as that in Hawthorne's 'The Celestial Railroad' (1843) or Thoreau's *A Week on the Concord and Merrimack Rivers* (1849); and their collective effect, unavoidably acceded to, is to speak the measure of human confusion—about a sealed and finally undecipherable universe, a historic Christian ethics impossibly at odds with human nature, and an inherited world of language in which Ambiguity of necessity subordinates all before it. Little wonder that Melville describes his company of passenger-readers as a 'piebald parliament' a 'pilgrim' parade:

As among Chaucer's Canterbury pilgrims, or those oriental ones crossing the Red Sea towards Mecca in the festival month, there was no lack of variety. Natives of all sorts, and foreigners; men of business and men of pleasure; parlor men and backwoodsmen; farm-hunters and fame-hunters; heiress-hunters, and still keener hunters after all these hunters. Fine ladies in slippers, and moccasined squaws; Northern speculators and Eastern philosophers; English, Irish, German, Scotch, Danes; Santa Fé traders in striped blankets, and Broadway bucks in cravats of cloth of gold; fine-looking Kentucky boatmen, and Japanese-looking Mississippi cotton-planters; Quakers in full drab, and United States soldiers in full regimentals; slaves, black, mulatto, quadroon; modish young Spanish Creoles, and old-fashioned French Jews; Mormons and Papists; Dives and Lazarus; jesters and mourners, teetotalers and convivialists, deacons and blacklegs; hard-shell Baptists and clay-eaters; grinning negroes, and Sioux chiefs solemn as high-priests. In short, a piebald parliament, an Anacharsis Cloots congress of all kinds of that multiform pilgrim species, man. (8)

Aboard the *Fidèle*, thus, a 'congress' of passenger voices, each to be matched (and clearly overmatched) by the avatar voices, and they, in turn, matched and at the behest of the book's ostensible authorial voice, and behind all of these, deafeningly silent and wrily just out of reach and hearing, Melville's own: such the layers of voicing in the text. To embark upon *The Confidence-Man*, book and Mississippi journey, entails entering more than usually upon a process of reading as listening and hearing, and of listening for and hearing as much what is *not* being said as what is—for the gaps, that is, between speaker and message and that being spoken and that being meant. The narrative thereby in every sense offers a 'parliament' and 'congress' of speaking voices; and also an invitation to the reader to make of himself the most utterly alert and cautious listening-post.

3

The larger design of *The Confidence-Man* so indicated in the two opening chapters, it remains only for Black Guinea's list to set the narrative's talk even more actively into imaginative motion. Each guarantor of Black Guinea's identity will propose

a validation—of Guinea himself (though as what we might
well ask), of the proposition that the world *is* what it seems and
harbours no discrepant, untoward or 'black' secrets, and that
Charity everytime will win over No-Trust and dourest scepticism. Such the 'word' to be supplied by the guarantors;
nothing, of course, could be further from what the narrative
actually reveals: more contrary, ventriloquial argument, more
cleverly equivocal and misapplied quotation, more interpola-
tions and dubious acts of commentary and parables which
might better be construed as anti-parables (those of Goneril
and China Aster particularly). All, to one or another degree,
point to the Word as Apocrypha, from which at Midnight, the
very witching hour, there will quite literally be extracts (about
another Jesus, another 'wisdom' (275), that of Jesus, Son of
Sirach). In 'giving their word', their living spoken word and
their word as 'credit', Guinea's guarantors—whether each a
different avatar or incarnations of some single master-voice—
draw out by their sure, plausible, sweetest confidence a
darkness everywhere within and about them, as complex as
the Gordian knot aboard the *San Dominick* in Melville's 'Benito
Cereno' or as the black human knottedness of Guinea himself.
The list runs as follows:

> 'Oh yes, oh yes, dar is aboard here a werry nice, good
> ge'mman wid a weed, and a ge'mman in a gray coat and white
> tie, what knows all about me; and a ge'mman wid a big book,
> too; and a yarb-doctor; and a ge'mman in a yaller west; and a
> ge'mman wid a brass plate; and a ge'mman in a wiolet robe;
> and a ge'mman as is a sodjer; and ever so many good, kind,
> honest ge'mmen more abord what knows me and will speak for
> me, God bress 'em; yes, and what knows me as well as dis poor
> old darkie knows hisself, God bress him! Oh, find 'em, find
> 'em,' he earnestly added, 'and let 'em come quick, and show
> you all, ge'mmen, dat dis poor ole darkie is werry well wordy of
> all you kind ge'mmen's kind confidence.' (12–13)

First, Guinea himself speaks in the fake, obsequious voice of
'Puttin' On Ole Massa', a voice self-protectingly used by
slaves before their white owner-enslavers, and which Melville
previously deployed with Fleece, the *Pequod*'s black cook, and
more menacingly with Babo in 'Benito Cereno'. Each guarantor

(the only two we don't meet are the 'ge'mman wid a yeller west' and the 'ge'mman as is a sodjer', unless Melville intended the ex-prisoner from the Tombs who masquerades as a Mexican War veteran to be one of the avatars) indeed proves 'werry well wordy'. The play of sound and meaning— wordy-worthy, 'kind ge'mmen' and 'kind confidence'—all enwrapped within Guinea's fawning could hardly better anticipate the massive duplicities of voice ahead. Guinea's plea for 'confidence', cast as sickening, parodic slave-argot, carefully paves the way for the further plausibility to come, against which even the book's toughest Nay-Sayers, the Wooden-legged Man, the Miser, the 'invalid Titan in home-spun' (96), and above all, Pitch, the inveterate boy-hater and seeming misanthrope, all finally prove insufficient match. And no one of Guinea's list more cajoles, or better and more plausibly argues for universal confidence, than the Cosmo-politan, the 'ge'mman in a wiolet robe', the ultimate up-holder of the 'worth' of all things—'talk', mankind, the universe, God. By his every ingratiating word he at once arouses doubt and seduces; a nimble, obfuscatory Giver of Dark yet by the same measure and given the darkness all about also the Great Enlightener. He it is, the Masquerade finally played through and the *Fidèle*'s voices at last hushed on this apocalyptic All Fool's Day, who says to the 'clean, comely old man' (273), armed with his counterfeit self-protection and thereby the very image of an aged but still unseeing Adamic humankind, 'let me extinguish this lamp' (286), a voice almost weary of its own ventriloquial exertions and of the gullibility it has elicited aboard this Mississippi and world craft.

The voices which buzz about Black Guinea, furthermore, indicate the colloquia still in store: first the Doubters, begin-ning with the Wooden-legged Man, a Hawthorne-like 'dis-charged custom-house officer' (11) who thinks Guinea 'a sham' (11), 'some white operator' (13) and his believers a 'flock of fools, under this captain of fools, in this ship of fools!' (15), in essence a voice of refusal; then, the Believers, 'the young Episcopal clergyman' (12), ingenuous and willing to think the best, and in turn the merchant whom the Confidence-Man as John Ringman ('the ge'mman wid de weed') will dupe

169

remorselessly by his tale of Goneril, and the 'soldier-like Methodist' (13), a one-time 'volunteer chaplain to a volunteer rifle-regiment' (13), Melville's pillorying embodiment of the Christian militarist who true to his moral paradox shifts from Believer to Doubter and designates Guinea 'some sort of Jeremy Diddler' (16). Playing across these voices, the text offers four others, each choric and interjectionary and provoked by the Wooden-legged man's jibes and general scepticism. In turn they read 'We ain't agoing to trust him' (15), 'What an example' (16), 'Might deter Timon' (16) and 'Something queer about this darkie, depend upon it' (17), a typical spectrum of Trust and No-Trust, which chime in and out of the comments of the cripple and of Guinea himself. An addendum is given in the voice of a 'gruff boatman' (18) who proposes Guinea find his guarantors himself, a nice touch if Guinea is but one and all the guarantors. Guinea's reply is to invoke 'dat good man wid de weed' (18), and he, as Chapter IV comes up, duly adds his 'voice' to the fray, a further voice as his name suggests to 'ring' the changes but whose tale of Goneril we don't actually hear until Chapter XII (and then in the voice of some apparently omniscient authorial 'we', 64). What the Goneril episode entails, as it were, is more silent voicing taking up from where the Mute left off; Melville makes us wait on and witness in rising impatience its impact on Mr. Roberts, the Country Merchant. This entangling, tangled weave of voices, ranging from confidence to doubt, surprise to bravado to Pitch-like unsurprise, sets the pattern to follow: more voicing and voices, all at cross-purposes and each designed to outmanoeuvre and undercut its predecessor. Indeterminacy so becomes the operating principle—indeterminacy of meaning, character, words and universe—and all nothing other than perfectly determined by Melville as artist, the directing hand behind his Masquerade and each competing voice of Confidence and No-Trust.

In these interlinking verbal encounters, too, Melville sets up the paradigm for those to follow: in turn, the 'ge'mman in a gray coat and white tie', the undissuadable, darkly Mrs. Jellybyish agent for a 'Widow and Orphan Asylum recently founded among the Seminoles' who would 'quicken' 'missions' as he says 'with the Wall Street spirit' (45), the Man of

Charity perfectly doubled as the Man of Business; the 'ge'mman wid a big book', the 'president and transfer-agent of the Black Rapids Coal Co.', whose successive enrolment of the Merchant and the Miser (and by implication others) amounts to a signing-on for Hell; the 'yarb-doctor', whose bland, all-natural physic and general rhetoric of the infinite curability of all ailments (by such medicine as his 'OMNI-BALSAMIC REINVIGORATOR' and 'Samaritan Pain Dissuader') charms even the Injured Soldier, the Old Miser and almost the 'ursine', nay-saying Pitch; and the 'ge'mman wid a brass plate', the Agent of the 'Philosophical Intelligence Office' who finally does win through Pitch's resistance, sells him a 'boy', and promptly disembarks at Devil's Joke (146), his confidence work triumphantly dispatched.

Each of these proves a masterly adept in the 'business' of persuasion, patient, ingenious, and utterly able to grasp and exploit the other point of view. By their insistent spirit of uplift—American to the core yet also universalized—they elicit time and again conspicuous human frailty, whether in the form of greed, the willingness to believe the best, the hope of robust good health and eternal vigour, even the wish for Everlasting Life. They work their rhetorical spells half as New World sermonists and half as the eternal huckster, salesmen of an American metaphysic of hope; and their appeal everywhere falls on ready ears, frontier 'passengers' in search of balm, gold, easy solutions. If they, in turn, pursue false goods—spiritual, material or cosmic—they do so as clients who can neither refuse the blandishments before them nor keep up their doubts; Pitch himself, after holding out, also finally falls into the trap.

The final apotheosis arrives in the Cosmopolitan, Melville's sublime, costumed and confidence-spouting pentecostalist who indeed 'speaks in tongues' and offers himself as the perfect Emersonian Representative Man ('Francis Goodman'), New World Plausibility and ready fraternity made incarnate. But though his every word sounds the note of Charity and Trust, he serves, too, as precisely Pitch's 'most extraordinary metaphysical scamp' (155), the ultimate vanquisher, or so it would seem, of the Barber's No-Trust Universe (a feat which also gets him out of paying for a shave), the avatar who twins

171

within his own person the fulfilment of our wish-to-believe and the trickster deity who takes every advantage of that impulse in order to indict humankind for all other related self-deceptions. Whether in the matter of the Moredock Indian-hating parable, or the play-within-a-play charade with Charlie Noble, or the Emerson-Thoreau Mark Winsome and Egbert parallel of the Master and Practical Disciple and the subsequent charade on Friendship and Self-Reliance acted out between them, he continues like a metronome to speak the language of Transcendental hopefulness. And he does so against all the evidence—Pitch's doubts, the Titan's groan, the China Aster and Indian-hating stories, the Barber's shrewd but unavailing sense that he is being taken for a ride and the Old Man's pathetic trustfulness. As he 'kindly' leads the old man away, having hinted that Jehovah himself might be nothing other than the ultimate godly reference-point for all false confidence, he keeps up the rhetoric of hope. But to hand are only the Apocrypha, the sleepy cabin voices, useless devices like the Counterfeit Detector and the excremental life-preserver, the young Faustian boy peddler and his sales-pitch and the 'waning lights' (286) of the *Fidèle*. His is the last voice we hear, except for Melville's apparent own, plausible to the end, calling for Trust yet arousing as always nothing less than No-Trust.

4

Deceptive and double as are the avatar voices, from the Mute's and Guinea's through to that of the Cosmopolitan, so to add complication overlaying them are others, those of the five parables and those of the pseudo-authorial Chapters XIV, XXXIII and XLIV. The former have provoked considerable critical attention: the Goneril story as a false allegory, the opposite of its appearance and actually a parody of ceremonial grief and mourning used to win the cash (and sympathy) of the unwary listener; the Cripple's story as a comment on those formulas of charitable appeal which best flatter the *largesse* of the alms-giver; the Indian-hating as a frontier chronicle adapted to indict all forms of chronic Absolutism, whether Indians as Devils or other moral and theological systems of

Heaven and Hell; Charlemont's story as an inverse Prodigal Son parable; and the China Aster narrative as that of the trusting light-giver 'betrayed by friends' and in part a cautionary tale like 'Bartleby' of the artist plunged into dark and death by the refusal to be 'credited'.[6] Although each needs its context to be read with a due regard for its inlaid ironies, in sum these stories all contribute to *The Confidence-Man's* general strategy; they 'say' what they don't mean, and hide what they most purport to reveal.

No less applies to the three authorial interfoliations. Chapter XIV takes a rather beady aim at notions of consistency of character in fiction, full of inventive double-talk about 'flying-squirrels' (77) and the metamorphoses of the caterpillar. The purpose ('Worth The Consideration Of Those To Whom It May Prove Worth Considering' as the chapter-heading puts it) of Melville's first digression surely has to do with parodying all notions of 'rules', art regulated by inherited Aristotelian *dicta* or the like. In Chapter XXXIII ('Which May Pass For Whatever It May Prove To Be Worth'), Melville takes the matter further; art as more real than life, and life as itself nothing less than art. The speculation goes as usual several ways at once, though the voice behind the chapter comes as close as any to Melville's own in the observation that Fiction 'should present another world, and yet one to which we feel the tie' (207). Chapter XLIV ('In Which The Last Three Words Of The Last Chapter Are Made The Text Of Discourse, Which Will Be Sure Of Receiving More Or Less Attention From Those Readers Who Do Not Skip It') returns to notions of 'character' in fiction, arguing for character as located in time, mutability and shifting viewpoints ('like a revolving Drummond light') rather than as some static, merely spatial, entity.[7] The point, to be sure, ties into a far wider literary-critical debate about how fictions—and the characters which inhabit them—go about their imaginative business. But true to form, Melville also slyly makes his observations 'fictions' in their own right, in part a justification for his self-acknowledging fictional 'man-show' (270), in part a display of how even supposed critical discourse can be a fiction.

In other words, the voicing in these three chapters, as much as it would seem to direct us towards a grand authorial Theory of Fiction, operates also as but one further instance of Melville's sleight-of-hand. No less than each avatar voice, or the voice in play throughout each story-parable, or the passenger voices, this 'authorial' voice solicits and at the same time mocks our readerly confidence. 'The Author' plays one more co-partner in the overall Masquerade. He purports to be authoritative, but on patient deliberation, he amounts to nothing other than a created, fictive voice. The true authorial voice we never actually hear for it lies as always 'off' and 'without', the voice of Melville's creative consciousness so deviously responsible for all the startling ventriloquy in evidence at every turn in *The Confidence-Man*.

NOTES

1. All page references throughout are to Elizabeth S. Foster (ed.), *The Confidence-Man: His Masquerade* (New York: Hendricks House, 1954).
2. These in sequence are 'Bartleby', 'Benito Cereno', 'The Lightning-Rod Man', 'The Encantadas; or, Enchanted Islands' and 'The Bell-Tower'.
3. 'Self-erasing' is R. W. B. Lewis's phrase, part of his account in the Afterword to the Signet paperback of *The Confidence-Man* (New York: New American Library, 1964) and republished in his *Trials of the Word: Essays in American Literature and the Humanistic Tradition* (New Haven and London: Yale University Press, 1965).
4. Hawthorne's *Journal*, 12 November 1856. Reprinted in Jay Leyda (ed.), *The Melville Log: A Documentary Life of Herman Melville, 1819–1891* (New York: Harcourt, Brace and Co., 1951), Vol. 11, p. 529.
5. See, for instance: Edward H. Rosenberry: 'Melville's Ship Of Fools', *P.M.L.A.*, LXXV (December 1960), 604–8; Walter Dubler: 'Theme and Structure in Melville's *the Confidence-Man*', *American Literature*, XXXIII (November 1961), 307–19; Philip Drew: 'Appearance and Reality in Melville's *The Confidence Man*', *English Literary History*, Vol. 31, No. 4 (December 1964), 418–42; Ernest Tuveson: 'The Creed of The Confidence-Man', *English Literary History*, Vol. 33, No. 2 (June, 1966) and the relevant chapters in H. Bruce Franklin: *The Wake of the Gods: Melville's Mythology* (Stanford University Press, 1963); Edgar A. Dryden: *Melville's Thematics of Form: The Great Art of Telling the Truth* (Baltimore: Johns Hopkins, 1968); Warwick Wadlington: *The Confidence Game in American Literature* (Princeton University Press, 1975); John G. Blair: *The Confidence Man in Modern Fiction* (London and New York: Vision, Barnes and Noble, 1979) and, to be sure, Elizabeth S. Foster's Introduction to *The Confidence-Man* (op. cit.).

6. Typical critical accounts include: Oliver S. Egbert: 'Melville's Goneril and Fanny Kemble', *New England Quarterly*, XVIII (December 1945), 489–500; Roy Harvey Pearce: 'Melville's Indian-Hater: A Note on the Meaning of *The Confidence-Man*', *P.M.L.A.*, LXVII (December 1952), 942–48; Hershel Parker: 'The Metaphysics of Indian-Hating', *Nineteenth-Century Fiction*, XVII (1963), 163–73; Carolyn Lury Karcher: 'The Story of Charlemont: A Dramatization of Melville's Concepts of Fiction in *The Confidence-Man: His Masquerade*', *Nineteenth-Century Fiction*, 21 (June, 1966), 73–84; Dan G. Hoffman: 'Melville's "Story of China Aster"', *American Literature*, XXII (May 1950), 137–49. For fuller bibliographies see *Modern Fiction Studies*, Vol. 8, No. 3 (Autumn 1962); *Studies in the Novel*, Vol. 1, No. 4 (Winter 1969); and the Annotated Bibliography in Hershel Parker (ed.), *The Confidence-Man*, The Norton Critical Edition (New York: W. W. Norton, 1971).

7. The subject is given lively critical analysis in, for instance, W. J. Harvey, *Character and the Novel* (London: Chatto and Windus, 1965).

9

Melville's Poetry

by ANDREW HOOK

1

A recent collection entitled *New Perspectives on Herman Melville* contains no essay on Melville's poetry; indeed the book's index suggests that no contributor, in writing about Melville's fiction, found it necessary to make any allusion whatsoever to the fact that Melville wrote poetry as well as novels and short stories.[1] What does this ignoring of Melville the poet imply? That it is impossible to offer a new perspective on Melville's poetry? Given the ingenuity of contemporary critics this is hardly likely. Much more probable is the implication that there is no need for a new perspective on Melville's poetry. The poetry, that is, is an irrelevance, a distraction, a minor after-thought. Melville's stature and reputation as a major artist, it is implied, rests fairly and squarely on his achievement as a prose writer; it is the novels and stories that count— the poetry is . . . well, nowhere, not merely out of perspective, but out of sight.

The question that follows asks itself. Is this assessment a fair and acceptable one? Whatever the opinion of a small band of Melville critics and scholars, there can be no doubt it does reflect a general literary and critical consensus. As everyone knows, Melville was the great forgotten man of American literature in the later nineteenth and early twentieth centuries. *The Oxford Companion to American Literature* informs us, however, that after his rediscovery in 1920 'the former neglect was atoned for by a general enthusiasm'. This is true. But he would be a bold, not to say foolhardy, literary historian who would argue that that 'general enthusiasm' extended to Melville's work as a poet. Of course Melville rapidly emerged as a major figure. And once American literature at last acquired enough respectability to become a suitable subject for academic study, Melville's place was secure, indeed central, within all courses, seminars, special subjects, and the rest, in any way concerned with American fiction, nineteenth-century American writing, the classic American novel, or whatever. On how many of these courses, however, did Melville's poetry appear? To my knowledge, precious few. If the appropriate test of Melville's poetic standing is switched from appearance on courses to published scholarly and critical output, the result is very much the same. Since the Second World War, the amount of scholarly and critical writing about American literature has been immense; no national literature has been studied with comparable thoroughness and amplitude. Writing about American writing became a vast, expanding industry. If the harsher economic climate of the 1970s and '80s has produced any downturn, it has only been at the margins, as volumes like the annual *American Literary Scholarship* show. In all this mass of intellectual energy and endeavour, Melville of course has been a mighty focus of attention. Melville the man, that is; Melville the novelist; Melville the short-story writer; Melville the thinker, the Seeker after Truth. Not, however, Melville the poet. In the checklists and bibliographies, amid the great oceans of Melville criticism and scholarship, essays and studies on Melville's poetry stand out like lonely desert islands.[2]

For a variety of reasons, this is surprising. American literature in the nineteenth century is not rich in poetry of major or even minor interest. Despite the massive critical industry just alluded to, which we can be sure has left few pages of the works of American poets unturned, little has emerged to subvert the conventional view that only in Walt Whitman and Emily Dickinson did nineteenth-century America produce individual, distinctive, and major poetic voices. Of course there are others of interest: Poe, Emerson, Bryant, Tuckerman, for example. But the overall poetic achievement remains—particularly in the context of the originality and vitality of nineteenth-century

177

American fiction—remarkably slim. Melville's poetry, therefore, has not been neglected because of the strength of the competition.

Perhaps Melville's basic mistake was to work initially in prose. Whatever was the case during his lifetime, his fiction now attracts so intense and fascinated an interest, that his poetry is almost denied the right to exist. It should never have happened; Melville ought to have gone on writing more novels, more short stories. By choosing to write poetry, it seems, Melville, disappointed and creatively exhausted, was in some way denying himself, reneging, giving up. On the face of it, of course, this is absurd. Much more natural would have been the assumption that the stature of Melville's fiction would guarantee equal interest in his poetry. That the novelist had written it should have been enough. This is the rule that seems to operate in the case of most poet-novelists; Scott, Emily Brontë, Meredith, Hardy, Kipling, Lawrence—the stature of none of these as writers of prose fiction seems in any way to have detracted from the interest taken in their poetry. And, to be fair, such attention as has been paid to Melville's poetry certainly originated in the idea that the poems could be seen as illuminating attitudes, ideas, themes and preoccupations of the novelist. The poems were still very much a coda to the novelist's career, but at least the coda could be revealing. Despite this attention, the heart of the matter is that for all the scale of the critical and scholarly industry surrounding the works of Melville, interest in the novelist's poetry remains surprisingly muted: a minnow in an ocean of whales.

What conclusions may we come to? I think there can only be one. Melville's poetry is set aside, paid little attention to, scarcely allowed to exist, because it is thought to be bad. Or, at the very least, too consistently minor to deserve to be kept very much in mind. This is why we can get on with our Melville courses and studies without taking account of Melville's poetry.

These of course are splendid circumstances for the revisionist critic. How grand it would be to step forward and announce to a surprised audience that the critics had got it entirely wrong—that Melville was after all a great poet. Unfortunately it cannot be done. In 1960 Walter Bezanson wrote that 'We have not lived long enough with the idea that [Melville] was a poet at all to decide justly how good a poet he was.'[3] Bezanson of course dissociated himself from the old myth that poetry was 'a left-handed venture for Melville', but his hesitation over the actual worth of the poetry was not uncharacteristic of the tone of those critics and scholars who did take an interest in Melville's poetry. Robert Penn Warren, for example, in an important and pioneering essay, published in 1946, felt obliged to concede that Melville failed to learn his trade as a poet, and that his poetry as a result remained 'poetry of shreds and patches'.[4] Even earlier, F. O. Matthiessen, one of the seminal critics of nineteenth-century American literature, wrote that Melville's poetry 'though very illuminating for his inner biography, adds little to his stature as an artist'.[5] By the 1960s and '70s, however, a few critics were prepared to advance Melville's claims as a poet with a greater degree of confidence. Building on the hints provided by Warren in particular, a case begins to be made to explain the apparent clumsiness, the irregularities, the lack of fluency and polish, in so much of Melville's verse. But the reservations remain. In 1962 Richard Harter Fogle describes Melville's verse as 'experimental and uneven'. 'Only infrequently,' he writes, 'do we find a poem of Melville's completely satisfying.'[6] And even William Bysshe Stein, perhaps the most enthusiastic and committed revaluer of Melville's poetry, is compelled, in the Introduction to his study, to look to a future when 'eventually' Melville's poetry 'is bound to be read with more pleasure and understanding'.[7] Back in the 1950s, Randall Jarrell, distinguished poet and critic, wrote that Melville's poetry 'has been grotesquely underestimated'. He was sure that in the long run, despite 'the awkwardness and amateurishness of so much of it', it would be 'thought well of'. In a parenthesis, however, he guesses that 'in the short run it will probably be thought entirely too well of.'[8] Clearly this has not in fact happened. And Jarrell's parting shot—'Melville is a great poet only in the prose of *Moby-Dick*'—would still be generally seen as being right on target.

If, then, one concedes that Melville is not a truly great poet, strangely neglected, what remains? In my view, a great deal. The poetry that a great novelist writes over the last thirty years of his life cannot be without interest. Critics of that

179

novelist neglect such writing at their peril. A novelist who stops writing novels and turns instead to poetry does not thereby provide evidence that he is suffering from creative exhaustion. That the poetry that Melville produced in the second half of his life does not equal in imaginative range and vitality the achievements of the earlier part of his career does not mean that the poems do not merit attention. Who would argue that Shakespeare's late romances do not deserve to be read because they are not the great tragedies? The comparison may not be as arbitrary as it seems. Randall Jarrell encompasses more or less the entire case against Melville's poetry when he refers to its 'awkwardness and amateurishness'. But are these not the very deficiencies that a range of Shakespearean critics and scholars have detected in the late plays? May it not be as likely in Melville's case as in Shakespeare's that the characteristics in question arise from changed priorities?

The opening stanza of a poem by Melville entitled 'A Utilitarian View of the Monitor's Fight' goes as follows:

> Plain be the phrase, yet apt the verse,
>   More ponderous than nimble;
> For since grimed War here laid aside
> His painted pomp, 'twould ill befit
>   Overmuch to ply
> The rhyme's barbaric cymbal.

Rather like George Herbert in his 'Jordan' poems, Melville here seems to be establishing an aesthetic of undecorated plainness. War has ceased to be romantic and colourful; the poetry of war should follow suit even if the result includes a degree of 'ponderousness'. What is certain is that Melville's verse is anything but 'nimble'. On the other hand, the stanza endorsing plain-ness is itself far from being entirely 'plain'. It is full of poeticisms of word-order and word-choice, and conventional poetic imagery. None the less, Melville has asserted that his theme demands an unconventional, unromantic style. That theme here is war—the *Monitor* was the North's first ironclad warship in the Civil War—but war or conflict in some form is a perennial Melville theme. Hence perhaps it is not surprising that a romantic mellifluence and smoothness are not characteristic of Melville's poetry as a whole. Sophisticated versions of this point have certainly become the standard defence of Melville's poetic style. Most critics are agreed that Melville's rejection of the smoothness and fluency, the metrical and rhythmical regularity of most of his contemporaries, was a deliberate act. Robert Penn Warren, in his 1946 essay, argued that 'the violences, the distortions, the wrenchings in the versification of some of the poems' was less the result of poetic ineptitude than of an attempt to create 'a nervous, dramatic, masculine style'. Similarly, apparently alarming shifts of tone may also be deliberate: an attempt to produce a poetry 'of some vibrancy, range of reference, and richness of tone'.[9] Richard Harter Fogle agrees. Ungainliness and irregularity in metre, rhythm, and stanzaic form, are all deliberately sought. And Fogle's conclusion reads very much like a definition of what Warren famously and influentially called 'impure' poetry:

> Melville's departures from regularity . . . are connected with his instinct for dramatic complexity and contrast, and with his desire to explore all the potentialities of the situation he has established in his poem, even if they should lead him to discordance and contradiction.[10]

Walter Bezanson implies that it was just these elements of discordance and contradiction that explain Melville's failure to appeal to his own contemporaries. In a poetic climate dominated by 'elderly gentlemen-poets' (William Cullen Bryant, J. G. Whittier, Samuel Longfellow, J. R. Lowell, O. W. Holmes) and 'a middle-aged coterie of gentility' (Bayard Taylor, E. C. Stedman, Richard Stoddard, Thomas Bailey Aldrich)[11] Melville's puzzling roughness and disharmony were bound to appear unacceptable and ill-judged. But it is William Bysshe Stein who has gone furthest in insisting on the deliberate unconventionality, and 'unVictorian-ness' of Melville's verse. The 'hobbled metrics', 'stumbling rimes', and 'contorted language' of Melville's poems are part of a design. Melville, Stein assures us, had come to believe that 'the measured euphony of verse belied experiential reality, and as a consequence he finally settled upon ugly discordance and incongruity—in metre, rime, image, symbol, and language—as the indices of truth in the finite world.'[12]

All of these critics make sensible and telling points. Bezanson's

181

reminder of what mainstream American poetry was like in the post-bellum period is particularly pointed. Presumably no one would imagine that when Melville turned to poetry—after *Moby-Dick*, *Pierre* and *The Confidence-Man*—he could conceivably have written in a mode or style even remotely like that of his genteel and complacent poetic contemporaries. None the less there are limits. Stein may be right about the particular poetic forms which he alleges Melville came to see as 'the indices of truth'. It is the absence of any kind of external evidence which makes one hesitate. Stein's formula, indeed, would seem to be capable of rationalizing, or explaining away, more or less any poetic mode, however apparently 'amateurish'. Which is what makes it genuinely surprising that he is prepared to dismiss out of hand easily the longest, most ambitious, and most demanding poem that Melville ever wrote. *Clarel*, for Stein, is characterized by 'grotesque inversions, tortured ellipses, banal rimes, expedient archaisms, distorted word forms, and limping rhythms'. 'Stiff, stuffy, and stultifying,' he concludes, 'the style is out of key with the subject of the poem.' The tetrameters in which the poem is written produce a monotony which 'not even the most beguiling sophistries can justify'.[13] It is precisely the point at which the honest defence of the apparent oddities, deficiencies, irregularities, of Melville's poetry—in terms of the demands of his themes, and his own individual artistic integrity—is in danger of passing over into 'beguiling sophistries' which is so difficult to establish.

This, however, is not a problem peculiar to Melville. It rises in relation to perhaps the greatest of the nineteenth century's poet-novelists: Thomas Hardy. And indeed the problems of form and style are only one of the areas that align these two great writers with each other. There are obvious parallels in the artistic biographies of the two: both devoted their creative energies to poetry after long careers as novelists. And both are supposed to have made the switch because of the reading-public's misunderstanding of and lack of sympathy for their fiction. The two writers' shared distaste for many of their own society's attitudes and habits of mind provides another obvious link: the often complacent liberal progressivism and optimism of the Victorian period was to the taste of neither writer. But perhaps the parallels—or their true significance—go deeper. The notion that Hardy turned back to poetry in a fit of pique over the public's response to *Tess of the Durbervilles* and *Jude the Obscure* has never been wholly compelling. More persuasive is the view of those scholars, like Ian Gregor, who maintain that Hardy abandoned the novel after the experiment of *Jude the Obscure* because he sensed that the new society coming into being at the opening of the twentieth century demanded a new kind of novel; the inheritance of Wessex provided him with no way to meet that demand.[14] In Melville's case too, the notion that he abandoned fiction only because, after *Moby-Dick*, the reading-public turned against him, has never seemed to be wholly convincing. It is no doubt perfectly true that he was under heavy pressure to earn a better living than he seemed able to do as a writer; but he was only an 'unsuccessful' writer because he insisted on writing the kinds of book he wanted to write. And surely at least part of the truth is on the side of those who argue that in *Pierre* and *The Confidence-Man* Melville had written himself into a corner; if reality is as treacherously ambiguous as these books suggest, what truth is left for art and the artist to communicate? These points of course relate to Melville's decision to accept a full-time appointment in the New York Custom House in 1866—a decision which has normally been seen as meaning that an exhausted Melville had given up the struggle to be a professional American writer. Such a view is only possible if the assumption is made that Melville's poetry does not count. In fact, between his 1866 appointment and his death in 1891, Melville published four volumes of poetry, as well as writing another substantial body of poems that remained unpublished. So it cannot be argued that he ceased to write. What is true is that in all this long period he wrote—with the one exception, right at the end of his life, of *Billy Budd*—no more prose.

What lay behind this change? As has been indicated, the traditional view is that after *The Confidence-Man* Melville was emotionally and imaginatively exhausted, effectively finished as an author. His poetry, it follows, is an afterthought of little significance. Bezanson, on the contrary, sees the poetry as highly significant; but he speculates that the switch from prose to poetry was a question of a loss of strength and energy.

'Probably a theory that poetry demanded less energy', he writes, 'was at the root of his otherwise willful abandonment of prose.'[15] This may well be true. But the causes of Melville's physical and spiritual exhaustion may include factors other than the failure of his later novels to appeal to the reading-public. Melville, that is, may have been as deeply disappointed by America's failure as by his own. The end of the 1850s and the opening of the next decade saw the imminence, and then the outbreak, of the Civil War. As his poetry proves, the War made an immense impact on Melville. Perhaps it was that impact that was in fact decisive. It is a critical commonplace to say that Melville's novels reveal him as deeply hostile to mid-nineteenth century American society—to its bourgeois, common sense philosophy, its naïve optimism, its superficiality, and moral complacency. Yet he was equally capable of responding imaginatively to the transcendent democratic idealism of the American experiment. That experiment seemed to end in ruin with the firing of the first guns at Fort Sumter. History was confirming the failure of hope Melville had already adumbrated in his fiction.

Melville did not relish being proved right. *Battle-Pieces*, his collection of Civil War poems, emphasizes the enormous cost in blood and suffering experienced by both sides in the conflict. And his patriotic pride in the North's victory is increasingly muted. In the conclusion to the impressive prose Supplement, which he published along with the poems, he asked only that America learn the lesson of the war; if learning that lesson would not amount to its justification, at least then the war would have served some purpose. 'Let us pray', writes Melville, 'that the great historic tragedy of our time may not have been enacted without instructing our whole beloved country through terror and pity; and may fulfillment verify in the end those expectations which kindle the bards of Progress and Humanity.'[16] Those 'expectations' were not in fact destined to be fulfilled (which could hardly have surprised Melville)—essentially because America refused to be instructed by what Melville saw so clearly was 'the great historic tragedy' of his time. Once the war was over, the South's secession defeated, the Union reaffirmed, the whole effort of 'official' American culture seems to have been directed towards persuading American society that nothing had changed. The threat to the United States had been beaten off, and the old order had been re-established. The values and ideals of the republic had been sorely tried; but in the end they had triumphed. The status quo therefore prevailed. What this meant in literary terms was that American authors, in the post-bellum period, went on writing as though the war had never occurred. On one level, this is why Daniel Aaron's study of American writers and the Civil War is appropriately entitled *The Unwritten War*. On another, this is why American literature took so long—until the 1880s and '90s—to register, in any comprehensive way, that American society in the post-bellum period was undergoing the most rapid and ruthless process of social, economic, and industrial transformation that the world had ever seen. More significant still was the reluctance of those who controlled America's culture and its institutions to admit that this process of change, originating in the Civil War years, involved in any way the defeat of republican America's democratic ideals. On the contrary. For most of the period 1865–1900 America's cultural establishment—religious, philosophical, educational—was more than ready to defend what the booming industrial, business interest was doing to American society as a whole. Hence those Americans who, while the Civil War was still going on, or in the immediate post-bellum years, had any sense of what the future would bring, were clearly few in number. President Lincoln was one.[17] Melville was another. In a poem called 'Bridegroom Dick' (1876), Melville alluded to the Civil War and the profit-making it encouraged:

> In mart and bazar Lucre chuckled the huzza,
> Coining the dollars in the bloody mint of war.

But in his poetry as a whole, the theme of an America corrupted by materialism and utilitarianism, and descending into civic barbarism, is a recurrent one. Bezanson reminds us that Melville's job as an official in New York's Custom House placed him in a context where the spoils system and the political racketeering it encouraged operated in a peculiarly blatant manner. Melville was in a position to see the corruption of post-bellum American democracy at first hand. That this

185

was the lesson that America had learned from the bloody battlefields of a tragic and fratricidal civil war, must have been, for him, a final disillusionment. All around him, in the 1860s and '70s, in the behaviour of politicians, business leaders, and the rest, was overwhelming evidence that his darkest and bleakest views on the inevitably fallen nature of mankind were correct. Perhaps it is here, then, that we find a deeper reason for Melville's turning away from fiction. There was no longer an audience for what he wished or needed to write. Even before the Civil War, American society had not been ready to listen to what he wished to say to it. What chance was there in the masquerade that was the reality of post-bellum America? Particularly after *Battle-Pieces*—which was hardly a popular success—Melville turned to poetry because he could regard it as a more private art. In the Romantic and post-Romantic age, the poet wrote for himself, rather than for an audience; poetry was an art, above all, of self-expression. Just such an art served Melville's creativity in the long, last period of his life.

2

Nonetheless, in my view, *Battle-Pieces and Aspects of the War*, the first and most public of his volumes of poetry, published in 1866, remains the best and most satisfying of his four volumes. The poetry is public, of course, both in the sense that its focus is on the historical fact of the recent Civil War, and that Melville, as the prose Supplement makes clear, has a view on the war and its aftermath that he is anxious to convey to his readers. This volume is published with a purpose; it says something that Melville believes is vitally important, not just for himself, but for the nation. Melville's later poetry seems rather to speak only to himself. The themes that he takes up in that poetry are still general, objective, universal even, but the approach is much more individual and eccentric; communication is a lesser consideration. The knowledge that he was not writing for an audience perhaps even encouraged the 'amateurishness' of Melville's verse. But the case for the superiority of *Battle-Pieces*—it is not a fashionable case among those who care about Melville's poetry—is made on other grounds. *Battle-Pieces* has an emotional depth and fullness that sets it apart. The

Civil War mattered enormously to Melville; the emotions it evoked were, as one would expect, more complex than simple, but they were deep and powerful. The later poems may be more skilful—or at least some of them—but to me at least they often lack a comparable emotional charge and weight.

The poems in *Battle-Pieces* are of various kinds; many are narrative, some dramatic; many focus on particular episodes or incidents or figures in the Civil War; the land and sea battles, famous in Civil War history, tend to recur. Melville's approach to these topics is usually contemplative or meditative. The lyrical is the poetic mode with which he seems always to have felt least at ease. What the poems do have is a weightiness which persuades us that Melville is doing much more than exploiting the circumstances of history. The tone of the poems is equally varied; occasionally it is one of patriotic exultation, more often one of horror at the nature of a fratricidal war; sometimes there is hope for the future:

> Faith in America never dies;
> Heaven shall the end ordained fulfill.
> We march with Providence cheery still.
>
> ('Lee in the Capitol')

More often, doubt and despair prevail. Melville's emphasis falls increasingly on the cost, the losses and suffering entailed by the war, rather than on anything achieved by it. Slavery is referred to early on:

> I muse upon my country's ills—
> The tempest bursting from the waste of Time
> On the world's fairest hope linked with man's foulest crime.
>
> ('Misgivings')

But hardly recurs. This is why the overall impression created by the volume is an elegiac one. For Melville the Civil War is in the end an American tragedy; even its successful outcome may promise nothing good:

> Power unanointed may come—
> Dominion (unsought by the free)
>   And the Iron Dome,
> Stronger for stress and strain,
> Fling her huge shadow athwart the main;
> But the Founders' dream shall flee.
>
> ('The Conflict of Convictions')

187

The 'Iron Dome' is the dome of Congress in Washington which Melville had seen while it was being reconstructed. But in this version, rather than a guarantor of freedom and democracy, the dome has become a menacing, stern, and fearful image of something closer to tyranny.

Unlike Whitman, Melville had little or no first-hand experience of the war. Only once, in 1864, did a visit to Virginia bring him into the war zone. The poems in *Battle-Pieces* are therefore largely retrospective, few of them written earlier than 1865, and for their historical detail they rely on printed sources: mainly the multi-volume compilation of newspaper and other reports called *The Rebellion Record*. Melville disdained any overall design in the composition of the poems, but in the published volume they do fall into a broad chronological pattern, moving from the opening of the war to its close. Within this simple pattern, certain themes recur. One of the most powerful of these is the dark and sinister knowledge that war brings: Melville is one of the earliest writers to see war as revealing the kind of truth that most of the time we prefer to ignore or set aside. War, for Melville, brought out in stark terms that dark side of experience which he spent much of his artistic career trying to persuade himself was not the only true side. Thus in 'The March into Virginia' he writes of the innocent gaiety with which the soldiers entered the battle:

> So they gayly go to fight,
> Chatting left and laughing right.

War inevitably teaches a sharp lesson:

> But some who this blithe mood present,
>   As on in lightsome files they fare,
> Shall die experienced ere three days be spent—
>   Perish, enlightened by the vollied glare.

The enlightenment that experience brings has nothing to do with innocence or joy. The theme recurs in 'The College Colonel' in which Melville contrasts the hero's welcome, offered to the returning officer at the head of his worn and tattered troops, with the bitter knowledge that two years of fighting has actually brought him:

It is not that a leg is lost,
　It is not that an arm is maimed,
It is not that the fever has racked—
　Self he has long disclaimed.
But all through the Seven Days' Fight,
　And deep in the Wilderness grim,
And in the field-hospital tent,
　And Petersburg crater, and dim
Lean brooding in Libby, there came—
　Ah heaven!—what *truth* to him.

What truth that is, is imaged in a sombre poem called 'The Armies of the Wilderness' where the blasted landscape mirrors the primal evil of war:

The wagon mired and cannon dragged
　Have trenched their scar; the plain
Tramped like the cindery beach of the damned—
　A site for the city of Cain.
And stumps of forests for dreary leagues
　Like a massacre show.

That truth is the shark that 'glides white through the phosphorus sea' ('Commemorative of a Naval Victory') and it is the same truth which destroys the alien figure of the prisoner-of-war:

Listless he eyes the palisades
　And sentries in the glare;
'Tis barren as a pelican-beach—
　But his world is ended there.

Nothing to do; and vacant hands
　Bring on the idiot-pain;
He tries to think—to recollect,
　But the blur is on his brain.

Around him swarm the plaining ghosts
　Like those on Virgil's shore—
A wilderness of faces dim,
　And pale ones gashed and hoar.

('In the Prison Pen')

Of course for Melville the war does also reveal man's capacity for heroism and endurance on an enormous scale. And this is true even if war—particularly war at sea with the development of iron-clad vessels—has become more mundane and practical than in the colourful past:

> The gloomy hulls, in armor grim,
>   Like clouds o'er moors have met,
> And prove that oak, and iron, and man
>   Are tough in fibre yet.
>
> But Splendors wane. The sea-fight yields
>   No front of old display;
> The garniture, emblazonment,
>   And heraldry all decay.
>
> ('The Temeraire')

War may now be placed 'Where War belongs/ Among the trades and artisans' ('A Utilitarian View of the Monitor's Fight'), but loyalty and bravery—in both North and South—are in no way diminished. But always in *Battle-Pieces* Melville returns to the cost and waste of war. At the close of the inventively dramatic narrative 'Donelson', it is the deadly price of the Union victory that Melville registers:

> The death-list like a river flows
>   Down the pale sheet,
> And there the whelming waters meet.

In the end *Battle-Pieces* becomes what amounts to a political statement. Melville is appalled by those in the North who wish, after Lee's surrender, to continue a harsh and vindictive policy towards the defeated South. This is why the poems in *Battle-Pieces* pay constant tribute to the Southern soldiers' bravery and humanity. For Melville the war was less a struggle between right and wrong than between the right and the misguided. This is why there is no point in thinking in terms of punishing the South:

> What could they else—North or South?
> Each went forth with blessings given
> By priests and mothers in the name of Heaven;
>   And honor in all was chief.
> Warred one for Right, and one for Wrong?
> So put it; but they both were young—
> Each grape to his cluster clung,
> All their elegies are sung.
>
> ('On the Slain Collegians')

And this is why the two final poems in the collection—'Lee n the Capitol' and 'A Meditation'—both plead eloquently 'or forgiveness and reconciliation:

> When Vicksburg fell, and the moody files marched out,
> Silent the victors stood, scorning to raise a shout.

If the North refuses to adopt this attitude—and Melville pleads directly for it again in the splendid prose Supplement to the poems—then Melville's fears are those voiced by the questioning voice Lee hears in the 'charnel-fields' of the war: ' *"Died all in vain? both sides undone?"* '

3

Battle-Pieces was published in an edition of 1,200 copies. After two years only 468 copies had been sold. Nevertheless, compared with the degree of public interest shown in Melville's next poetic venture, *Battle-Pieces* was a success. *Clarel*, an extremely long narrative poem, published at the expense of Melville's uncle in 1876, was totally ignored by the reading-public in England and America. Nor is this at all surprising: *Clarel*, over 18,000 lines of it, is a difficult and demanding poem. Writing it seems to have taxed Melville's creative and psychic energies to the utmost. The tone of the author's note that prefaces the poem is tired and dismissive, while Melville's wife's letters suggest the burden which the work had become: 'this dreadful *incubus* of a *book*' she calls it, while hoping that its completion will lead to an improvement in Melville's 'mental health' about which she has 'the gravest concern and anxiety'.[18]

Clarel, A Poem and Pilgrimage in the Holy Land, is based on Melville's own experiences. In the autumn of 1856, before the publication of *The Confidence-Man*, Melville crossed the Atlantic to undertake an extensive European and Near Eastern tour. At the beginning of that tour he was reunited with Hawthorne, then U.S. Consul in Liverpool, and this was the occasion of the famous conversation between the two writers, recorded by Hawthorne, which has always been thought of as uncannily illuminating of Melville's mental and spiritual state at this time. Then it was that Hawthorne described Melville as neither able to believe 'nor be comfortable in his unbelief', constantly struggling with ultimate metaphysical questions, but never finding any kind of peace or rest. 'It is strange' writes Hawthorne, 'how he persists—and has persisted ever since I knew him, and probably long before—in wandering to and fro over these deserts, as dismal and monotonous as the sand hills amid which we were sitting.'[19] These words are strangely prophetic of what is to come in *Clarel*; the dismal and monotonous sandhills will become those of Palestine, rather than those near Liverpool, but the metaphysical deserts in which Melville will wander will be very much those that Hawthorne describes here.

At a literal level, then, *Clarel* draws heavily on Melville's three-week visit to Palestine in 1857. Melville found that experience disillusioning. In his Journal he commented: 'No country will more quickly dissipate romantic expectations than Palestine—particularly Jerusalem. To some the disappointment is heart sickening.'[20] In truth, however, there was nothing especially eccentric about this reaction. Nineteenth-century travellers normally found the Holy Land a somewhat dismal and disappointing experience. For Clarel, a young American divinity student already afflicted by doubt, this is certainly what it is. But it would be misleading to suggest that Melville's actual experience of the Holy Land is at the heart of the poem. The landscape, topography, and historical settings of the central events of the Christian story, are there—seen presumably as Melville saw them in 1857—but they are little more than a threat around which the poem is woven.

Clarel is a long narrative poem, with a plot—Clarel's abortive love-affair with a Jewish girl of American origins—and a wide variety of characters. But plot and characters, like the Holy Land travelogue dimension, are inadequately rendered to provide the poem with a firm and available structural basis. History grounds *Battle-Pieces* in reality, just as whales and whaling grounded *Moby-Dick*. *Clarel* is constantly dissolving its landscapes, incidents, and characters into a purer symbolism, allegory, or metaphysical searching. This is what makes the poem seem more private and personal than *Battle-Pieces*, despite the fact that its themes of faith and doubt, the complex history of Christianity, science and democracy, physical and spiritual love, are general and universal. In the end, Clarel's wanderings in the Holy Land simply become a spring-board from which Melville could once again explore the perplexing questions about human existence and its meaning, which Hawthorne in Liverpool saw as obsessing him, and which had appeared at the heart of his major fiction.

I have earlier referred to William Bysshe Stein's condemnation of the form and style of *Clarel*. And it is difficult to deny that Melville is indeed guilty of the 'countless infelicities of expression' with which he is charged. These in turn frequently lead to difficulty and obscurity. Bezanson quotes *The Westminster Review* when *Clarel* originally appeared: ' "Clarel" is a long poem of about twenty-seven thousand lines, of which we can only say that we do not understand a single word. Here is a specimen:

> Although he naught confessed,
> In Derwent, marking there the scene,
> What interference was expressed
> As of harsh grit in oiled machine—
> Disrelish grating interest.

> (II, xiv, 75)'[21]

Bezanson is convinced that the *Westminster* reviewer, by insisting that these lines are unintelligible, simply convicts himself of an inability to read poetry. It is possible, nonetheless, to have some sympathy with the nineteenth-century critic. The drift of meaning may be clear enough, but in my view at least, an obscuring awkwardness of expression remains. Certainly in passage after passage in *Clarel* its meaning has to be ravelled out—this is what makes one suspect that Melville had scant regard for an audience he did not expect to have. Yet *Clarel* cannot easily be set aside. Its earnestness and weight give it authority; and in the end it overcomes its own deficiencies and imposes itself as a major creative act. American poetry in the post-bellum period offers nothing of comparable substantiality; in England only *In Memoriam* and the more philosophical of Browning's poems provide appropriate parallels. The Melville who is present here is unquestionably the same Melville who wrote the major novels. And this is a question of much more than the sea imagery which to an

astonishing degree pervades the poem, or even of direct echoes
of the fiction (Palestine is on occasion made to share the
blasted landscapes of 'The Encantadas', Derwent, an Anglican
clergyman sometimes sounds exactly like Amaso Delano in
'Benito Cereno', and there are many other parallels of this
kind). The deeper links are in the way control of the poem
seems in danger of slipping away from Melville-Clarel—who,
like Melville-Ishmael, for lengthy periods becomes a rather
shadowy figure—and even from the toughly realistic characters (Rolfe, Vine), whom Melville would like to identify with,
to the Ahab-like extremists, men of total disillusionment and
monomania (Mortmain, Agath, Ungar). It is when these
monomaniac characters speak, that urgency and intensity
most commonly appear in the texture of the narrative. The
urgency and intensity in question, however, are essentially of a
destructive and negative quality. Despite this, Melville ends
his poem with a hint of hope:

> Then keep thy heart, though yet but ill-resigned—
> Clarel, thy heart, the issues there but mind;
> That like the crocus budding through the snow—
> That like a swimmer rising from the deep—
> That like a burning secret which doth go
> Even from the bosom that would hoard and keep;
> Emerge thou mayst from the last whelming sea,
> And prove that death but routs life into victory.

Whether the poem as a whole suggests that this, or any other
kind of victory, is likely to be attained is much less clear.

4

Melville published two further volumes of poetry: *John Marr
and Other Sailors* (1888) and *Timoleon* (1891). Both appeared in
private editions limited to twenty-five copies. Conventionally
these poems have been seen as reflecting a new-found wisdom
and acceptance of life. Melville's long drawn-out 'quarrel with
God' is at last over, replaced by a poised serenity of mood.
Stein, these poems' critical champion, does not entirely dis-
agree: the poems flower 'out of the rich soil of emotional and
spiritual contentment'.[22] But Stein correctly emphasizes the

particular nature of this 'contentment': Melville is as far away as ever from any recognition of the essential rightness of things. Outrage at the human condition has been replaced by acceptance of its futility. Certainly in *John Marr* little seems to have changed. The sea upon which men sail is as treacherous as ever. In 'The Haglets' the victorious warship is wrecked; some of the drowning sailors 'heaven invoke', 'but rings of reefs/ Prayer and despair alike deride.' In 'The Aeolian Harp at the Surf Inn' the harp is 'Stirred by fitful gales from sea':

> Listen: less a strain ideal
> Than Ariel's rendering of the Real.
> What that Real is, let hint
> A picture stamped in memory's mint.

The picture that follows is of another wrecked vessel, this one a sinister floating hulk, itself a greater hazard to other ships than even 'the sunken reef':

> O, the sailors—O, the sails!
> O, the lost crews never heard of!
> Well the harp of Ariel wails
> Thoughts that tongue can tell no word of!

Bleaker still is 'Far Off-Shore':

> Look, the raft, a signal flying,
> Thin—a shred;
> None upon the lashed spars lying,
> Quick or dead.
>
> Cries the sea-fowl, hovering over,
> 'Crew, the crew?'
> And the billow, reckless, rover,
> Sweeps anew!

Timoleon is a more varied and accomplished volume. It contains some of Melville's best known poems: 'Monody' (a tribute to Hawthorne), 'Art', 'After the Pleasure Party' and 'In a Bye Canal', distinguished by a single marvellously resonant image: 'I have been/ Twixt the whale's black flukes and the white shark's fin'—an image itself reminiscent of the pilot fish in 'The Maldive Shark' (from *John Marr*) who

195

> . . . lurk in the port of serrated teeth
> In white triple tiers of glittering gates,
> And there find a haven when peril's abroad,
> An asylum in jaws of the Fates!

Is this Melville's final image of the human predicament? Perhaps it is. But beside it should be placed another image from 'Pontoosuce', one of Melville's finest and most beautiful poems. 'Pontoosuce' begins by evoking a beautiful, autumnal landscape. But the poet's pleasure in the scene is abruptly dispelled by 'a counter thought', which becomes a kind of refrain in succeeding stanzas: 'All dies.' Not only the beauties of nature, the mighty trees, man himself:

> The poet's forms of beauty pass,
> And noblest deeds they are undone
> Even truth itself decays, and lo,
> From truth's sad ashes fraud and falsehood grow.

These dark meditations are in turn interrupted by the appearance of a visionary, female figure. She reassures the poet of the constant cycle of life recreating all things:

> Who sighs that all dies?
> Summer and winter, and pleasure and pain
> And everything everywhere in God's reign,
> They end, and anon they begin again:
> Wane and wax, wax and wane:
> Over and over and over amain
> End, ever end, and begin again—
> End, ever end, and forever and ever begin again!

(Is there a hint of hysteria in these repetitions?) In softer voice the figure tells the poet he should cease to grieve 'Since light and shade are equal set.' In the poem's final stanza the poet and his vision are momentarily united:

> With that, her warm lips thrilled me through,
> She kissed me, while her chaplet cold
> Its rootlets brushed against my brow,
> With all their humid clinging mould.
> She vanished, leaving fragrant breath
> And warmth and chill of wedded life and death.

196

Rather like Moneta in Keats's 'Fall of Hyperion', Melville's visionary figure seems to transcend life (warm lips, chaplet, rootlets, fragrant breath, warmth) and death (cold, mould, chill). Union with her is acceptance, in imaginative terms at least, of light and shade 'equal set', an equilibrium less fearful than that of the pilot fish among the shark's serrated teeth. Was Melville ever able to decide between these images? Perhaps that is the question that *Billy Budd, Sailor*, explores for one last time.

NOTES

1. See Faith Pullin (ed.), *New Perspectives on Melville* (University of Edinburgh Press, 1978).
2. Of Melville's major poetic work *Clarel*, Nina Baym writes: 'The poem receives only cursory treatment in most of the general studies of Melville and is omitted in several of them. There are not a half dozen published articles on the work. . . .' See 'The Erotic Motif in Melville's *Clarel*', *Texas Studies in Language and Literature*, 16, 316.
3. See Walter E. Bezanson (ed.), *Clarel, A Poem and Pilgrimage in the Holy Land* (Chicago and New York: Hendricks House, 1960), p. x.
4. Robert Penn Warren's essay, 'Melville the Poet' has been reprinted in Richard Chase (ed.), *Melville, A Collection of Critical Essays* (Englewood Cliffs: Prentice Hall, 1962), pp. 144–45. For this reference see p. 148.
5. F. O. Matthiessen, *American Renaissance* (New York: Oxford University Press, 1941), p. 494.
6. Richard Harter Fogle, 'Melville's Poetry', *Tulane Studies in English*, 11–12 (1961–62), 81.
7. William Bysshe Stein, *The Poetry of Melville's Late Years* (Albany: State University Press of New York, 1970), p. 3.
8. Randall Jarrell, *Poetry and the Age* (New York: Knopf, 1955), p. 101.
9. Warren, op. cit., p. 146.
10. Fogle, op. cit., p. 86.
11. Bezanson, op. cit., p. xl.
12. Stein, op. cit., p. 4.
13. Ibid., p. 11.
14. Ian Gregor, 'Jude the Obscure' in Maynard Mack and Ian Gregor (eds.), *Imagined Worlds* (London, 1968), pp. 237–56.
15. Bezanson, op. cit., p. xxxii.
16. The Supplement to *Battle-Pieces* is printed in full in Howard P. Vincent (ed.), *Collected Poems of Herman Melville* (Chicago and New York: Hendricks House, 1947), pp. 460–67.

17. In a letter to W. R. Ellis, written before the end of the Civil War, Lincoln spoke of how, as a result of the war, 'corporations have been enthroned, and an era of corruption in high places will follow, and the money power of the country will endeavour to prolong its reign by working upon the prejudices of the people until all wealth is aggregated in a few hands and the Republic is destroyed.'
18. Quoted by Bezanson, op. cit., p. xxxviii.
19. Bezanson, op. cit., pp. xiii, xiv, quotes Hawthorne's account of his meeting with Melville in full.
20. Bezanson, op. cit., p. xx.
21. Ibid., p. xli–ii.
22. Stein, op. cit., p. 12.

10

From Empire to Empire:
Billy Budd, Sailor

by H. BRUCE FRANKLIN

Toward the accomplishment of an aim which in wantonness of atrocity would seem to partake of the insane, he will direct a cool judgment sagacious and sound . . . whatever its aims may be—and the aim is never declared—the method and the outward proceeding are always perfectly rational.

—*Billy Budd, Sailor*

I have to be heart and soul in sympathy with the people who are talking about the horrors of nuclear war and the fact that we should do everything we could to prevent such a war from happening. . . . I would hope that some of these people, however, who are insisting on some of these things would realize that I'm with them as to the need to do something to lessen the possibilities, but I would ask them to consider that no matter how sincere and well intentioned, only in this position do you have all the facts necessary to base decisions upon action, and therefore I would ask then trust and confidence that feeling as sincerely as I do, that they would allow us to take the actions that we think are necessary to lessen this threat.

—President Ronald Reagan, 20 April 1982

Indeed it is the very rationality of the discourse that masks and marks the craziness of the thought!
—Robert Jay Lifton and Richard Falk, *Indefensible Weapons: The Political and Psychological Case against Nuclearism* (1982)

Looking backward from the late twentieth century to *Billy Budd, Sailor*, we may misplace the tale in history. Our perspective distorts historical time, an effect exaggerated by the setting of the story in 1797 and our tendency to think of Melville as a pre-Civil-War author. Recent years almost always seem longer, more eventful, and generally more important than earlier years. So the years between the 1980s and 1891, when Melville finished working on the tale, make *Billy Budd* seem more remote than it is, while the years between 1891 and 1797 seem to collapse into each other, wiping from our awareness the history of the nineteenth century. But *Billy Budd* actually stands midway between us and the period of its action, turning the shaping events of the late nineteenth century into a nexus joining our age with the outcome of the American and French revolutions. To read *Billy Budd* as a work of its own time is to discover that it is a work of our own historical epoch, created in the smoke-filled dawn of the twentieth century amidst the events that would soon lead to the First World War.

Between 1886 and 1891, while Melville was composing *Billy Budd*, the United States, having fulfilled its manifest destiny to conquer the continent from ocean to ocean, now contemplated a globe being divided and redivided by the great European empires. America's puny little navy could hardly lead the nation into a global destiny, especially while the country was hemmed in by the indomitable fleet and world-wide empire of Great Britain. To become a world power, America would need both overseas colonies and a large peacetime navy. Indeed, these two were inseparable, for a military fleet was necessary to seize and hold colonies, and these colonies provided bases indispensable to maintaining such a fleet. The crucial question being debated was this: what would be the consequences for the American republic and its democratic ideology, both founded in a revolution against imperialism and the standing armies indispensable to imperialism, if the nation were to rule overseas colonies and maintain a large, permanent, peacetime navy?

This fateful debate was central to two profoundly important works of the period. The first was Captain Alfred Thayer Mahan's *The Influence of Seapower upon History, 1660–1783*, published in 1890, which 'was to have as profound an effect on the world as had Darwin's *Origin of Species*'.[1] Writing as head of the Naval War College, and minimizing the contradictions that he conceded between a large standing navy and democracy, Mahan helped chart America's future course into imperialism and militarism. The second work, completed the following year, was *Billy Budd, Sailor.*

The priceless currency of Melville's tale is implicitly acknowledged by the great debate raging since 1950 about its meaning. But the time has come for us to move beyond this debate, for it tells us far more about our epoch and about the terrifying values of those who misread the story, than it does about Melville's meaning, which is fundamentally unambiguous. This is not to deny the profundity or the complexity or the richness of the story. Quite the contrary, for the murky fog of supposed ambiguity—generated mainly by the confusion (or worse) of some academics—has tended to obscure the luminous insights dramatized by *Billy Budd* and thus to deprive us of its guiding light as we try to steer out of the deadly straits toward which Melville saw us heading. One of the more appalling symptoms of our predicament is the spectacle of some modern readers, apparently intelligent, humane, learned, and well-intentioned, fulfilling the prophecy of the story by exalting precisely the conduct and values against which Melville desperately warns. The fact that such people can argue that Captain Vere incarnates 'virtue' or Melville's one authentic 'hero' merely displays the treacherous, insidious character of some of the ethical norms of our society and the function of Vere's intellectual counterparts today. This should be no great surprise, for the '*Bellipotent*' is becoming as apt a name for America as for the warship of the eighteenth-century captain.

This is no mere literary or academic matter. For example, Hannah Arendt, the anti-revolutionary political philosopher revered in certain circles, finds her personification of ' "virtue" in the person of Captain Vere', and argues that 'the virtuous man, Captain Vere', must 'punish the violence of absolute innocence'—that is, must kill Billy Budd, who embodies 'absolute good'—since 'absolute, natural innocence . . . is "at war with the peace of the world and the true welfare of

201

mankind".'[2] This is central to her argument, which she somehow manages to read into *Billy Budd* as well as history, that 'the Rights of Man' constitute an 'absolute' which 'spells doom to everyone when it is introduced into the political realm'.[3]

To hear clearly what *Billy Budd* says to us, we must, once and for all, settle the noisy, misleading debate about whether Melville condemns, approves, or is ambiguous about Vere's killing of the morally innocent Billy Budd in order to preserve order on the *Bellipotent*. To remain deaf to Melville's judgement of this quasi-legalized murder, one must ignore all five of the following: (1) the text of the story; (2) the entire corpus of Melville's work; (3) Melville's own experience as a sailor; (4) the historical context; (5) the massive body of evidence and analysis produced by the majority of Melville scholars since 1950.[4] Those dozens of articles and books cannot be summarized here. But before we resume our exploration of *Billy Budd*'s historical message, just consider these twenty-two points:

(1) The story, not entitled *Edward Vere, Captain*, glorifies Vere's victim, *Billy Budd, Sailor*, designated 'the main figure'[5] of a tale in which he appears from beginning to end. Vere, a late addition in the composition, is not even mentioned in seventeen out of the thirty chapters.

(2) Budd is one of three embodiments of the truly heroic figure, 'the Handsome Sailor', who appears first in the dedication to Jack Chase, Melville's actual shipmate and Handsome Sailor virtually deified in *White-Jacket*, and then in the colossal opening image of the Black African, a godlike man, combining 'strength and beauty', the 'champion' of his shipmates, workers of 'such an assortment of tribes and complexions' that they could serve as the 'Representatives of the Human Race'.

(3) To think that Melville at all condones Vere's action one must divorce the story from Melville's actual life as a foretopman on a man-of-war, recalled not only in the dedication to Jack Chase but also in the overtly autobiographical details woven into the narrative. For example, if Billy Budd must be hanged, then Jack Chase should also have been hanged, for he openly and with full intent defied his captain and the Articles

of War, deserting his ship to fight for Peruvian independence—because of his devotion to 'the Rights of Man'. Yet even the vicious Captain Claret has enough sense to give him no harsher punishment than a mild verbal rebuke. In Melville's imagination the hanging of the Handsome Sailor is no mere metaphor. Would he have admired or been ambiguous about a captain who executed another incarnation of Jack Chase?

(4) Those who (like Milton Stern) argue that *Billy Budd* is the product of 'an old man's quiet conservatism' and that Melville in his 'old age'[6] here renounces his earlier values should re-read *John Marr and Other Sailors*, published in 1888, including poems like 'Bridegroom Dick', in which 'the formidable Finn' threatens officers and attacks the Master-at-arms, only to be released with a mere threat of a flogging by the 'magnanimous' captain.

(5) Vere explicitly repudiates the Rights of Man, the dictates of conscience, nature, and any law or truth higher than the most ruthless code of military justice, a code denounced systematically by Melville in chapter after chapter of *White-Jacket* as 'bloodthirsty' and 'tyrannical'. For example, in Chapter 71 he brands the American Articles of War a detestable importation 'even from Britain, whose laws we Americans hurled off as tyrannical, and yet retained the most tyrannical of all'. After arguing that these laws are useless in enforcing discipline, he directly annihilates Vere's main argument to his drumhead court:

> Nor . . . is the general ignorance or depravity of any race of men to be alleged as an apology for tyranny over them. On the contrary, it cannot admit of a reasonable doubt, in any unbiased mind conversant with the interior life of a man-of-war, that most of the sailor iniquities practised therein are indirectly to be ascribed to the morally debasing effects of the unjust, despotic, and degrading laws under which the man-of-war's man lives. (Ch. 72)

(6) Throughout Melville's works, his loathing of war and imperialism is expressed in key images that recur in *Billy Budd*. This central point is explored in depth in Joyce Adler's marvellous book, *War in Melville's Imagination*.

(7) Vere orders the atrocity most passionately excoriated in

White-Jacket, flogging a sailor—for precisely the same offence for which White Jacket himself was sentenced to be flogged. Billy's thoughts on witnessing this flogging are identical to Melville's recorded thoughts on witnessing his first flogging. White Jacket was prepared to murder his captain, if necessary, to preserve his humanity against this barbarous practice, which Melville himself helped stop in the U.S. Navy. White Jacket is saved only by the personal intervention of Jack Chase.

(8) Vere demands of his officers and himself that 'the heart', 'the feminine in man', 'must here be ruled out' so that they can kill Budd (271–72). But Melville had always chosen the heart. As he put it in his famous 1851 letter to Hawthorne: 'I stand for the heart. To the dogs with the head!' This allegiance is repledged throughout *Billy Budd*, from the very words of dedication to Jack Chase: 'that great heart'.

(9) In order to effect his will and carry out his snap judgement that he must hang Billy, Vere himself actually must violate the very code which he claims to be enforcing. Vere had no authority to administer a punishment greater than twelve lashes, his drumhead court is illegal, and a case such as this had to be submitted to higher levels.[7]

(10) Some attribute this to Melville's alleged ignorance of the British naval code of the period, though he did research on this question while working on the story. However, Vere's own officers are aware of what the code does dictate, that they are supposed to 'postpone further action' in such a case until 'they rejoin the squadron, and then refer it to the admiral' (234), and they, as well as other officers later, believe that Vere acts improperly.

(11) Vere's procedures are compared to those of 'Peter the Barbarian', the infamous Russian czar (242).

(12) Melville compares Vere's procedures with the hanging of three men on the U.S. brig *Somers*, which he had unequivocally denounced (see, for example, *White-Jacket*, Chs. 70 and 72), though in that case there was some evidence of a planned mutiny.

(13) Vere's action, and his entire argument to his drumhead court, is based on a fear of an imminent mutiny. But we readers of this 'Inside Narrative' never see the faintest hint of

any such possibility. Discipline is only breached *after* Billy's execution.

(14) Vere's drumhead court, all British naval officers, all familiar with the recent mutinies in the British navy as well as the situation on the *Bellipotent*, each hand-picked by Vere himself as most likely to support his prejudgement, do not agree to have Billy hanged until Vere manipulates, tricks, and coerces them with a combination of his authority over them, his better-trained intellect, and rhetoric.

(15) Although Vere's verbal adroitness (the opposite of Billy's tongue-tied innocence) overwhelms this trio of naval officers, to trained students of rhetoric his devious methods are blatantly specious. In a detailed analysis, William Shurr has demonstrated that Vere's verbal manipulation 'must be one of the most wicked uses to which rhetoric has ever been put'.[8] It's shocking to find English professors taken in by these old tricks, but then rhetoric is no longer a required part of our curriculum. (A class hour spent analysing Vere's methods is a fine educational experience.)

(16) The core of Vere's argument is that 'Nature', 'the heart', and 'the conscience' must all be subordinated to the particular order embodied by the British King and British Empire. This is the king and empire from which America had just won its freedom.

(17) This very king was a notorious madman. Vere's own argument inadvertently recalls that one of George III's most famous symptoms of insanity was his obsession with making buttons, giving him the sobriquet of 'The Button Maker'[9]: 'But do these buttons that we wear attest that our allegiance is to Nature? No, to the King' (267–68).

(18) On one hand, this displays what James Farnham has called Vere's 'existential failure': 'Vere hides inside his uniform. . . . He reverts to a clothes philosophy, to the pleasing untruth that the clothes, in this instance the gold buttons on an officer's uniform, define the man. . . .'[10]

(19) It also points to the horrendous fallacy in Vere's historical position. As Edgar Dryden has demonstrated at length, 'The appalling truth of *Billy Budd* is not that innocence must be sacrificed to maintain the order of the world, but rather that innocence is destroyed by the forces of chaos and

darkness masquerading as "measured forms"."[11]

(20) Except for his dying murmur of 'Billy Budd, Billy Budd', Vere's last quoted words sum up the philosophy he embodies: ' "With mankind," he would say, "forms, measured forms, are everything; and that is the import couched in the story of Orpheus with his lyre spellbinding the wild denizens of the wood" ' (333). This grotesquely perverted view of poetry, music, imagination, and beauty is contradicted on every level—aesthetic, ontological, and ethical—by the form and content of *Billy Budd, Sailor.*[12]

(21) These 'forms, measured forms' are immediately repudiated by the narrator's dismissal of 'the symmetry of form attainable in pure fiction' (335).

(22) Those ignorant sailors—whom Vere so deeply fears and so disdains that he hangs 'an angel of God' to keep them in line—have the last word. The final words of the tale are in the formless art of a 'rude' ballad, made by the 'tarry hand' of 'another foretopman'—obviously Melville himself, who had, like Budd, been a foretopman.

Those who argue that Vere incarnates 'virtue' or that Melville is ambiguous about his actions base their case upon a few isolated passages, taken quite out of context. For example, they cite the two references to Vere's character as 'exceptional' (81; 214), ignoring the two references to Claggart's character as 'exceptional' (125; 129). The passage cited most frequently as approving of Vere's action (282–83) actually displays its practical error, unless one is such a landlubber as to believe that a wise captain increases the speed of his ship in a dense fog.[13] Vere uses a 'fatherly' 'tone' (225) to Billy, but as a father his rôle is likened to Abraham, though Vere actually sacrifices ' "my boy" ' (225), and not to God but to Mars. Vere and Budd are referred to as 'two of great Nature's nobler order' (289), but that term is a synonym for human beings and, as such, flatly contradicts Vere's contemptuous definition of ' "mankind" ' as mere disorderly animals for whom ' "forms, measured forms are everything" '.

Vere does have many positive qualities, but these serve to strengthen Melville's case against the system he serves and to heighten the emotional horrors of his decision. If he were an especially tyrannical, unjust, irrational, brutal, or ignorant captain, his act could be ascribed to his personal character rather than to the military and imperialist institution of which he is, by his own argument, merely an officer.

Only two men in the ship are 'intellectually capable of adequately appreciating the moral phenomenon presented in Billy Budd' (141). One is Claggart, who 'could even have loved Billy' (178). The other is Vere, whose wilful sacrifice of the transcendent being he recognizes as 'an angel of god' becomes an overwhelming heart-rending loss of freedom, love, and human possibilities. If Vere were a mere stage villain, his act would evoke more anger than anguish. But to argue that therefore Melville must condone or admire his act is tantamount to saying that Shakespeare condones or admires Othello's murder of Desdemona, an act also made more appalling because of the finer qualities of the murderer.

There is only one ambiguity about Vere: is he sane or mad? Insofar as the story focuses on Vere, it is the study of an apparently rational, humane man who can argue with learning, calm, and some plausibility that the most ethical course of action is to kill the most innocent and beloved person in your world to preserve the military law and order necessary for monarchy and empire.

The question of Vere's sanity is raised privately by the ship's surgeon. Immediately Melville asks each reader to answer this question 'by such light as this narrative may afford' (237). Here we should ask another question: what is our rôle as readers? All of Melville's fiction after *Moby-Dick* asks the readers to penetrate beneath the surface appearances to hidden reality. *Billy Budd* is no exception. Melville gives us something to work with, and that is Claggart, a mystery that he explores for us and explains as deeply as possible. Claggart is like one of those sample answers on our standardized tests. Vere is the problem to be solved.

Melville's sample solution is given at length in his disquisition on 'Natural Depravity'. Talking about the obvious example of Claggart, he frames a general definition which fits Captain Vere much more precisely. The best examples of this depravity 'invariably are dominated by intellectuality' (131). 'Civilization, especially if of the austerer sort, is auspicius to it. It folds itself in the mantle of respectability.' Clearly all this applies to the 'austere' and bookish, highly civilized Captain who equates himself with his officer's uniform. Now listen carefully to this definition, and match it point by point with Captain Vere:

> It is not going too far to say that it is without vices or small sins. There is a phenomenal pride in it that excludes them. It is never mercenary or avaricious. In short, the depravity here meant partakes nothing of the sordid or sensual. It is serious, but free from acerbity. Though no flatterer of mankind, it never speaks ill of it.
>
> But the thing which in eminent instances signalizes so exceptional a nature is this: Though the man's even temper and discreet bearing would seem to intimate a mind peculiarly subject to the law of reason, not the less in heart he would seem to riot in complete exemption from that law, having apparently little to do with reason further than to employ it as an ambidexter implement for effecting the irrational. That is to say: Toward the accomplishment of an aim which in wantonness of atrocity would seem to partake of the insane, he will direct a cool judgement sagacious and sound. These men are madmen, and of the most dangerous sort, for their lunacy is not continuous, but occasional, evoked by some special object; it is protectively secretive, which is as much to say it is self-contained, so that when, moreover, most active it is to the average mind not distinguishable from sanity, and for the reason above suggested: that whatever its aims may be—and the aim is never declared—the method and the outward proceeding are always perfectly rational.[14]

Essential to these men is some secret passion, a force driving their will, which dominates their conscience. Using as metaphor the profession Melville found most contemptible, the very one Vere assumes at the crux of the trial, he tells us that 'Claggart's conscience' was 'but the lawyer to his will' (150). And what was Vere's secret passion, that degrades his conscience to the rôle of lawyer? It is precisely the motive that Melville in *White-Jacket* ascribes to the entire officer class, the motive that impels them to seek what all the sailors and other common people dread, what Melville labels the greatest of all evils: war. That motive is *ambition*, for war offers them the possibility of 'glory' and 'promotion'.[15] Hence the officers have an objective interest as a 'class' in the 'slaughtering of their fellow-men'.[16] Finally, at Vere's death, we discover that his 'spirit . . . 'spite its philosophic austerity may yet have indulged in the most secret of all passions, ambition' (338).

Melville spells out this message most directly in *White-Jacket* in explaining why naval officers rejoice 'when all the world wailed':

> I urge it not against them as *men*—their feelings belonged to their profession. Had they not been naval officers, they had not been rejoicers in the midst of despair. (Ch. 49)

And his conclusion indicated why these men are so dangerous:

> Standing navies, as well as standing armies, serve to keep alive the spirit of war even in the meek heart of peace. In its very embers and smoulderings they nourish that fatal fire, and half-pay officers, as the priests of Mars, yet guard the temple, though no god be there.

In 1891, as America prepared to embark on its global pursuit of imperial power, Melville understood even more clearly the dreadful consequences.

Claggart, the evil head of the secret police, is no mystery to us. First came Vidôcq, Claggart's contemporary, like Claggart a former criminal, who set up the first modern secret police force, in Paris. A century later there were the secret police whose machinations led to the Haymarket bombing and the railroading of the workers' leaders in the ensuing trials, part of the immediate background of *Billy Budd*.[17] And now we are in an epoch when the secret police are ubiquitous within our society, with 'dirty tricks' that make Claggart look like a boy scout and gigantic covert operations aimed at 'neutralizing' all those who oppose the latest wars conducted by our global empire. But Claggart, as head of the ship's secret police, was, after all, merely an agent of Vere who himself is merely an agent of the Empire. Billy's blow against Claggart, as Vere instantly recognizes, is an attack on the very foundations of that Empire.

Now we can see *Billy Budd* as an epiphany of the interlocked history of the late eighteenth century, the late nineteenth century, and the late twentieth century. The forces served by Captain Vere did indeed triumph over the hero of *The Rights of Man*. The British Empire, temporarily set back by the

American revolution, was soon moving ahead full speed, in tides of blood, everywhere on the planet, using its almost total hegemony over the seas to extend its rule to over a quarter of the world's population, mostly non-white.

While feudalism was being replaced by capitalism, and Vere's aristocratic class, with its ancient blood lines, was being replaced by men like Claggart, rising by their wits and cunning from unknown origins to the key places of power,[18] the industrial revolution was transforming mercantile capitalism into industrial capitalism. Industrial capitalism demanded colonies and provided the means to acquire them: steamships, instantaneous communication, new weapons of unprecedented destructive power, armies of desperate unemployed men.

Let us not forget that Melville first made his mark as one of the boldest anti-imperialist writers of the century. His outrage focused on the islands of the Pacific, where 'the civilized white man', whom he brands 'the most ferocious animal on the face of the earth',[19] was using warships and missionaries to enslave the so-called 'savages' and 'barbarians'. All this is compressed into the passages after Billy is equated with 'those so-called barbarian' peoples who 'stand nearer to unadulterate Nature' (307). He receives the Christian chaplain of the *Bellipotent* just as missionaries were 'received long ago on tropic isles by any superior *savage*, so called—a Tahitian, say. . . .' (310). In a stunning comparison that foreshadows the opening section of Conrad's *Heart of Darkness*, Melville reminds the English imperialists (and their American descendants) that their ancestors were once treated as they now treat such illiterate 'barbarians' as common sailors and Pacific islanders:

> And, as elsewhere said, a barbarian Billy radically was—as much so, for all the costume, as his countrymen the British captives, living trophies, made to march in the Roman triumph of Germanicus. Quite as much so as those later barbarians, young men probably, and picked specimens among the earlier British converts to Christianity, at least nominally such, taken to Rome (as today converts from lesser isles of the sea may be taken to London). . . . (307–8)

Between 1797, when Vere kills Budd, and 1886, when Melville began writing the story, the British Empire had seized many Pacific islands, Trinidad, British Guiana (Guyana), Saint Lucia, Malta, Dominica, Gambia, Sikkim, Singapore, North Borneo, Malacca, Penang, the Gold Coast (Ghana), Assam, Mauritius, Sierra Leone, many Atlantic isles including the Ascension and Falkland (Malvinas) Islands, Aden, New Zealand, Hong Kong, Natal, Sind, the Punjab, Burma, Bahrain, Nagpur, Nigeria, Baluchistan (southeastern Afghanistan), Basutoland, Fiji, Cyprus, British Honduras (Belize), Somaliland, the Seychelles, Bechuanaland (Botswana), and Egypt. By the time he had finished, Britain had also conquered Southern Zambezia (Zimbabwe), Zululand (part of South Africa), Sarawak, Kenya, Zanzibar, Northern Zembezia (Zambia), Nyassaland, and Uganda.

Looking with late twentieth-century American eyes at Great Britain, we tend to see our historic ally with whom we united in World War I, the invasion of the Soviet Union, World War II, and the post-war global crusade against communist revolution and national liberation movements. But Great Britain looked very different to late nineteenth-century American eyes.

The American revolution against Great Britain was still perceived as the foundation of national identity (Melville's vision is dramatized in *Israel Potter*, a work directly relevant to *Billy Budd*). Fifteen years after the action of *Billy Budd*, the nation's next formal war began, partly as a result of British warships impressing seamen from America's merchant fleet, an image evoked by Billy's impressment from *The Rights of Man* by *H.M.S. Bellipotent*; the indomitable British fleet brought an invading army to burn America's capital city. By 1849, in *Mardi*, Melville was allegorizing Great Britain as the arrogant world empire of Dominora, ruled over by 'rapacious' King Bello, with 'his territorial acquisitiveness, and aversion to relinquishing stolen nations' (Ch. 146). In 1866, Melville attributed the secession of the South to a conspiracy between England and the slave-owners. 'The arts of the conspirators', he argues in the 'Supplement' to *Battle-Pieces*, 'entrapped' the majority of the white people of the South 'into the support of a war whose implied end was the erecting in our advanced century of an Anglo-American empire based upon the systematic degradation of man.'

The British Empire to which Captain Vere sacrifices Billy Budd was neither abstract nor remote for Americans in the 1880s and 1890s. By then, the British global empire had become so overwhelming, and its operations in the Western Hemisphere so threatening, that many Americans expected yet another attempt at crippling the United States.

For example, on 27 July 1890, the *New York Times* ran 'A Stranger at Our Gate', a 2,000-word article by William Drysdale arguing that 'Great Britain is no longer a distant power across the seas, but a powerful nation with intrenchments thrown across our front yard, ready to interfere with our ingress and egress whenever opportunity may offer':

> This offensive line—for I can hardly regard it as a defensive line—is maintained at almost fabulous expense, and there is a reason for its existence. . . . A map of America with all the British possessions printed in black would be as dark as a thunder cloud. . . . Is England a friendly nation? I read every day of the war ships she is sending up to Behring Sea, and of the fleet she is concentrating at Halifax, and again ask the question. I see those guns she is pointing at us all along our shore, and leave the question for you to answer. . . . The British army officer can sit down and tell by the hour why the Confederate Army should have whipped us, and explain how it happened that they didn't, without mentioning that their not doing it was no fault of the British government.

When Drysdale traces the offensive line from the fortifications along the Canadian border to the island fortress at Bermuda down through the British colonies strung from the Caribbean to British Honduras, he names the powerful warships manning the line along 'our coast'. The most potent of these is the *Bellerephon*.

In fact, between 1886 and early 1891, the very years when Melville was writing *Billy Budd*, Great Britain and the United States were frequently close to armed hostilities. Especially dangerous were the confrontations in the Bering Sea, where Canadian ships manned by British subjects were often seized in waters claimed by the United States, while British warships steamed to the area and American warships, hastily rigged with new armour and long-range cannons, raced to meet them.

On 5 January 1891, for instance, the headline of the *New York Times*, one of the least bellicose newspapers of the day, blared 'IS IT WAR OR BLUSTER', while below appeared a box listing the number of guns, the number of men, and the speed of each ship in the opposing war fleets. On 7 January, the lead story discussed Canadian preparations for war with the United States, and compared the possible military scenarios with the War of 1812. On 18 January, an article entitled 'England In Our Waters' warned against our lapses in naval power, and traced the history of our conflicts with Great Britain back to 'the deadly apathy' that allowed the 'riveting of the chains of British oppression' in the eighteenth century.

I am not implying that *Billy Budd* is some kind of anti-British or jingoistic diatribe. For *Billy Budd* was written just as America was about to transform into a world empire resembling the British empire against which it had rebelled. The story foresees the consequences of unbridled militarism and imperialism, which obliterate the rights of man not only in the colonized lands but also among the people forced to do the fighting and colonizing. By going a century into the past to explore the consequences of the triumph of militarism and imperialism in England, it foreshadows the century of the future, with the consequences of the triumph of militarism and imperialism in America.

By destroying Billy Budd and what he embodies, Claggart and Vere clear the decks for British world hegemony. The struggles taking shape as Melville wrote his story were struggles contesting that hegemony, struggles that were to culminate in the aptly-named First World War.

By the late 1880s, there was very little of the non-white world left for the imperialist powers to carve up. Hence there were already emerging the inter-imperialist rivalries and alliances characteristic of the period through the Second World War. Hints of this appear in the coverage of the Anglo-American crisis of early 1891.

For example, the story under that 5 January 'IS IT WAR OR BLUSTER' headline lamented the collusion between the British and German Empires in denying Pacific colonies to the United States and implied that they might be about to gang up militarily against the U.S. Pacific fleet: 'The intimation that the British fleet is to be complemented in the North Pacific by the fleet of the German Empire does not strike as improbable any one who has been aware of the persistency with which Great Britain and Germany have operated in the Pacific.' On 7 February, in an editorial on German colonial aspirations, the *Times* pushed for turning this alliance into a rivalry, with the explicit aim of checking British global ambition:

> We may apply a slang phrase in sober reality to the aspirations of Great Britain in saying that the "wants the earth," of which she has already selected for herself the most eligible of the portions not inhabited by civilized men. . . . In BISMARCK'S time Germany showed a disposition in the affair of the Kameruns, in the affair of Samoa, and in several minor affairs to take what she wanted without reference to the desires of England, and the world was treated to the novel and refreshing spectacle of England being successfully bullied, as she has been in the habit of bullying alike inferior powers and "natives" when the question was of adding to the British possessions or of extending British markets.

When the wish came true, America was in a position to ally with Britain to advance its own global ambition.

By 1891, pro-imperialist and pro-militarist forces were on the ascendancy. Seven years after Melville stopped working on *Billy Budd*, America was to launch its manifest destiny of the twentieth century by picking on the weakest of the European empires, waging war against Spain in order to assume its colonial rôle in such places as the Philippines, Puerto Rico, Central America, and Cuba.

Melville's imagination gives us images that keep expanding to encompass our historical reality. For example, we can see Vere's ceremony of militaristic order, the lines of men on the decks of the *Bellipotent*, lengthening into those endless lines of perfect order in the giant Nazi rallies. The guns of the *Bellipotent*, those 'seventy-four beauties' called 'the fighting peacemakers', evolve into 'Little Boy' and 'Fat Man' and their endless descendants, Minutemen, Titans, Poseidons, Tridents, Pershings, MIRVs, MARVs, and the one recently named 'the Peacekeeper'.[20]

Those who command the war machine can sound just as urbane, calm, prudent, reasonable, and sensible as Captain

Vere while they explain that their strategy known as MAD Mutually Assured Destruction) is now our best defence, hough even greater security lies in a race for indomitable power in space. Operating from Vere's insane premises, they have within their hands the authority and means to turn the entire planet into the sterile, lifeless, inorganic mass that is the *Bellipotent*'s final triumph of order and measured forms: 'And the circumambient air in the clearness of its serenity was like smooth white marble in the polished block not yet removed from the marble-dealer's yard.'

In *Billy Budd, Sailor*, the last words, though funereal, belong to the nemesis of the despots and empires, with their implacable captains and machines of war—the common people they oppress. If we comprehend Melville's story, we may improve our chances of bringing about a happier ending.

NOTES

1. Louis M. Hacker, Introduction to Alfred Thayer Mahan, *The Influence of Sea Power upon History, 1660–1783* (New York: Sagamore Press, 1957), v.
2. Hannah Arendt, *On Revolution* (New York: Viking, 1965), 79.
3. Ibid.
4. My analysis is deeply indebted to the pioneering works of 1950–60, whose arguments still stand unrebutted: Joseph Schiffman, 'Melville's Final Stage, Irony: A Re-examination of *Billy Budd* Criticism', *American Literature*, 22 (May, 1950), 128–36; Arthur Sale, 'Captain Vere's Reasons', *Cambridge Journal*, 5 (October, 1951), 3–18; Leonard Casper, 'The Case Against Captain Vere', *Perspective*, 5 (Summer, 1952), 146–52; Karl E. Zink, 'Herman Melville and the Forms—Irony and Social Criticism in *Billy Budd*', *Accent*, 12 (Summer, 1952), 131–39; Merlin Bowen, *The Long Encounter* (University of Chicago Press, 1960). The great scholarship of Harrison Hayford and Merton Sealts' edition of *Billy Budd, Sailor (An Inside Narrative)* (University of Chicago Press, 1962) found fresh evidence in the process of Melville's composition. Some more recent splendid contributions to our understanding of *Billy Budd* and to my own analysis include: Edgar Dryden, *Melville's Thematics of Form* (Johns Hopkins University Press, 1968); William H. Shurr, *The Mystery of Iniquity: Melville as Poet, 1857–1891* (Lexington: University Press of Kentucky, 1972); A. Carl Bredahl, Jr., *Melville's Angles of Vision* (Gainesville: University of Florida Press, 1972); Christopher W. Sten, 'Vere's Use of the "Forms": Means and Ends in *Billy Budd*, *American Literature*', 47 (March 1975), 37–51; Marvin Mandell, 'Martyrs or

Murderers? A Defense of Innocence', *Midwest Quarterly*, 18 (1977), 131–43; Marlene Longenecker, 'Captain Vere and the Form of Truth', *Studie. in Short Fiction*, 14 (1977), 337–43; Miriam Quen Cheiken, 'Captair Vere: Darkness Made Visible', *Arizona Quarterly*, 34 (1978), 293–310 Stanton Garner, 'Fraud as Fact in Herman Melville's *Billy Budd*', *Sar Jose Review*, 4 (1978), 82–105; C. N. Manlove, 'An Organic Hesitancy. Theme and Style in *Billy Budd*' in Faith Pullin (ed.), *New Perspectives or Melville* (Kent State University Press, 1978), pp. 275–300; Rowland A. Sherrill, *The Prophetic Melville* (Athens: University of Georgia Press 1979); James F. Farnham, 'Captain Vere's Existential Failure', *Arizona Quarterly*, 37 (1981), 362–70; Joyce Sparer Adler, *War in Melville's Imagination* (New York University Press, 1981); Christopher S. Durer, 'Captain Vere and Upper-Class Mores in *Billy Budd*', *Studies in Short Fiction*, 19 (1982), 9–18. Brook Thomas' '*Billy Budd* and the Judgment of Silence', *Bucknell Review* (1982), 51–78, is a penetrating reading that exposes the hidden political agenda of deconstructive approaches to the story.

5. Hayford and Sealts, leaf 48. Future references are by parenthetical notation of the leaf number in this edition.
6. Milton Stern, Introduction to his edition of *Billy Budd, Sailor* (Indianapolis: Bobbs-Merrill, 1975), viii, xvii, xxi.
7. See Hayford and Sealts, pp. 175–83, and C. B. Ives, '*Billy Budd* and the Articles of War', *American Literature*, 34 (1962), 31–9.
8. Shurr, pp. 251–52.
9. Garner, p. 98.
10. Farnham, p. 367.
11. Dryden, p. 215.
12. For a wonderful analysis, see Longenecker, pp. 338–42.
13. Garner, p. 95.
14. Leaves 132–34. Vere's precise fit was first noted by those pioneering articles of the 1950s, but is usually ignored by Vere's apologists.
15. *White-Jacket*, Ch. 49.
16. Ibid.
17. See Robert K. Wallace, '*Billy Budd* and the Haymarket Hangings', *American Literature*, 47 (1975), 108–13.
18. For a discussion of Vere and Claggart as representatives of the two classes contending for the rule of England see Durer, pp. 10–14.
19. *Typee*, Ch. 17.
20. The MX missile was named the 'Peacekeeper' only because its original name—the 'Peacemaker'—was deemed too close to 'pacemaker' (*New York Times*, 23 November 1982).

Notes on Contributors

HAROLD BEAVER is Professor of American literature at the University of Amsterdam. He has contributed five editions of Melville and Poe to the Penguin English Library and has just completed a book, based on past essays and articles, *The Great American Masquerade*.

HERBIE BUTTERFIELD is Reader in Literature at the University of Essex. He is the author of a book on Hart Crane, a monograph on Robinson Jeffers, and miscellaneous shorter pieces on various other American writers, including Poe, Hawthorne, Longfellow, Henry James, Willa Cather, and Hemingway.

H. BRUCE FRANKLIN is Professor of English and American literature at Rutgers University, Newark, New Jersey. His most recent books are *Prison Literature in America* and *Robert A. Heinlein: America as Science Fiction*.

RICHARD GRAY is Reader in Literature at the University of Essex. He has edited two anthologies of American poetry, a collection of essays on Robert Penn Warren and (in the Critical Studies series) *American Fiction: New Readings* (1983). He is also the author of *The Literature of Memory: Modern Writers of the American South* as well as essays on American poetry and fiction.

ANDREW HOOK is Bradley Professor of English literature at Glasgow University. His American interests are reflected by his books, *Scotland and America 1750–1835* (1975) and *American Literature in Context, 1865–1900* (1982) as well as by articles on Anglo-American literary relations.

JAMES H. JUSTUS, Professor of English at Indiana University, has written on such American authors as Charles Brockden Brown, Hawthorne, Kate Chopin, Hemingway, Faulkner and other twentieth-century writers of the American South. His most recent book is *The Achievement of Robert Penn Warren* (1981).

A. ROBERT LEE teaches American literature at the University c Kent at Canterbury. He is editor of the Everyman *Moby-Dick* (1975 and three previous collections in the Critical Studies series, *Blac Fiction: New Studies in the Afro-American Novel Since 1945* (1980) *Nathaniel Hawthorne: New Critical Essays* (1982) and *Ernest Hemingway New Critical Essays* (1983). He has recently published a B.A.A.S pamphlet *Black American Fiction Since Richard Wright* (1983) an essays on Chester Himes, Richard Wright, Emily Dickinson an Robert Penn Warren.

ERIC MOTTRAM is Professor of English and American literature i the University of London, at King's College. He has publishe books on Kenneth Rexroth, Paul Bowles, Allen Ginsberg an others, and, with Malcolm Bradbury, edited and contributed to th *Penguin Companion to American Literature* (1971). He has written widel on nineteenth-century and twentieth-century America. His las three books of poetry were *Elegies, A Book of Herne* and *Interrogatio Rooms*.

WILLIAM WASSERSTROM is professor of English at Syracus University and has published widely on American literature an social issues. Among his books are *The Time of the Dial, A Dia Miscellany, Heiress of All the Ages, Civil Liberties and the Arts* and *Th Legacy of Van Wyck Brooks*.

218

Index

Index

Moore, Maxine: *The American Almanac*, 31, 39
Morewood, Sarah Huyler, 68, 69
Morgan, Pierpont, 102
Mosher, Bernard, 89

Nabokov, Vladimir, 132; *Pale Fire*, 124, 132
Newton, Sir Isaac, 156

Odyssey, The, 75
Olson, Charles, 9, 12, 94, 97, 102, 108; 'A Later Note on Maximus Letter No. 15', 93; *Archaeologist of Morning*, 13; *Call Me Ishmael*, 7, 8
Ortega y Gasset, Jose: *History as a System*, 120
Orwell, George: *Nineteen Eighty-Four*, 104

Pavese, Cesare, 10
Poe, Edgar Allan, 33, 35, 105, 138, 177; *Eureka*, 76; *The Narrative of Arthur Gordon Pym*, 32
Pound, Ezra: *The Cantos*, 76
Proust, Marcel: *A la Recherche du Temps Perdu*, 76
Pynchon, Thomas: *Gravity's Rainbow*, 76, 92

Rabelais, 36, 98
Reagan, Ronald, 199
Reich, Wilhelm, 95
Richardson, Samuel: *Clarissa*, 76
Rieff, Philip, 102
Rockefeller, John D., 102
Ross, Harold, 91
Rousseau, Jean-Jacques, 17
Rowe, John Carlos, 135
Russell, William Clark, 10

Sachs, Viola, 74; *The Game of Creation*, 89
Scott, Sir Walter, 98, 178

Shakespeare, William, 8, 71, 93, 123, 180, 207; *As You Like It*, 163; *Hamlet*, 106; *King Lear*, 106; *Macbeth*, 98; *Othello*, 106; *Romeo and Juliet*, 119
Shaw, Judge Lemuel, 26
Shelley, Mary, 104
Shelley, Percy Bysshe, 104
Spenser, Edmund, 29; 'Bowre of Blis', 36
Stedman, E. C., 181
Stein, William Bysshe, 179, 182, 193
Stern, Milton R., 203
Stevens, Wallace, 131, 152
Stoddard, Richard, 181
Stowe, Harriet Beecher, 142

Taylor, Bayard, 181
Tennyson, Alfred Lord: *In Memoriam*, 193
Thoreau, Henry David, 20, 70, 142, 172; *A Week on the Concord and Merrimack Rivers*, 166; 'Civil Disobedience', 110
Thurber, James, 91
Tolkien, J. R., 29
Tuckerman, Frederick, 177
Twain, Mark, 11, 143, 159; *Huckleberry Finn*, 11

Updike, John, 8; *Hugging the Shore*, 13

Warren, Robert Penn, 11, 179, 181; *Selected Essays*, 13
Weaver, Raymond, 69, 88, 137
Whiston, William, 35
Whitman, Walt, 70, 142, 177, 188; *Leaves of Grass*, 76
Williams, William Carlos: *Paterson*, 76

Zukofsky, Louis, 94

221

CELEBRATE THE GOSPEL OF JESUS

Melvin E. Banks, Sr., Litt.D.
A. Okechukwu Ogbonnaya, Ph.D.

Urban Ministries, Inc.
Chicago, IL

Publisher
Urban Ministries, Inc.
P.O. Box 436987
Chicago, IL 60643-6987
1.800.860.8642

First Edition
First Printing
ISBN: 0-940955-61-X
Catalog No. 6-5210

Unless otherwise noted, Scripture texts are taken from the
King James Version of the Bible.

To Mrs. Olive Banks
for thirty years of dedication
to helping others learn to
Celebrate Jesus

TABLE OF CONTENTS

INTRODUCTION

Celebrate the Gospel of Jesus is a compilation of studies dealing with lessons from the life of our Lord Jesus Christ. We are being called to celebrate the Good News in the various acts performed by our Lord. For those of us who have willingly responded to the Good News, we call you to celebrate the Good News of His birth and the Good News of His forgiveness. As we study, we are being led into the rhythm of joy which may have accompanied His teaching and His action. Yes, even in the announcement of His death there is cause for celebration, for you see finally, humanity can be freed from the prison of guilt and shame. What would you do if you were healed of leprosy? What would have been your response if you were there when the angels sang "glory in the highest"? How your heart would have leaped, if you followed Jesus through the dusty roads of Galilee and saw His compassion for the lowly and outcast. Celebrate the Gospel of Jesus is designed to help churches and individuals get deeper step-by-step into the life of our Lord, and to lead them into celebrative joy for all that He has done.

We invite you to follow as we look into the celebrative power of Jesus' messianic identity as articulated by Peter, to share in the celebration of the angels and the shepherds at the birth of our Lord, to enter into the blessedness of Mary as she accepts the natal mandate from above. For those who may feel that there is no reason to celebrate because of contexts of historical existential despair—if you have been struggling with a weight of pain that makes it hard for you to celebrate—the affirmation of the care of Jesus can still lead you to celebrate even in the midst of the storm. There is also Good News in service, for in service we share in the very servant-hood of Jesus. It calls for celebration. The privilege of participating with the God of the universe in service is cause for celebration. If you have been marginalized or have barriers between you and God and others around you, we invite you to experience the boundary-breaking Good News of Jesus. When your sin seems ready to crush you under its heavy weight, you can experience forgiveness which Jesus offers. When your lack and your needs are just coming faster than you can think, we want you to know that Jesus is enough. As sure as the sun rises, the night will fall. When the night time of the soul falls upon your weary soul, hear the Lord as he says, "I am the light of the world." Here is the Good News. Here is cause for celebration. Here we lift our highest praise and celebrate the goodness of our God. Let's celebrate!

We hope that this work will help you as you celebrate the gospel of our Lord this year. Our final aim is that all celebration will result in the salvation of the lost and ultimately to the glory of the Lord God and Father of our Saviour Jesus Christ.

A. Okechukwu Ogbonnaya
Dr. Melvin Banks
Chicago 2000

Chapter One

GOOD NEWS: JESUS IS THE MESSIAH

BASED ON MATTHEW 16:13-23

Matthew 16:13-23

When Jesus came into the coasts of Caesarea Philippi, he asked his disciples, saying, Whom do men say that I the Son of man am? [14] And they said, Some say that thou art John the Baptist: some, Elias; and others, Jeremias, or one of the prophets. [15] He saith unto them, But whom say ye that I am? [16] And Simon Peter answered and said, Thou art the Christ, the Son of the living God. [17] And Jesus answered and said unto him, Blessed art thou, Simon Bar-jona: for flesh and blood hath not revealed it unto thee, but my Father which is in heaven. [18] And I say also unto thee, That thou art Peter, and upon this rock I will build my church; and the gates of hell shall not prevail against it. [19] And I will give unto thee the keys of the kingdom of heaven: and whatsoever thou shalt bind on earth shall be bound in heaven: and whatsoever thou shalt loose on earth shall be loosed in heaven. [20] Then charged he his disciples that they should tell no man that he was Jesus the Christ. [21] From that time forth began Jesus to show unto his disciples, how that he must go unto Jerusalem, and suffer many things of the elders and chief priests and scribes, and be killed, and be raised *again the third day. 22 Then Peter took him, and began to rebuke him, saying, Be it far from thee, Lord: this shall not be unto thee. 23 But he turned, and said unto Peter, Get thee behind me, Satan: thou art an offence unto me: for thou savourest not the things that be of God, but those that be of men.*

The identity of Jesus has been a thorn in the side of academicians in our age. Their continuing story is recorded in countless volumes, beginning with a book written by Albert Schwietzer titled *The Quest for the Historical Jesus* to some modern works, one of which is called *The New Quest*. In fact, European scholars have always assumed that Jesus was European and with the return of exiled Israelites from Europe, this idea has even become entrenched. But the identity of Jesus is not just a problem for scholars, it has also been a problem for non-scholars. In the West where everything good has been defined as "white," the question of the color identity of Jesus has become crucial as we seek to win people of color to the way of Jesus. The color identity of Jesus may have been settled by the vote of the Roman Catholic church to portray Jesus as Black. But the fact is that in most Eastern Orthodox churches many of their icons are Black including the Lord Jesus Christ. The West's grip in anti-African sentiments has robbed it of the opportunity to get to know Jesus just a little better. The identity of the Lord involves more than His color, it has to do with His character, His mission, and His purpose.

The quest to discover the identity of our Lord was the subject of a short story written by Richard Wright about a young boy who painted Jesus Black (*Uncle Tom's Children*, 1938). Today, in many circles, this may not be as big an issue as it was in the Untied States in 1938. In that era, this young boy's painting was done at a time when a picture of a Black Christ was not at all acceptable. In the story, the Black principal at the boy's school failed to get a major promotion because he dared to place the painting in a school-wide competition. His White supervisor exploded with anger. He could not understand why the principal commended the child instead of reprimanding him. For these people, Africans could not be true humans. How could they think God could even be close to them, let alone take on their identity? Today, controversy continues about the identity of Jesus Christ; even with the turn to a more accurate understanding of Jesus' racial identity, the controversy will continue. But a study of geography, anthropology, and the Bible leads to the conclusion that Jesus was not the White person so typically portrayed in most Bible art. And this affirmation is especially important to young people of African descent. However, the question Christ wants us to clarify in our minds and hearts is not how He looks, but who He is. One may indeed argue that knowing what He came to do for us is more important than how we depict Him. But the danger of such dismissal is that when people find out that they have been deceived, we may lose our witnessing edge.

Before Jesus came to earth, the Jews had a definite idea of the Messiah and what He would accomplish. Jewish history is replete with prophets who told of a Majestic Messiah who was to restore Israel to its rightful political place. According to the Prophet Isaiah, the long-awaited Messiah would occupy the earthly throne of King David. The prophet wrote, "He will reign on David's throne and over his kingdom, establishing and upholding it with justice and righteousness from that time on and forever" (Isaiah 9:7, NIV). The scribes of Jesus' day had completely overlooked Isaiah's assertion that God's Servant, the

Messiah, would suffer and die (Isaiah 53). During Peter's time, Israel was ruled by Herod the Great, a usurper to the throne and a puppet of Rome. The people believed the Messiah would assume the throne of David and overthrow the Roman oppressors. He would restore Israel to her past glory. Many of those who accepted Jesus as Messiah expected Him to establish His throne at this time.

Peter, the main character in the text for this study, was introduced to Jesus by his brother Andrew (John 1:40, 41). Andrew had listened to Jesus' teaching and believed Him to be the Messiah. Andrew immediately went and found Simon Peter, telling him, "We have found the Messiah" (1:41, NIV). He took Peter to meet Christ, and Peter also believed. Later, by the Sea of Galilee, Christ approached the brothers about a total commitment. Peter and Andrew were tending to their fishing enterprise when Jesus said to them, "Follow me, and I will make you fishers of men" (Matthew 4:19). Jesus needed a group of men in His ministry who would travel with Him, learn from Him, and be able to carry on in ministry once He left earth. Peter and Andrew responded immediately to Jesus' call. They left their business and followed Him (v. 20).

One day, Jesus and His disciples were traveling toward the region of Caesarea Philippi. When they reached the outskirts of this city, Jesus asked His disciples an important question, "Whom do men say that I the Son of man am?" (v. 13) The 12 men threw out various names they had heard circulated throughout the cities. Some were saying Jesus was John the Baptist whom Herod had beheaded (v. 14). When Herod heard of the things Christ did, he also feared that Jesus was John returned from the dead (Mark 6:14). Another of the disciples piped in, "Others say Elijah" (Matthew 16:14, NIV). Malachi prophesied that Elijah would return before the coming of the Messiah (Malachi 4:5). Therefore, some thought Jesus was Elijah. Still others believed He was Jeremiah or one of the prophets (Matthew 16:14). Because of His strong, exhorting message and His compassion toward the people, some believed Jesus was Jeremiah; while others compared Him to the great prophet Elijah because they performed similar miracles. Because Jesus' appearance was more lowly than expected, He was believed to have been just a prophet, or even John the Baptist who was also clothed modestly and appeared to be unassuming.

In this passage, knowing who Jesus is relates to sharing in His power. One of the highest commemorative honors given to a Roman authority was to have places, children, and buildings named after him. Caesarea Philippi was named for two prominent Roman rulers: Caesar Augustus and Philip the Tetrarch. The influence of Greek and Roman culture was everywhere, and pagan temples and idols abounded. It was here that Jesus, disregarding all of this Roman fanfare, audaciously asks about His own greatness. He wanted to know what the disciples thought of Him. Primarily Jesus wanted to know if they really knew Him. His reference to Himself as the Son of man (unlike the Gospel of Mark's usage to indicate the humility and suffering) implies exaltation and glory.

This chapter explores the identity of Jesus and the good news inherent in that identity for us. Not only does the question of identity come from the mouth of the Master Himself, but He tells us what benefits await those who know who He is.

The account in Matthew 16:13-23 takes place on the way to Caesarea Philippi after the Lord has rebuked the Pharisees and Sadducees for their quest to understand the weather patterns of the earth but failing to understand the signs of the coming of the kingdom of God. As He leaves that confrontation with the leaders of Israel, He warns His disciples about the leaven of the Pharisees and Sadducees. Of course, being people who thought mainly in physical terms about spiritual truths, they immediately thought that Jesus was speaking of food. But Jesus promptly reminds them of the miraculous feeding of the five thousand and the four thousand (vv. 8-9). When Jesus asked the question "Whom do men say that I am?" The emphasis on the interrogative pronoun "who" (Greek *tis*) questions the ideas that people have about Jesus. One could change it to mean "Do these people really know who I am?" The people had tried to crown Jesus King because He fed them. They had accused Him of being demon-possessed. Even His own parents had tried to take Him and lock Him up because He presumed to speak for God. Who do they really think He is? Do they really think that He was like every man? How do they describe Him? But even within this question is the question of "Why?" Why do they come to Him? Why do they call on Him? Why do some love Him and others want to kill Him? Note that question is not, "Who does God think Jesus is?" but who do humans think He is?" The word answer refers to something someone says as the result of a prolonged gaze. Having seen Jesus in a variety of contexts, what is the disciples' verdict? This question also includes the existential question of purpose. The disciples have looked at Jesus with astonishment, as at someone remarkable, but do they really know who He is? Do they now have a spiritual and dynamic understanding of who He is, or are they caught up in merely mechanical expressions of what it means to be the Messiah? Is their identification of Him based on the passive or casual influence of other peoples' opinions or observations? Or is it a result of true spiritual insight based on knowledge?

Our understanding of who the Lord is should not be merely the passive reception of tradition. To know who the Lord Jesus truly is we must search intensively. The significance of an earnest desire to know the Lord will be seen in our continued inspection of biblical and historical facts. How can anyone know who Jesus is when they have spent all their time watching Him from a distance? How can anyone really know who He is when they make decisions based on what appears instead of what is revealed? "Whom do men say that I the Son of Man am?" . . . . is therefore a question that hits at the heart of the world's understanding or misunderstanding of the Person and purpose of Jesus Christ. The disciples answered Jesus' question with the common view that Jesus was one of the great prophets come back to life. But it is interesting that given Jesus' reference to the "son of man" that they did they not mention Ezekiel whom they believed to be one of the great transitional prophets of Israel. In Deuteronomy 18:18, God promised to raise up a prophet from among the people like Moses. But here they did not even mention Moses. Jesus was "Emmanuel" right in the presence of the people, but they were oblivious to the fact that He was God incarnate. They would rather see Him as a dead prophet reincarnated than believe that indeed He was the One whom God had promised them. This halfway acquiescing is so typical of human beings; Jesus was great, but not as great as the Messiah would be. They were willing to give Him credit for being one of their most respected prophets, but they were not willing to accept that He was the Son of man or the Son of God.

Many in our world today, still, are reluctant to move beyond a mere human description of who Jesus is. Many are willing to grant Him the status of a prophet but unwilling to crown Him Lord. Many would have Him be a messenger but not the Son of

God. Many would have Him be a miracle worker but not the Saviour. Many will call Him good but not God. Who do the people around you say that He is? Some even want to make Him a politician but refuse to grant Him access to their heart and soul. Some would have Him as their provider and bread-maker but not the Bread of Life that comes from heaven. Some would have Him as an acquaintance but not get intimate with Him. Some acknowledge Him on Sunday, but fail to make Him Lord of their life on Monday through Saturday. However, we cannot let these half-baked opinions of His identity fool us. These responses all fell short then, and they still miss the mark even today. Any opinion of who Jesus is that is not based on the Word, no matter how liberating, how scholarly, or how rhetorically sweet, is not good news but bad news, and stands under the judgment of God.

How do we know that all those responses were unsatisfactory? The fact that Jesus proceeded to ask "But whom say ye that I am?" suggests that all the other responses fell far short of describing His identity. His use of the word "but" suggests that it does not matter what others thought of Him. Their opinions did not count because they did not know Him. They had not walked with Him. They were not His friends. What did these disciples who have walked, talked, and eaten with Him think about Him? The question was directed to all of them. One can almost hear the deafening silence.

Church people also have their cliches about the identity of Jesus. We say things like: "He is my friend." "He is my provider." " He was a great man." But if we stop there, we are no better than those who watch Jesus from afar. The good news is not that Jesus is our friend. We can have friends who are no help to us when we are in trouble. The good news is that Jesus is God in the flesh and that He is able to save and to protect to the utmost.

The question Jesus asked the disciples is the most far-reaching and personal question that can be asked: "Whom say ye that I am?" (v. 15) This question is critical because their response to it relates to their own salvation. What a person believes about Jesus is a prelude to his or her willingness to trust Him for salvation. Faith in Jesus Christ determines whether one receives eternal life or eternal damnation. The issue is not what others think about Jesus but what you think about Him. What's important is not so much what others say about Jesus but what you say about Him. Your salvation hinges on what you believe.

Although the disciples had seen Jesus perform miracles, cast out demons, and control nature, they still were unsure of His identity. Jesus wanted to know if they knew Him and believed in Him. Can you imagine the disciples timidly looking at each other. What if they said the wrong thing?

The affirmation exploded from Peter's heart to his lips. Without hesitation he responded, "Thou art the Christ, the Son of the living God" (v. 16). Jesus gave Peter an "A+" for correctly identifying Him as the Christ, the Son of the living God. He called Peter "blessed" (v. 17), because the truth which he spoke did not come from his own reasoning or superior intellect. The heavenly Father had disclosed this information to Simon Peter and enabled him to make the great confession that Jesus was not just the Son of man, but He was the Son of the living God. Such a confession signifies that Jesus not only has dominion over the earth, but the power which comes because of His relationship with the living Creator of the earth. Jesus was the Messiah, the Christ, the Redeemer of Israel, sent by the ever-present, living God of Israel. The importance of Peter's confession lies in the fact that if the disciples were going to be Jesus' spokespersons after the resurrection they would have to be convinced of the Lord's identity.

In response to Jesus' personal question, "Who do you say that I am?" Peter confessed Jesus as Divine and as the promised and long-awaited Messiah. If Jesus were to ask you this question, how would you answer? Is He your Lord and Saviour? Peter said directly "Thou art the Christ." His response showed that he knew without a doubt that Jesus was the promised Messiah, the Son of the living God. To Peter, Jesus was more than a human friend, a miracle worker, or another prophet; indeed, He was more than man. He was the anointed, the Messiah.

In those days, just as in these, there were many so-called messiahs and would be saviours. If Peter had stopped there the others could have said "So, what else is new?" Many have been anointed. In fact, the tradition of anointing was so strong that on one occasion when asked the people "Whose son is the Messiah?" their response was that he was the son of David. They were still thinking in terms of the anointing of a human person with oil for a specific work. True, Jesus was human and, as such, the Son of man. But it must be remembered that He was also the only begotten Son of God. Peter described the identity of Jesus as "the Son of the living God." The idea is that although many people have been anointed, but here we have the "Son." By being Son, He is the very essence of anointing. He comes directly from the God who anoints and is of the very nature of that God. Peter's statement is replete with implication. He has just equated Jesus not just with the warrior king of Israel who will deliver them in battle but with the God of Israel by calling Him "the Son of the living God." He is not a son of an idol that cannot move. He is the Son of the living God which immediately makes Him the life giver. The revelation that this Galilean with a sun-baked face is the Son of the living God who now walks in this valley of the shadow of death with us, is good news. That the One who shares the very nature of the Most High, even the God of Israel, will come to us earthly creatures, that is truly good news. To say that Jesus is the Messiah, as Peter said, was to declare that hope has come down. To say that Jesus is the Son of the living God is to say that we too can now stand in the presence of life.

Watch Jesus' response to Peter's insight into His identity. His first statement is not "Peter you are right" but "Blessed art thou." Why is Peter blessed? Because God thought well of him to reveal this insight unto him. First, he had just been blessed by faith which acknowledges whom God sent to save the world. Peter is blessed because in this response, he has entered into intercourse with realms of divine wisdom. For Peter to see the identity of this One who holds the mystery of godliness, this mystery must first inhabit him. For him to speak a heaven-sent word to the Word made flesh, he himself must be inhabited by that word. For Peter to cut through all the confusing traditions of the ages, he must have been lifted to a higher plain. Jesus' statement in verse 17 "for flesh and blood hath not revealed it unto thee, but my Father which is in heaven" suggests that a special transaction had taken place between Peter and the heavenly realm, of which even Peter himself may not have been quite aware. This piercing through the veil of ignorance, this kind of cutting down of the tree of darkness, this piercing of the divine sun into this vale of confusion, can only come through revelation. Yes indeed, Peter was blessed to have his eyes opened to the very appearance of God in this world. If you and I will cut through this confusion, this present darkness, cross this vale of

ignorance, and know who Jesus truly is, we must be open to revelation from the Father. Blessed are those who are ready for revelation.

Jesus also gave Simon a new name. In ancient times among
the Igbos of West African, when one is initiated they receive a
secret name which bears their true destiny and it was kept secret
until such a time as their purpose is manifested. For those of us
who are children of modernity, names may not be important.
They may have significance mainly as cataloging instruments.
But among the Africans a name embodies the divine destiny of
its bearer. In many African cultures, if you were to find the true
identity of someone, you could participate in their power and
their destiny. By acknowledging the true identity of Jesus, Peter

was now a candidate for sharing in the very destiny of Jesus. Not only does Jesus pronounce a blessing on Simon for knowing His identity, He gave him a name bearing his destiny. He called him Peter. He called him a rock, signifying his participation with Jesus as the true and eternal Rock, the precious cornerstone and foundation of our faith. Those who know the nature and destiny of our Lord share in his nature and destiny. It is good news to know the identity of the Lord Jesus, for then we can also share in His nature.

The identity of Jesus is good news to the Church and the world. It is based on Jesus' identity that the Church is built. In Matthew 16:18, after the revelation of the identity of Jesus, we have the first occurrence of the word "church" in the Bible. The Greek word for "church" is ecclesia and means called out assembly. The word as Jesus used it here conveys the prediction that all believers (Jew and Gentile) would be joined together in unity. The Apostle Paul described this group as a "body" having many members (1 Corinthians 12). Jesus was doubtlessly referring to the Church when He said believers would be the light of the world (Matthew 5:14). Jesus' identity as the Son of the Living God who died for our sins is the basis of the Church, a group of diverse people coming together in faith to create a community of love.

Furthermore, Jesus says to Peter because you know my identity, whatever you bind on earth is bound and whatever you loose is loosed. This declaration of authority which the Lord invested upon Peter is given to all who are willing to move from merely humanizing Jesus to acknowledging His divine essence. When we come to know the identity of Jesus and acknowledge His status as the Son of the living God, we receive His blessing, we receive a new identity, and we receive spiritual power to bind and loose. We read "then Jesus said, Thou art Peter, and upon this rock I will build my church" (v. 18). There is much theological controversy surrounding this verse. However, we can agree that it points to the blessing that follows one who acknowledges the true identity of Jesus. Peter's participation in the work of Jesus is quite clear. The Bible records that Peter did open the door of faith to the Jews on the Day of Pentecost (Acts 2:14-41), to the Samaritans (Acts 8:14-25), and also to the Gentiles (Acts 10:34-48). His role in opening the doors of the church at Pentecost shows him participating with Christ to reach the world. His role in opening the door for evangelizing the peoples outside of Israel also shows his understanding of the nature and purpose of the Lord to offer salvation to all.

Jesus assured Peter and the other disciples that even though the forces of evil would be arrayed against the Church, they would not prevail. The Lord promised to give Peter the keys of the kingdom of heaven. The keys mentioned in Matthew 16 refer to the exercise of spiritual authority—to open the doors of God's kingdom. When Jesus affirmed Simon Peter and his statement and called him "blessed," this word does not merely denote happiness, but is equivalent with having God's kingdom in one's heart and produces satisfaction which comes from God and not the world. Simon, as the son of Jonah or Bar Jonah, was probably an abbreviated manner of stating that Simon's father was named John. However, Simon was no longer Simon Bar Jonah; his name was now simply Peter. He was no longer the infantile disciple wondering who Jesus was, but he was now securely grounded in the knowledge of the Messiah. Jesus promised to secure the Church on Peter's solid confession, not just on Peter. The Greek word for "rock," petra, is feminine and does not refer to Peter, but to his statement. Jesus declares that neither Hades, nor Hell, nor any entity will be strong enough to defeat His Church.

Many scholars believe that the keys represent God's delegated authority to carry out church discipline (Matthew 18:15-18). This is conveyed in the phrase "binding and loosing" (see 16:19), which means forbidding and permitting. The Church, as God's representative on earth, exercises full spiritual authority according to His Word. The decisions made on earth would be in keeping with decisions already made by God, indicated by the Greek perfect tense for "shall" used in verse 19. Jesus closed this question-and-answer period about His identity by telling the disciples that although they knew He was the Messiah, the time had not yet come for others to know. The disciples, those closest to Jesus, must first be sure of who He was, before others are made aware of Him. After making His statements concerning the Church, Jesus told the disciples not to tell anyone who He was. Peter's confession of faith opened the door for him to receive blessings from God. He was then given the keys to open the doors of blessings to others. It is only after opening the door of our heart, through faith in the Word of God and the identity and finished work of God's son, that we come to know Jesus as the Christ, the Son of the living God.

Peter, like all of us, had the tendency to confuse his own thoughts with divine thoughts. After Peter had announced His identity, Jesus went a step further and declared His work. Jesus pointed out that He would suffer and die, and that Jerusalem, the center of Israel's religious life, would be the place of His death and resurrection (v. 21). Since the disciples now knew that He is the Messiah, Jesus tells them what the Messiah must do. Jesus the Messiah did not come to overthrow the Roman government and establish a Jewish political kingdom. Instead,

Christ came to suffer, die, and be raised. Jesus inferred that Jewish leaders would be involved in His suffering and imminent death. Going to Jerusalem related to with Matthew's use of Jesus' Jewish genealogy as the Great Jewish King, the Messiah, must always be associated with the city of David. Just as Matthew's Gospel recorded how Jesus was part of the lineage of David, Jesus' face must always be toward Jerusalem, the city of David.

Upon hearing this, Peter, like the others, was thoroughly confused. They expected the Messiah to overthrow the Roman oppressors, then reign gloriously on earth. He was not supposed to suffer and die. Peter expressed his confusion and concern: "Never, Lord! This shall never happen to you!" (v. 22, NIV). Peter loved Jesus and sought to protect Him from His own grim prophecy. But Jesus immediately responded, "Get thee behind me, Satan: thou art an offence unto me: for thou savourest not the things that be of God, but those that be of men" (v. 23). Even though Peter understood that Jesus was God who had come down to earth to dwell among them, he could not bring himself to agree with Christ's stated mission. Moreover, he took upon himself to determine what His destiny must be. Because Jesus had just affirmed to Peter that he would share in His power, Peter now assumed that this power meant that he could control the plan of God in the life of the Lord. In Peter's mind, this power was meant to give pleasure and, therefore, anything that seemed to imply pain was not allowed.

How often do we use the very power which God has given us to attempt to hinder the will of God? How easy it is for those who have been empowered by the Lord to cross over into the demonic process. Sometimes what makes absolute sense to us may stand in the way of God's purpose. Those who are given power to lead the church of the Lord must be very careful. How many times do we find people who have been given authority to participate in God's work taking responsibility upon themselves to tell God and others how the Church must carry out its mission? Watch out for power, it can make us do strange things. If we are not careful, it can become power "not to do" instead of power to do God's will. If unguarded, it can even become the power to stop others from doing what God is calling them to do instead of empowerment to help them accomplish God's will for their lives.

Note that Peter's statement does not come from hatred or anger, but rather from love. However, this love which seeks to hinder the way of God and sees life mainly from a human perspective is not of God. Peter "loved" Jesus so much that he would stop Him from doing the will of God. How do we respond when God calls someone we love to do what may not be popular or may not meet with our emotional pleasure? Is it not amazing how from this human desire to protect loved ones from pain or persecution, sometimes, ironically develops in opposition to God's will?

Jesus strongly rebuked Peter because, like Satan, Peter tried to interrupt God's perfect plan to save humanity. Peter "the rock" had become Peter "the stumbling block." The one who moments before had proclaimed divine revelations was now thinking like the devil. When Jesus spoke about His coming trials, Peter forsook God's perspective and evaluated the situation from a human point of view. Peter was like so many of us who have no problem accepting God's will during times of blessing, but see things only from our own perspective during times of testing. Peter never failed to follow Jesus, although he often stumbled. He is an excellent example for all believers to persevere in Christ—even in times of apparent failure. Peter was still grappling with his image of a conquering Messiah. He was also torn between his own desires for Jesus to remain with him and the other disciples. According to Peter, Jesus should stay, especially now that they knew who He really was. Thus, Jesus the Christ, Peter's Messiah, was not supposed to suffer and die. Peter even stated that the living God should not let this occur.

This passage in Matthew shows the dual nature of spirituality and humanity in Peter. First, he was the solid rock who boldly declared that Jesus was the Messiah. Next, he was the stumbling block who could not discern God's will. Therefore, he was referred to as "Satan" because his statement offered the temptation that the Messiah go against the will of God. Peter's fear of what was to come overshadowed his discipleship to the Christ. In spite of Peter's failure at this point, the good news is that Jesus did not reject him but instead continued to help him along the way. Peter's confession of the identity of Jesus became the rock to which he will return again and again. No matter what happens to you and I in our journey, sometimes we may be up and at other times we may be down, but in every situation, we must continue to affirm the identity and purpose for which our Lord came into this world. We must continue to do so even when it involves emotional pain or even the loss of our own power. For, when all is said and done, the good news is that Jesus is who He is. Because He is our Messiah, He will do all things well. Our Saviour will make all things beautiful, just because He is who He is. Our Deliverer will rebuke every pretense to power just because He is who He is. Our Redeemer will draw us in and cover us from our misunderstandings and our tendency to misuse the very same power that He gives us, because He is who He is. We must always keep in mind who He is. Jesus Christ, the Son of the Living God, is our good news in this bad news world.

Chapter Two

BLESSED ART THOU

BASED ON LUKE 1:26-38

Luke 1:26-38

*A*nd in the sixth month the angel Gabriel was sent from God unto a city of Galilee, named Nazareth, [27]To a virgin espoused to a man whose name was Joseph, of the house of David; and the virgin's name was Mary. [28]And the angel came in unto her, and said, Hail, thou that art highly favoured, the Lord is with thee: blessed art thou among women. [29]And when she saw him, she was troubled at his saying, and cast in her mind what manner of salutation this should be. [30]And the angel said unto her, Fear not, Mary: for thou hast found favour with God. [31]And, behold, thou shalt conceive in thy womb, and bring forth a son, and shalt call his name JESUS. [32]He shall be great, and shall be called the Son of the Highest: and the Lord God shall give unto him the throne of his father David: [33]And he shall reign over the house of Jacob for ever; and of his kingdom there shall be no end. [34]Then said Mary unto the angel, How shall this be, seeing I know not a man? [35]And the angel answered and said unto her, The Holy Ghost shall come upon thee, and the power of the Highest shall overshadow thee: therefore also that holy thing which shall be born of thee shall *be called the Son of God.* [36]*And, behold, thy cousin Elisabeth, she hath also conceived a son in her old age: and this is the sixth month with her, who was called barren.* [37]*For with God nothing shall be impossible.* [38]*And Mary said, Behold the handmaid of the Lord; be it unto me according to thy word. And the angel departed from her.*

Imagine being a young girl in a society that regulates marriage and childbearing with strict laws. Three decades ago America embraced similar rules. During that time, abortions were illegal. Premarital and extramarital relations were not the norm. A young woman who became pregnant outside of wedlock was shunned. The man who was responsible was expected to marry the young girl—it was the only honorable thing to do. Often parents would send their children away until the child was born. The "illegitimate" children born out of wedlock were affected as well. They were often considered to be mistakes and misfits and frequently had a rough way to go in life. As a result, a woman would never desire to be an unwed mother. It was too difficult.

Now think of the ecstatic response of a woman who discovers that she is pregnant because she has aligned her will with God's plan for her life and not because of sin. Such was the case with Mary, the mother of Jesus. She became "with child" and her pregnancy was holy. Her condition was not the result of promiscuity. It was a result of her willingness to align herself with God's plan for the salvation of the world. In every situation we find ourselves in, like Mary, we must learn the importance of yielding our lives to God and responding in whole-hearted agreement with and obedience to His will.

Luke's Gospel is set in the context of the events of the times. John the Baptist is born in the days of Herod the Great, who ruled from 37—4 B.C. When Judea encompassed the entire area of Palestine. John's parents represent Jewish piety at its best. Zechariah, his father, is a member of one of the 24 divisions of the priesthood. John's mother, Elizabeth is also of priestly descent. Although they are righteous before God, they had not received the blessing of a child (Luke 1:6-7).

Zechariah belonged to the section of Abia. Every direct descendant of Aaron was automatically a member of the Levitical priesthood. Because there were many priests, they were divided into 24 sections. During the Passover, at Pentecost, and the Feast of Tabernacles all priests served. In addition, each division served twice a year for a period of one week. On this day, the lot fell on Zechariah to burn the incense. He was serving his turn as priest in the temple when the angel appeared to him announcing that he and his wife would have a son who was to be named John. However, Zechariah had doubts that he and his wife would have a son and because of his unbelief he was stricken speechless. Elizabeth conceived and went into hiding, and Zechariah was silent, waiting in expectation for the child. When the child was born, Zechariah received a great vision concerning his son. He prophesied that John would be the prophet and forerunner who would prepare the way of the Lord.

John was born from the priestly family of Aaron and Abijah (1 Chronicles 24:10). He grew up very conscious of the requirements of the law. In the plan of salvation, he was just the right person to serve as the forerunner of the Saviour. Six months have passed since Gabriel's announcement to Zechariah. Now the Lord sends His messenger on another mission. This time Gabriel goes to a house in Nazareth, not to an aged man but to a young and vibrant maiden (Luke 1:26-28). The promised child to Zechariah and Elizabeth was in answer to many prayers; the promised child given to Mary was a total and complete surprise.

A child born of a virgin—here is something all together new.

Gabriel is mentioned four times in Scripture. In the Old Testament, he was sent to explain the visions which Daniel saw (Daniel 8:16; 9:21). His first appearance is as a man in a vision (Daniel 8:16). He is called "the man Gabriel" and explains to Daniel the vision of the 70 weeks (9:21). In the New Testament, Gabriel was sent to announce the birth of John the Baptist (Luke 1:11-20), and now he was sent by God to the little village of Nazareth to announce the most glorious event of human history. In Luke 1:26-38, he announces the birth of a Son to Mary. Gabriel stands in the presence of God (1:19) and can therefore provide reassurance to mortals: "Do not be afraid, for your prayer is heard (v. 13); "Do not be afraid, Mary for you have found favor with God" (v. 30).

Nazareth was a small, insignificant village in lower Galilee, with a population of about a hundred people. Nazareth is first mentioned as the home of Mary and Joseph at the time of the annunciation. Although Nathanael asked "Can anything good come out of Nazareth?" (John 1:46), God sent Gabriel to convey a message to a virgin girl named Mary in this village.

The angel Gabriel congratulated Mary and told her to rejoice because she had found favor with God. Mary wondered what the angel's message could mean. Why had she found favor with God? Perhaps Mary had found favor with God because of her purity. She was a virgin waiting to be married. "To be chosen by God so often means at one and the same time a crown of joy and a cross of sorrow. God does not always choose a person for ease and comfort and selfish joy, but for a great task that will take all that head and heart can bring to it. God chooses a person to use that person" (William Barclay, The Gospel of Luke, Philadelphia: The Westminster Press, 1975, p. 8).

Sometimes it seems like our blessing is mixed up with something that, instead of bringing joy, unfolds an ever-flowing stream of pain. Mary receives the announcement of Jesus' birth (vv. 28-33) while she was already "pledged to be married to Joseph" (v. 27). But the angel said to her, "you will conceive in your womb and bring forth a son and you shall call His name Jesus" (v. 31). This was a frightening experience for Mary, because she knew the consequences of not being pure for her marriage. The marriages in antiquity were the result of an agreement between families, not individuals, and were parentally-arranged. Marriage contracts required extensive negotiation in order to ensure that families of equal status were being joined and that neither took advantage of the other. A couple thus betrothed did not live together, though a formal divorce was required to break the now public agreement. If the man to whom a girl was betrothed should die, in the eyes of the law, she was a widow. Once two people were betrothed, there was a bond between them which nothing but death could break. In spite of her pledge to Joseph, God chose Mary to bring forth His Son, the Saviour of the world. She was "the virgin" of prophecy (Isaiah 7:14). The mother of the divine-human person whom Isaiah said was to be "a child" (human) and "Son given" (divine) (John 3:16; 2 Corinthians 9:15). "And He shall reign over Israel forever; His Kingdom shall be forever; His Kingdom shall never end!" (Luke 1:33, LB)

Mary did not find favor with God because she was perfect or unusual, but because she was simply a yielded vessel. The same question may be asked of us today: How can we find favor with God? It is not who we are or what we have that causes us to find favor with God. We find favor with God through humility, a willingness to listen, and obedience to His Word. In other words, we find favor with God by being yielded vessels, willing to do His bidding. God uses simple ordinary people to carry out His will. Mary was a simple, young virgin girl waiting to be married to Joseph and God chose her. She simply yielded to the will of God for her life. When Gabriel spoke to her, she responded by saying, "Let it be according to your word" (v. 38). There are others throughout the New Testament that God chose in spite of themselves.

Saul of Tarsus was a Jew who literally wasted the Christian Church (Acts 8:1). But God chose him, in spite of himself, to minister to the body of Christ. When Saul saw the brightness of God's glory, he fell to the ground. He heard the voice of Jesus asking why he was persecuting Him. Saul was confused because he thought he was doing the will of God. But when he found that he was not doing God's will, he humbled himself and said, "Lord, what wilt thou have me to do?" (Acts 9:6). Saul obeyed and became the Apostle Paul who went about doing the will of God. He had found favor with God.

Martha's sister, Mary, found favor with Jesus by humbly seating herself at His feet. She anointed Jesus' feet with an expensive oil of spikenard and wiped them with her hair (John 12:3). Because of her humility Mary, the sister of Martha, found favor with Jesus and she is remembered throughout the Christian arena even until today. We don't always know the unique will of God for our lives, but we can find His favor by becoming yielded vessels, and keeping ourselves humble and obedient to His Word as Mary did. God has outlined in the Bible all of the commandments and principles that He wants us to follow—line upon line, precept upon precept.

David found favor in God's eyes because he was willing to do God's will. David understood that God could not fail and that God would never fail him. As a result of David's faith and adoration, God caused him to be blessed and become one of the most revered men in Bible history. The only time David ceased to have God's favor was when he stopped following the will of God. The consequences of sin included losing the throne for a period of time and losing the opportunity to see the temple built.

Mary's blessing came to her before she could actively pursue it or set out a strategy for being blessed. Without solicitation, heaven opened up and into her life came an angel with a message of blessing "Blessed art thou." This did not happen as a result of Mary's instant obedience and unconditional faith, since she did not immediately believe. In fact, she was stunned and the first thing came into her mind was "This can't be."

Too often, instead of being like Mary, we choose to make the same mistake David made. We may fail to enjoy some blessings from God because we are often blinded by our own fallen frailties. Sometimes our sinful rationalizations may lead us down the path of disobedience to the will of God and result in the loss of blessings or increase planned for us by God. But in this passage, it is clear that Mary's merit is not the foundation for the favor which God bestows upon her. Yes, there are blessing which come as a result of our obedience and submission. But as believers in Christ, we of all people know that we cannot find favor with God based on our own merit. When all is said and done, even our submission must be seen as enabled by God's grace. Most of our blessings have come to us not because we have worked hard for them, but because God who will have mercy on whom He will have mercy has chosen to shower us with His blessings.

There is the false belief that Mary was favored because she was the most righteous of all women who dwelt in the land. If that was the case, did God choose Jacob because he was more righteous than Esau or were they chosen before they even knew who they were? Here indeed is the greatness of the Lord revealed: He has blessed us as He blessed Mary, and although we may try hard to explain it, the explanation is not in us.

Sometimes, it seems that we are in a position which makes it almost seem impossible for blessings to come by us. This may be a result of our physical condition, our progeny, our class, our gender, or even our culture. Mary responds to Gabriel (vv. 34-37) with a question: "How can this be seeing that I do not know a man." We may have similar questions. "How can I be blessed when I do not have any money?" "How can I be blessed when I do not have the requisite education according to the standard for success set forth by the world?"

Mary asked the angel, "How can this be since I have not known a man? The angel replied, The Holy Spirit shall come upon you and the power of God will overshadow you" (vv. 34-35, NKJV). Christ was placed in the womb of the virgin by a creative act of God, through the power of the Holy Spirit (Matthew 1:18-20). The eternal Son of the Most High, through divine intervention, united himself with human nature as seed in the womb of the virgin. Therefore, the Baby that was born to Mary was holy. Deity and humanity united to redeem the human race.

Often we encounter situations we don't quite understand and it is necessary for us to ask questions. It can be the loss of a loved one, a job, or finances. It can be overwhelming to hear of some unexpected event that occurs without warning. It does not matter whether it is good news or bad news. The question of how or why will emerge. Mary also asked the question, "How can this be?" After hearing the angel's news, Mary was in a state of confusion and asked the question to determine what was expected of her. It is human nature to want to know the reasons for things. However, we should not doubt God's goodness. Whatever God does is right. God does not chide us for asking questions. But He is disappointed if we conclude that He has forsaken us. By asking questions, we are able to understand what is expected of us. Questions are necessary and the only unanswered question is the question that is not asked.

Mary's reply to the angel was given in the language of faith and humble admiration. She did not ask for a sign to confirm the message. She simply said, "Let it be to me according to your word" (v. 38). Mary of Nazareth surrendered to the will of God. Her response is a model for all believers. She accepted the will of God for her life in humble obedience and without controversy. She glorified God by singing, "My soul magnifies the Lord and my spirit rejoices in God my Savior" (vv. 46-47). Like Mary, we can allow the Word of God to guide our desires and responses.

Joyful acceptance of God's will is a lesson we all can learn as believers in Christ. Many times we say, "Lord have your way in my life," and when God's will is not what we expected, we begin to complain. We sing "Order My Steps" and as soon as He orders them we groan and question His will. Very often, we struggle with the will of God for our lives because we do not want to obey.

There are several stories in the Old Testament of people who defied the will of God. Our first parents, Adam and Eve, did not accept the will of God for their lives and disobeyed God (Genesis 3:1-6). Abraham and Sarah were promised a son, and they could not wait for God's will to be fulfilled, as a result Ishmael was born (Genesis 16:1ff). Saul, the first king of Israel, also disobeyed God (1 Samuel 15:1ff). These are just a few examples, there are others. It is important for us to realize that God is in control of our lives, and He allows us to be exposed to diverse situations to build our spiritual character. If we would graciously accept God's will, we can say to God as Mary said, "Let it be unto me according to your word."

Chapter Three

GOOD NEWS: JESUS IS BORN

BASED ON LUKE 2:4-20

Luke 2:4-20

And Joseph also went up from Galilee, out of the city of Nazareth, into Judaea, unto the city of David, which is called Bethlehem; (because he was of the house and lineage of David:) ⁵ To be taxed with Mary his espoused wife, being great with child. ⁶ And so it was, that, while they were there, the days were accomplished that she should be delivered. ⁷ And she brought forth her firstborn son, and wrapped him in swaddling clothes, and laid him in a manger; because there was no room for them in the inn. ⁸ And there were in the same country shepherds abiding in the field, keeping watch over their flock by night. ⁹ And, lo, the angel of the Lord came upon them, and the glory of the Lord shone round about them: and they were sore afraid. ¹⁰ And the angel said unto them, Fear not: for, behold, I bring you good tidings of great joy, which shall be to all people. ¹¹ For unto you is born this day in the city of David a Saviour, which is Christ the Lord. ¹² And this shall be a sign unto you; Ye shall find the babe wrapped in swaddling clothes, lying in a manger. ¹³ And suddenly there was with the angel a multitude of the heavenly host praising God, and saying, ¹⁴ Glory to

God in the highest, and on earth peace, good will toward men. [15] *And it came to pass, as the angels were gone away from them into heaven, the shepherds said one to another, Let us now go even unto Bethlehem, and see this thing which is come to pass, which the Lord hath made known unto us.* [16] *And they came with haste, and found Mary, and Joseph, and the babe lying in a manger.* [17] *And when they had seen it, they made known abroad the saying which was told them concerning this child.* [18] *And all they that heard it wondered at those things which were told them by the shepherds.* [19] *But Mary kept all these things, and pondered them in her heart.* [20] *And the shepherds returned, glorifying and praising God for all the things that they had heard and seen, as it was told unto them.*

Luke painstakingly recreates the social history for the reader. He tries to show us what was taking place at the time of the birth of Jesus in both the Hebrew and Gentile communities and the Roman Empire. Luke ties the birth of Jesus in Bethlehem to the figures of Herod the Great, Caesar Augustus, and Quirinius under whom the census took place. Luke's Gospel is written mainly for Gentiles. Theophilus, to whom it is addressed, is a Gentile, as is Luke himself. Because Luke is one who understands the ways and thoughts of the Gentiles and the Person and work of Jesus Christ, he writes so that the Gospel can be understood by Gentiles.

For two centuries, African Americans were slaves with seemingly no hope for deliverance. As they toiled in wretched conditions, they sang songs and prayed prayers, hoping for relief. God heard their cries, and He allowed someone to rise among them. Her name was Harriet Tubman and she was known as the "Moses" of her people. Tubman was born in slavery and experienced many hardships. Unlike some who had accepted their lot, she longed for freedom. And God did indeed allow her to escape the bonds of slavery. She enjoyed her freedom, but she couldn't forget her brothers and sisters who were still in bondage. She returned to the South many times and led her people to freedom, just as Moses had done in Egypt for his people. The slaves were clever. They included coded escape signals in their songs. After dark, "Steal Away" was the song used to signal slaves to move to a meeting place from which they would escape to the North by the Underground Railroad. Harriet Tubman helped more than 300 slaves escape to freedom this way. And though she only delivered a relatively few from the bonds of slavery, her heroic deeds focused attention on the need for emancipation. Moses, Harriet Tubman, Martin Luther King, Jr., and others were powerful leaders who were led by God. Each came to lead a particular people at a particular time by the power of the One who came before them, who was from eternity, without whom they could do nothing. Without the coming of Jesus, their own coming would not be good news.

The coming of Jesus is truly good news. Jesus came for **all** people and His great work has and will be felt throughout all eternity. Our lesson today calls our attention to the birth of Jesus, the Saviour for the world. Even at the turn of this new millennium, no one can truly argue that the coming of Jesus Christ, the Son of God has not changed the world. We cannot explain away the important role that His humble birth has played in the formation and reformation of human historical and existential consciousness. This good news of our Saviour's birth caused some who heard it to break forth into shouts of praise for what God had done and is doing in human lives. What good news it is that God will help us in our weakness! What good news it is to know that God will share His life with us!

It was prophesied in Isaiah 9:6-7 that a child would be born to implement a righteous government that would be based on divine judgment and justice. Through God's divine providence, Caesar Augustus issued an imperial enrollment decree for all to be counted. Joseph and Mary had to go Bethlehem to register because Joseph was from the lineage of David. "The journey from Nazareth to Bethlehem was 80 miles in length. The accommodations for travelers were in any case most primitive. The town was crowded and there was no room for Joseph and Mary." While there, the time came for Mary to give birth to the Child that would be the Saviour of the world. Finding no room in the inn, and with Mary's delivery time being near, they were compelled to stay in a stable. After Mary gave birth to Jesus, she wrapped Him in swaddling clothes and laid Him in a manger. In the meantime, the angel of the Lord made the announcement to some shepherds to go to the city of David and see "a Saviour, which is Christ the Lord" (Luke 2:11).

Bethlehem was crowded, and everything was in an upheaval because of the registration. But Jesus was coming to town and there was no room to receive Him. This is so like our lives. Often, we are so taken up with our personal agendas that we neglect to recognize the presence of Jesus. We look for Him in the wrong places and He is not there. He is most at home with humble people, those who take time to let Him into their daily activities. He is with the people who have room for Him in their hearts. He is with the person who hears the voice of the Lord through the Word that points to Jesus. The shepherds were eager to listen to the voice of the angels directing them to go where they would find Jesus. Humble people listen to those who are directing them to where they can find Jesus. He is waiting for us with open arms.

Luke 2:8-14 describes the angels' poignant and exhilarating

pronouncement of the divine birth. That the pronouncement
came to shepherds is significant because it points to King
David's origin as a shepherd. Also, "the shepherds were despised
by the orthodox good people of the day. Shepherds were quite
unable to keep the details of the ceremonial law; they could not
observe all the meticulous hand-washing rules and regulations.
Their flocks made far too many constant demands on them; and
so the orthodox looked down on them as a very common people" (William Barclay, *The Gospel of Luke*, Philadelphia: The
Westminster Press, 1975, p. 22). This is particularly interesting
given the fact the Israelite ancestors were nomadic shepherds.
The shepherds' humble lifestyle offers encouragement to those
who lack religious status. The shepherds' lifestyle is also typical
of the life Jesus would lead during His ministry on earth. Jesus
would be unorthodox, not too concerned about hand washing,
and would circulate with the common people. His life would
mirror the lives of the shepherds.

The shepherds were overtaken with excitement when the
announcement was made to them by the angel. They immediately went to Bethlehem to see that the birth of Jesus was true.
They found the baby just as the angel announced. The fact that
the angelic announcement came to shepherds is significant. A
shepherd cares for flocks of sheep. He leads the sheep to pasture,
to water and, at night, to the fold for safety. The shepherd is
responsible for protecting the flock from wild animals. The
shepherd motif typifies the role of Jesus as Saviour. He was born
to be the Messiah, to lead the "flock," God's people, and to serve
the flock as the Lamb of God. Jesus referred to Himself as the
"good shepherd" (John 10:11). Unlike many of us today who
would probably question any miracle we might be privileged to
witness, the shepherds humbly accepted the angel's message and

acted immediately. They went to Bethlehem to see the Baby Jesus. The fact that the shepherds found Jesus lying in a manger was their confirmation that Jesus was the expected Messiah who was prophesied by the Prophet Isaiah: "For unto us a child is born, unto us a son is given; and the government shall be upon his shoulder" (Isaiah 9:6a).

This good news came to shepherds who were among the poor of the society. Shepherds were usually excluded from the religious ceremony of the temple. They were not sufficiently well-dressed for the finery and pageantry of the religious class. With no homes to call their own, tending the wealth that belonged to those who through legalism excluded them from the religious sanctuary, they were among the least of the house of Israel. Smelly, sweaty, and sometimes uncouth in their language and manner, shepherds were not welcome guests at the homes of the rich. But this news came to them. To these religious and social outcasts came good news. Can we grasp how God in this passage turns human pretensions upside down? These who until now were thought to be unfit to share in the things of the kingdom, by being exposed to the good news of the birth of this Child, have moved from being the bane of religious mockery to possessors of heaven's treasured gifts.

Categorized by earthly lords and ladies as perpetual outsiders, they now are taken as insiders with God sharing in divine secrets hidden even from the wise, from the foundation of the earth. Is it not like God to choose the foolish things of the world to confound the wise? Is it not like God to choose the simple things to confound the profound? Is it not like the Lord to choose the poor to shame those who are lost in their riches? In their everyday experience, the shepherds knew how they were perceived. They were seen as rooms without windows but by revealing to them the good news, God turns them into an open place of blessing. No more enclosed beings going around in cycles of poverty and shame, required to bow their heads; they now become embodiments of God's infinite future. As candidates of the good news they moved from their living as beings of the night into God's light.

Notice that Luke states that they were "keeping their flock by night." He could have said simply that they were keeping their flock, but he did not. If we understand that this was not just physical night but in a world such as that in which Luke wrote, this night signals something more. Caught in the night, they were filled with fear; the King James Version states "they were sore afraid," enclosed and blinded by the night. This "night" could be an intentional systemic deprivation of justice or other such basic human need as was so common in those days and is still common today. Shepherds lived in constant fear for their lives. Even a light from God in the middle of the night would have signaled the nearness of pain, the nearness of trouble. Are there many of us, who because we have been in the night so long that even when good things begin to happen we still are in the habit of walking in our past fear?

This good news of Jesus cuts at the heart of our cosmic temerity and personal phobias. It dethrones barriers created by religiously bound systems, class-informed relations, gender-generated gaps, and racially assigned geographic limitations. For those who will receive it, this good news has the potential for removing inhuman categorization of one as "less than"—less than human, less than sacred, less than heavenly, or even less than God intended. How does one caught in fear receive courage? How does a people caught up in marginality receive hope? Of course, by replacing bad news with good news.

People who are caught in the grip of fear cannot receive good news. In order to prepare the shepherds for the good news brought by the angels, there needed to be a breakthrough. This breakthrough can only be effected by the entrance of God into our circumstance. In this passage, we read "and the glory of the Lord shone around them." We could also see it as the light of God piercing through their night, the sun of the most high cutting through their thick darkness with its dynamic rays of hope. There had to be exposure in the light before the angels could effectively deliver the good news. Before the angels could communicate, with them, something must come alive that allows them to hear and to receive and to act in accordance with the good news.

When the glory of the Lord is revealed, when our night is cut through and our darkness is pierced by the light of God's presence, there results within us a response of joy. It's one thing to have personal joy which results from a meritorious act, but its another to have the joy that comes from an act freely given by another. This joy resulting from the good news is not worked for, it comes simply as a result of hearing from heaven. What joy, when we have waited in the night for so long and it seems that the voice of our God is lost in the vast expanse of time and space and then, all of a sudden, the divine voice breaks into our hearts! How can we fail to rejoice when we have walked in the wilderness for so long and God comes to us in the middle of the night with great news? It is good news to my soul that those who have been counted for destruction are now counted among those to be saved. It is good news that a world dying in its own filth receives a Saviour from the very bosom of the most High.

Note that the glory of the Lord results in joy and the joy is indiscriminate. The writer states that it is "great joy which shall

be for all people." Given the social condition of the shepherds, it would have been possible for them to imagine that such joy could not be for them. It may have been for other people. But "for all people"? That was radical and is still radical, even in today's world where democratic assumptions seem to be in fashion. Surely this joy could only be for those who are constantly in the temple. Or maybe it could only be for those who have kept particular aspects of the law. How can a people caught up in the struggle for the bare necessities of life be included in this joy? Such news! From a mere human perspective, such good news of joy belongs to those who live in palaces and dine in fine, expensive feast halls. For some believe that joy belongs to those who can buy it. Even for some of us who believe in God, it is easy to confuse joy with the ability to get what we want. The servicing of human desires at the oasis of our fallen nature seems to many to be the height of joy. But this Scripture passage makes it quite clear that this joy shall be for all people. This joy comes because now heaven turns earth towards heaven, and those who were down can now look up and live. We can now lift our night-blinded eyes and see. We can have great joy because the glory of the Lord has come down that we might rise on its wings into the very heart of God.

The second effect of this good news was that it gave them a voice. Transformed by God's message from a people without a voice, the shepherds became a people with a voice. This demonstrates the awesome nature of our God. In the presence of God, our tongues are loosed. People may have taken our voice from us, but when God's good news comes it restores our voice. Fear may have frozen our true voices but when God comes in with good news our voices begin to unthaw. We read "the shepherd said . . . ." If we are poor and marginalized as the shepherds were, the world seeks to silence our ability to speak. But when the glory of the Lord shines and we hear the good news of heaven telling us that we have been given a Saviour—someone who will take us from the margin to the center—we cannot help but break forth into speech.

But even the shepherds did not just receive their voices to hear themselves speak but to help the community move forward. Many of us use our voice mainly for our own self-aggrandizement. Those of us who have come to know the good news, can no longer speak mainly of ourselves. We must move from talking mainly about ourselves and our needs to spreading the good news to our community. When this good news comes we will find ourselves saying "let us." As hearers and recipients of the good news, we must move beyond the enclosed, fear-derived refuge of unrooted individuality to divine communal inclusion. As those who have received the good news of the Saviour's birth into our world, we must be willing to include others—our brothers, sisters, and yes even those who we now consider to be our enemies. This voice is given not so that we can tell others off but so that we can invite them to come with us to the place where we all can experience the Saviour.

This good news also results in the ability to walk. We cannot receive the good news and remain where we are. This good news results in movement. An example is seen in the traditional African response to the birth of a child. When a child is born and news reaches the home, there is a spontaneous response of dance. If indeed it is good news resulting in great joy, if indeed it is good news which loosens our tongue, if indeed it is good news for all people, then it must move those who believe it. We must join in the divine cosmic dance of joy.

Furthermore, this good news results in true insight. God's glory cannot shine without revelative knowledge. This good news reveals to us God's inner character and allows us to participate in the wisdom which has been hidden from the foundation of the world (Matthew 13:55; Ephesians 1:4). This good news when received and celebrated by us leads us to share its results in outreach and witnessing. We read that after the shepherds saw Jesus "they made known abroad." The shepherds relayed the angelic message concerning Jesus' birth (Luke 2:17).

Within this message, we hear another celebrative tone, not

just of joy but of "peace on earth."Although a form of joy can come from war, for example, those who vanquish others may take great joy in their looting and killing or those who oppress others may get some evil pleasure from watching their victims writhe in pain, this celebrative joy on the other hand is a joy informed by peace. But this peace is not just for those who stay on the mountain meditating and waiting for a final movement into nirvana no, this peace is for all on earth. Again the good news in the coming of Jesus is that this peace is inclusive of all the earth.

In our world today, many nations enjoy a so-called "peace" mainly by oppressing others and making sure that their neighbors do no have enough rest to enjoy life. It is a peace born not out of good news but out of lust and greed. But the divine peace of which this Scripture speaks arises from the very heart of God and freely flows to all who will receive it. This good news which results in peace for the earth does so because it affects the very will of the human being. But more than that, it is a deep peace because God now wills good towards humanity. The greatest need humanity has is to be at peace with God. God's good will towards humanity is revealed in the coming of His Son. The good news of Jesus' birth not only makes peace between us and God but also brings good will for one another which, when embraced, leads to peace on earth. True peace will never come until the good news of the Messiah is embraced and celebrated.

It is one thing to hear good news, and it is another thing to respond appropriately. We notice people whose responses always seem to be negative. Some are so caught up with bad news and the pain inflicted by its bearers that no matter what happens to them they think it must be more bad news. Our response to good news is often infected by our long interaction with bad news.

Thus, we may find ourselves responding negatively to news which is meant to evoke life and joy within our souls. May God help us. But note the response of the shepherd to this news. Their first response of course was fear which the angels quickly put to rest by emphatically presenting divine joy to them. Those who heard their message were utterly amazed at the events unfolding before their eyes.

Another person who embodies a powerful response to this good news is Mary, the mother of Jesus. Mary broke forth into divine praise when she received the good news of the coming of the Messiah into the world, "My soul magnifies the Lord, and my spirit has rejoiced in God my Saviour" (Luke 1:46-47). *Praise*. To praise is to extol and give thanks. Praising God is much more important than merely talking about God. God is our object of praise (Deuteronomy 10:21), and thereby the superiority and uniqueness of God's divine Person and activity are set forth. Praise attempts to describe God, but it can only offer a limited description.

There are eight instances in the New Testament that refer to the joyful praise of God through the hymns or prayers of individuals (Luke 2:20; Acts 3:8-9), a group (Luke 19:37), the community (Acts 2:47; Revelation 19:5), angels (Luke 2:13), or within a religious setting (Matthew 21:16; Luke 18:43). We honor God when we praise Him. Isn't that beautiful? Yes, Mary celebrated the will of God for her life. We must respond to the good news with our soul, spirit, and heart as Mary did. Mary kept the message in her heart (vv. 18-19). Indeed, Mary pondered many things in her heart (vv. 17-19). She constantly received and watched as prophecies were fulfilled through God's Son. We can learn much from Mary. We can learn to: meditate and ponder the message God gives us through His word; be obedient to the Word of God; celebrate the good news of our Lord and Saviour who has come into our lives.

The angels give us an added dimension to the celebration of this good news. While it is true that the angels are bearers of the good news as heaven's emissaries, they do not loose sight of the fact that the purpose of this good news is to bring glory to God (v. 20). The birth of Jesus Christ as the angels see it has two dimensions, one moving upward and the other descending even to the lowliest. First it sends forth glory to God, note that for the first time since Adam fell something is rising to the heavens from the earth that is not stained with sin and odious to the nostrils of God. And this is not a temporary good news that will be shattered again by human recklessness. No, this is the everlasting good news because Jesus is the fulfillment of God's promise. Here is the One of whom David wrote, "it is written of me, I delight to do thy will" (Psalm 40:8). Jesus brings glory to God because He is the Saviour of the world and because for the first time since Adam there is a human being who reflects divine perfection. He is the Saviour whom God Himself sent into the world.

We celebrate the good news that God gives us His Son so that whoever believes in Him can be saved (John 3:16b). Angels, focused on doing the total will of God and not confined to time and space, were used to announce the birth of Jesus. As they made the announcement, they celebrated by worshiping and glorifying God. To worship and praise God is part of their character. They joined with the heavenly host in saying: "Glory to God in the highest, and on earth peace, to men on whom his favor rests" (Luke 2:14, NIV). When the angels returned to heaven, the shepherds went immediately to Bethlehem to visit Jesus. How wonderful it would be if today we truly celebrated the birth of Jesus rather than mere human substitutes.

Chapter Four

GOOD NEWS: JESUS CARES

BASED ON MARK 4:37-41; 5:35-43

Mark 4:37-41

And there arose a great storm of wind, and the waves beat into the ship, so that it was now full. [38] And he was in the hinder part of the ship, asleep on a pillow: and they awake him, and say unto him, Master, carest thou not that we perish? [39] And he arose, and rebuked the wind, and said unto the sea, Peace, be still. And the wind ceased, and there was a great calm. [40] And he said unto them, Why are ye so fearful? how is it that ye have no faith? [41] And they feared exceedingly, and said one to another, What manner of man is this, that even the wind and the sea obey him?

Mark 5:35-43

While he yet spake, there came from the ruler of the synagogue's house certain which said, Thy daughter is dead: why troublest thou the Master any further? [36] As soon as Jesus heard the word that was spoken, he saith unto the ruler of the synagogue, Be not afraid, only believe. [37] And he suffered no man to follow him, save Peter, and James, and John the brother of James. [38] And he cometh to the house of the ruler of the synagogue, and seeth the tumult, and them that wept and wailed greatly. [39] And when *he was come in, he saith unto them, Why make ye this ado, and weep?* *the damsel is not dead, but sleepeth.* [40] *And they laughed him to scorn. But* *when he had put them all out, he taketh the father and the mother of the* *damsel, and them that were with him, and entereth in where the damsel* *was lying.* [41] *And he took the damsel by the hand, and said unto her,* *"Talitha cumi"; which is, being interpreted, Damsel, I say unto thee,* *arise.* [42] *And straightway the damsel arose, and walked; for she was of the* *age of twelve years. And they were astonished with a great astonishment.* [43] *And he charged them straitly that no man should know it; and com-* *manded that something should be given her to eat.*

If you were caught in a terrible rainstorm, can you imagine the storm ceasing because the mere voice of a man commanded it to do so? Or if a family member had just died, can you imagine a man taking your deceased family member by the hand and raising her back to life? In both of these crisis situations, it is pretty hard to imagine any human having the power to alter two natural events like a rainstorm and death. However, in our Scripture lesson we encounter a special human being who did make a storm stop and a dead person live. Let's notice His actions carefully because He has assured us that we as Christians can use His power to successfully confront critical situations we encounter (John 14:12). Are you a participant in the life of the Lord Jesus? Do you understand that His power is in action for you? As for me, I am convinced of His ability and willingness to calm the storms in our lives. All of us must determine to cast our cares upon Him.

We need His power. We must embrace His care. For you see, life is full of crises that often lead us to question ourselves, our friends, our loved ones, and yes, even God. Remember that during Jesus' earthly ministry, He encountered many instances where the people involved felt powerless. Whenever He encountered people struggling with powerlessness and lack of care, it served as an opportunity for Him to display divine power and care. Among the two most illustrative examples are those contained in Mark 4:37-41 and 5:35-43. These two portions of Scripture report the extraordinary nature of Jesus' power. They also chronicle the reactions of astonishment by those who witnessed the power of Jesus.

In Mark 4:37-41, we are told that a storm arose on the Sea of Galilee while Jesus and His disciples were sailing over to the other side. The Sea of Galilee had the reputation of having sudden tempestuous storms. We are not told the reason Jesus decided to cross the sea. In all probability, Jesus' power over the elements was more important than any other aspect of the story. Another important aspect of the story was the reaction of the disciples to the Lord's demonstration of His power over the forces of nature. The disciples' amazement at Jesus' power substantiates Jesus' identity as the Son of God.

In Mark 5:35-43, Jesus' ability to defy even death is recorded. The death of Jairus' daughter would have posed an unconquerable foe to any man or woman without a deep and unrelenting faith in God. However, death was no match for Jesus. We again read of the amazed responses of those who saw Jesus raising Jairus' daughter from the dead. The Word of God was written to prove that Jesus was God's Son. Without understanding this, our Scripture lesson cannot be fully comprehended.

There Will Be Crises

Jesus saw the need to sail across the Sea of Galilee in order to minister to the people in the country of the Gadarenes (5:1). At the beginning of the voyage, the sea was calm, but suddenly "there arose a great storm" (v. 37). The waves became so high

that water filled their boat and it began to sink. Though Jesus was on board fast asleep, the disciples became overwhelmed with the fear of drowning. The disciples clearly saw themselves in a crisis situation. Desperately needing someone to rescue them, they awakened Jesus and informed Him of their plight.

Similarly, in Mark 5:35-38, the rabbinic leader Jairus and his household found themselves in a crisis situation. While Jesus was on His way to Jairus' house to investigate and remedy Jairus' daughter's grave sickness, He was met by someone from the leader's household and was told that the young girl had just died. Everyone, particularly Jairus, was overcome with grief, but Jesus sought to console them by stating, "Be not afraid, only believe" (v. 36). Even more grief was exhibited after Jesus arrived at Jairus' house with only three of His disciples. Scripture states that many "wept and wailed greatly" (v. 39). They felt that death had put a period as the final punctuation to mark the end of the young girl's life, and there was nothing anyone could do to change it. What crisis situation has made you feel as though there was nothing anyone could do? Jesus has the power to help you in time of crisis. This power is able to turn your crisis into an opportunity for praise and joy (John 14:1, 27; 2 Corinthians 9:8).

The Sea of Galilee was also known as the Sea of Tiberias, Gennesaret, or Chinnereth. This body of water is about 8 miles wide and 15 miles long. Nine towns were located around the sea, including Capernaum and Bethsaida, where Jesus often ministered. The water is sweet and fishing was plentiful in Jesus' day. On its shores grew flowers, nuts, olives, figs, grapes, and palms. After Jesus was awakened by His disciples and told of the violent storm, He used His power to rescue His twelve followers. On the deck of the ship, He faced the turbulent wind and rebuked it. The wind obeyed. Then He spoke to the sea whose unruly waters battered the ship, and the sea hearkened to His command, "Peace, be still." The chaotic conditions which formerly surrounded the disciples suddenly disappeared. Jesus demonstrated that He was God in the flesh by His ability to control the forces of nature. How has Jesus demonstrated to you that He has power over everything?

Included among the forces of nature is humanity's most awesome enemy, death. Jairus and the members of his family recognized this fact and were crushed by it. However, Jesus, who held power over death, assured Jairus' household that "the damsel is not dead but sleepeth" (v. 39). In unbelief, they thought Jesus was joking when He suggested that He had power over death. Nevertheless, He took only Jairus, his wife, and three of His disciples into the girl's bedroom. Jesus demonstrated His power over death when He declared, "Talitha cumi" ("Damsel, I say unto thee, arise") (v. 41). Do we really believe that Jesus has the power to bring life into our dead situations? Can He make a way out of our dead ends? Can He cause our desert to bloom? Or are we like the people in Jarius' house? Although we may not laugh outright at the thought that our dead situations can be infused with life, somewhere in our mind, our enlightened rationality takes hold of us and we scoff: "Can He really? Does He really care if the young woman dies? Is there really somebody who cares enough to risk the scoffing of the world in order to show care for the suffering?" Or, if we are among those who believe, we wonder if such care and power includes us. We suppose that such displays are reserved only for those who may have lived right. We suppose that such manifestations are available only for those whose faith is like the rock of Gibraltar that never moves. Oh, but my friends, that manifestation flowing from the caring heart of our Saviour is for you, whomever you may be. It is for you, no matter how low your righteousness may seem at the present. Hear His word speak to your dead situation: "talitha cumi" arise and breathe.

Unbelief was not confined to the crowds of people who were gathered at the funeral of the young woman, crowds who had not yet met Jesus. Unbelief was also present in the hearts of the disciples who were part of Jesus' inner circle (4:40-41; 5:42-43). After the storm obeyed Jesus' command, and it was no longer an object of His attention, Jesus turned to His disciples and observed their unbelief. He proceeded to announce His disappointment in their failure to believe in God. Though He was asleep, Jesus wanted the disciples to believe that God would deliver them. When Jesus referred to "faith" (v. 40), He meant trust in God. Even disciples can be sometimes blinded by unbelief. Our unbelief sometimes comes from fear, and fear results from the sense that no one cares for us. For those of us who seem to live in the house of the disappointed, scepticism comes naturally.

The question of the disciples, "carest thou not that we perish?" is more than a passing interrogation from a frightened bunch of cowards. It is a fundamental question of human existence. Does any one care? Do my friends care? Does my family care? Does God care? Does heaven care when my life is on the brink and my soul seems to be tumbling down into what looks like an eternal abyss? Note that not even the disciples' close relationship with Jesus insulated them from this existential question. This situation with the disciples reveals the true picture of our own brokenness. We carry our experiences into other interactive contexts, even our interaction with the divine.

These experiences can cause us to make assumptions. Sometimes, we possess the assumption of faith, but many times we operate in the assumption of unbelief. Assumptions which grow out of fear have the tendency to lead us deeper into despair. When we do not believe that divine care is possible or that human concern is available, we tend to become obsessed with death. Here, the disciples connected the idea of care indirectly with the idea of life, and the idea of lack of care with the fact of death. Death is one of the events in human life when care is most needed. During the storm, the disciples faced the reality of their own mortality. Jarius' daughter actually experienced death. It should not be surprising then that the Holy Spirit chose both cases to show us the good news of divine care. For you see my friends, it is when our lives seem to be ending or slipping away that we most need care. It is during these times that God and humans must show the meaning of care. We find Jesus doing exactly that.

There are several effects of Jesus' care that are evident from these two Scripture passages. First, we see that His care has the power to effect peace. Indeed from the point of the view of the disciples in the tempestuous situation, there was no external or internal peace. But the peace that was manifested through the caring act of our Lord is peace which the world cannot give neither can it take away. During periods of struggle when we wage inner and external wars, when the storm is charging with all its pressure and not some threats of destruction, we can have peace. In fact, the presence of the Lord is, in itself, peace. Just as Jesus was the hidden key to peace for the disciples, so is He for us today. He continues to open the gate of heavenly peace for us. Jesus who sends us forth to preach peace, will He not also show us peace in the midst of our turmoil? He is the same Lord who commanded them saying "into whatsoever house ye enter, first say, Peace be to this house" (Luke 10:5, KJV). He is the Prince of peace. Because Jesus is your Lord, your peace is here for even now He speaks peace to your soul. If you have lost your peace somewhere along the way because of fear, remember that because the Master is your boat, tossed and shaken by the wind though it may be, your peace shall return to you.

So as you go out from your house or city, do not shake with fear for in the presence of the Lord the very ground upon which you step and even the wind that blows spell peace. You can have peace because you are in the presence of the Prince of Peace, and He cares for you. You are at peace, even in the face of judgment. The caring words of Jesus "Peace, be still" stilled the wind of the storm upon the sea and calmed the hurricane of fear in the existential core of His disciples. Oh how quickly a lack of faith in the presence of the Truth, in the presence of the Lord of life, can rob us of our birthright as sons and daughters of peace.

Was the storm the cause of the fear or was the fear already in the disciples? The storm may have only served to reveal the inner turmoil of their souls and their lack of faith in the protective power of the Saviour. Those who fail to receive, by simple faith, the presence of the Lord can hardly experience the peace of God. Can you hear the Lord in your situation say "Peace, be still"? Although it may seem like you are sinking into the very pit of hell, listen, yes listen, you can hear the caring voice of Jesus say "Peace, be still." Even when your fear explodes and thunders like a storm across the terrain of your existential field, if you listen, just listen, you can hear His voice calming the storm, speaking "Peace, be still." It can transform your situation. It can dispel the darkness. God's voice is calling forth the divine light and peace. Hear the Lord say to your situation, "Peace be still."

As we observe the command of our Master to the wind on the sea in Palestine, let us offer that same peace to others. Oh, that the way of peace may be known in the midst of our world's tumult. Let us receive God's words of peace, acquiesce to His serenity, and embrace His divine calm. Oh, that we may lay down the swords of our unbelief and lay down the stirring storms of our bitterness so that God might speak to us "Peace, be still." When we face those things that are beyond our control, we must commit them to Him and get out of the way so that He can rebuke them. The truth is that every situation must obey His voice. For our world to have peace, we must be willing and able to offer this divine peace to others so that they, too, can become children of peace. Once Jesus has spoken into the situations of our life, we become the embodiment of His peace.

We do not propose peace as merely a human phenomenon which may be reached by agreeing with the ways of wickedness.

God's peace does not mean "letting sleeping dogs lie." This is not a peace which calls us to sell our soul to evil to preserve tranquility. Although such peace may be quite successful, it is only temporary and offers no eternal value. It gives an outside calm, but stirs internal war. It gives with the right hand, but takes with the left hand. In contrast, the peace which Jesus gives, we are told in Scripture, passes all understanding. The Lord Himself says to us "My peace I give to you not as the world gives" (John 14:27, paraphrased). When our Lord speaks peace, a great miracle happens in the midst of life's storm.

In addition, the care of Jesus raises us from the dead. Note that Jarius' daughter was dead physically. Her body was lifeless and the Lord restored life even in the face of death. But the question we should also consider: Was she the only one in that house who was dead? Look at the tumult created by her death. There was weeping and wailing. But when Jesus came into the situation, He brought life. In a world that does not seem to care whether we live or die, when we find someone who truly cares, we stand in awe. We are left with gaping mouths and tongues that hang out in wonder. Can this really be? We may even whisper, "This is too good to be true." Similarly the disciples wondered, "What manner of man is this, that even the wind and the sea obey Him?" (Mark 4:41) However, when His words were backed by miraculous action their unbelief was transformed into "great astonishment" as they watched the miracle. Though Jesus instructed the observers of the miracle not to publicize it (Mark 5:43), it is apparent that everyone in the city witnessed the fact that the dead girl was now alive and well.

We must learn to be partakers of the life that Christ offers. Beloved, like Jarius' daughter, we all are subject to death. By virtue of our sins, we have been exposed to death. But through Christ, life has been given back to those of us who are believers. We were lost, mortified by the sinful life which we have led, but the caring love of our Master, Jesus the Christ, has brought life to our emaciated souls. We all were dead in trespasses and sins (Ephesians 2:1, 5; Colossians 2:13). We all need to receive the divine life and care available through Christ. He has stored up life for us in the recesses of His own divine life. Because Jesus cares for us, He gave His life for us and He shares His life with us. When Jesus comes into our situation, we are changed by the divine process from one thing into another (2 Corinthians 5:17). No longer is death the ending, instead it becomes the beginning of eternal life. When Jesus comes into our life, His presence gives birth to joy and joy gives birth to celebration. He is the creator of life (John 1:3).

In His care, there is life which cannot be touched by death. When the Lord comes in, we can say with the psalmist "I shall not die but live to declare the wonderful works of the Lord" (Psalm 118:17). The devil cannot take this life which we now live for God. Now that Jesus has come to us, let the old life sink that the new may rise, let death be swallowed up in victory, and let decay give way to spiritual germination for the Lord is in the house! We know that He cares and in His care we find life, joy, and peace. Jesus is the true life who has enlivened us (John 1:4). Shall we not hear His voice and cast our care upon Him? We shall cast our burdens upon Him; we shall call upon Him in the midst of the storm, we shall cast ourselves completely upon Him for "He cares for us" (1 Peter 5:7). The storm shall not blow us down, the rain flood shall not overflow us, for we are hidden in the care (Isaiah 41:10; 43:2). He cares for us. Yes, the Lord cares for us. Because He cares, He has raised us to victory. In His care, He saved both the disciples and Jarius' daughter. He also saved the crowd from their unbelief and the parents from their sorrow. He can do the same for you and I.

Chapter Five

THE GOOD NEWS OF SERVING

BASED ON JOHN 13:1-8, 12-17, 34-35

John 13:1-8

*N*ow before the feast of the passover, when Jesus knew that his hour was come that he should depart out of this world unto the Father, having loved his own which were in the world, he loved them unto the end. *² And supper being ended, the devil having now put into the heart of Judas Iscariot, Simon's son, to betray him; ³ Jesus knowing that the Father had given all things into his hands, and that he was come from God, and went to God; ⁴ He riseth from supper, and laid aside his garments; and took a towel, and girded himself. ⁵ After that he poureth water into a basin, and began to wash the disciples' feet, and to wipe them with the towel wherewith he was girded. ⁶ Then cometh he to Simon Peter: and Peter saith unto him, Lord, dost thou wash my feet? ⁷ Jesus answered and said unto him, What I do thou knowest not now; but thou shalt know hereafter. ⁸ Peter saith unto him, Thou shalt never wash my feet. Jesus answered him, If I wash thee not, thou hast no part with me.*

John 13:12-17

So after he had washed their feet, and had taken his garments, and was set down again, he said unto them, Know ye what I have done to you? [13] Ye call me Master and Lord: and ye say well; for so I am. [14] If I then, your Lord and Master, have washed your feet; ye also ought to wash one another's feet. [15] For I have given you an example, that ye should do as I have done to you. [16] Verily, verily, I say unto you, The servant is not greater than his lord; neither he that is sent greater than he that sent him. [17] If ye know these things, happy are ye if ye do them.

John 13:34-35

A new commandment I give unto you, That ye love one another; as I have loved you, that ye also love one another. [35] By this shall all men know that ye are my disciples, if you have love one to another.

Serving, for many of us, is not good news. In fact in our world today, the emphasis of various scholars, both religious and non-religious, seems to be on not-serving others. It is assumed that taking the posture of servant is dehumanizing. Maybe it is because history is so full of people forcing others to serve them. One cannot count the number of times that one race or nation concocted a theory of superiority through which they forced themselves upon others for the express purpose of placing them in perpetual bondage and servitude. Today children do want to serve their parents. Parents do not want to serve each other. Men do not want to serve women. Women do not want to serve men. And amazingly in many cases even the church does not take to the posture of servant-hood. This refusal to serve has even affected our willingness to serve God. It seems that God is now in the service of man instead of man being in the service of God. With the rise of the prosperity gospel, indeed God has now become the Servant Provider in the sky giving us whatever we believe we need. Our age seems to be experiencing a death of Christian service, directed both to God and to others. The concept of service is influenced by our ideological baggage of oppression and degradation. But the biblical view of service and servanthood can be freeing, exhilarating, and hope-inspiring. As Christians, our understanding of service and servanthood must derive from the Person and character of Jesus Christ as the servant of the Lord God who came to serve, not to be served. With honor, the Bible refers to Abraham, Jacob, Moses, and David as God's servants. Christ is called a servant in both the Old and New Testaments. Isaiah declares in announcing the Messiah's advent: "here is my servant" (Isaiah 53:11; Matthew 12:18). In the Old Testament, God continuously refers to Israel as "His servant" (Isaiah 41:8; 44: 21; 49:3).

In chapter 13 of John's Gospel, Jesus' public ministry has ended and He is alone with the twelve disciples. Of the Gospel writers, only John provides this intimate view of Jesus' private teaching and prayer (chapters 13—17). The 13th chapter records the events of the night before the Crucifixion including the eating of the Passover meal and the institution of the Lord's Supper (compare Matthew 26:17-29; Mark 14:12-25; Luke 22:7-38).

The story is told of a young man named Brian man who felt unloved because he was not given everything he wanted from his parents. He really was not that different from most of his friends who felt that somehow they were owed service by those around them. His parents had a truce in their house—they each did what they wanted and stayed out of each other's way. But they would not go out of their way to serve each other. For them it seemed that any sign of service meant that one was superior. Though they never articulated this unwillingness, it showed in simple things like bringing water to another at the table. But Brian's parents both tried to get him to serve them in little things. On the other hand, they gave him almost everything he wanted. His service did not grow from love or humility, but out of the spite they seemed to share one for another. Brian got married when he was only 19, trying to find "love," but what he was really looking for was for someone to serve him and all of his wishes. He wasn't ready for marriage—neither was his wife. Either of them was willing to serve. The lack of a servant attitude on their part resulted in a failed marriage. They could have learned from the servanthood of Jesus.

The Passover was the Jewish remembrance of God's great deliverance of their nation from slavery in Egypt. Moreover, it celebrates the fact that Israel was to be God's servant to the world. The event celebrated God's mighty act of passing over all of those who had put the blood of a lamb on their doors thus making them forever indebted to the Lord God. They were the only ones saved from the plague which killed all the first-born of Egypt (see Exodus 11 and 12). Thus their lives from that moment no longer belonged to them but to the God who saved them. During the Passover the Jewish people celebrate Israel's move from service through coercion and bondage to service that grows out of gratitude to divine care. It is fitting then that Jesus would use this time to teach a lesson about service to others. Passover was and is a time when the people of Israel serve God in gratitude and also serve their neighbors in the name of God. Jesus Christ is the fulfillment of this Old Testament remembrance and practice.

According to the Scriptures in 1 Corinthians 5:7, Jesus Christ is our Passover. Jesus Christ's sacrifice on the Cross and His resurrection provides the means of our deliverance from eternal death and provides access to God for believers. In this way, Jesus truly displayed the meaning of divine service. Even as He approached His own death, Jesus expresses love for His disciples continually through service. Jesus knew that His hour of death had come (cf. John 2:4; 7:30; 8:20), yet that in itself did not deter His focus on divine service. In this service, He gave His life. Jesus knew without doubt that He was the Father's unique Son with authority over all things, yet He had no problem serving for the purpose of the redemption of the world. Theologians often talk about redemptive suffering, but I am not so sure that is the suffering that redeems. Jesus' suffering results from service rendered. Thus, suffering is not the instrument of redemption, though suffering may accompany service. In the case of our Lord, it was redemptive service. Jesus' service to humanity led to His suffering. This suffering which comes to anyone who seeks to serve those who will not receive the service is a powerful tool for transforming one from enemy to friend. By taking upon Himself our sin and failure to serve God and others in whom God dwells, Jesus served us. By taking on the just punishment for our refusal of divine service, Jesus serves us as life-giver. By taking on our sickness, He serves us as healer. By serving us in the form of a Servant of servants, He raises us in divine service. Jesus is the serving One who liberates us from our infatuation with ourselves, and calls us to reach beyond the myopia of self-centeredness into a wider circle of divinely inspired self-giving.

By washing the feet of His disciples, Jesus clearly portrays the divine action of humble service for us (John 13:1-8). The disciples had been arguing among themselves about which of them was the greatest (Luke 22:24). As they entered the Upper Room for the Passover celebration, there evidently was no servant to wash their feet. They were dirty and uncomfortable. Even though the pitcher, water basin, and long linen cloth were all present, not one of the twelve would humble himself to do the dirty job. For to wash the feet of the rest was to declare oneself the servant of all, and that was precisely what each resolved that he would not do. They sat there looking at the table, looking at the ceiling, and arranging their dress. Not one would confess himself a bit inferior to the others by performing the slave's office of washing feet. Finally, the Lord Jesus got up from the table, picked up a towel, and began to wash the disciples' feet. Jesus the Lord washed the feet of His proud and selfish disciples—to demonstrate the nature of true love.

Jesus is the divine example of humble service (vv. 12-17). If the Lord had not proceeded to speak the words recorded here, Bible students would still, no doubt, record Jesus' humble service of foot-washing as an example. But our Lord intended to drive the lesson home to the twelve disciples. The proud, self-centered disciples needed to know about the true nature of love and service within the Christian community. Jesus knew that the lesson of love expressed in humble service would be necessary for the Church to exist and grow. Therefore, He explained His action so that they (and we) might see that spoken love must also be expressed.

It is possible to object to such debasement of service by one considered Master and Lord. In this story, Peter objected to the service offered by the Master (verses 6-8). Peter's first response is "NO." He insisted that the Master must not wash his feet. There have been many theories about the nature of feet, and preachers make flowery speeches about the awkwardness of feet and their lowly place in the body. Be that as it may, it is not the coarse nature of feet embraced by the dust of the earth that seems to bother Peter. Peter's response is a perfectly human response. He had responded that Jesus was the Messiah. This whole scenario was messing up Peter's well thought out system.

King, Messiah of Yahweh, Saviour, and Lord equals dignity and pomp. No menial labor for this One. Peter would rather wash the Master's feet because at least that gave him a special place in relationship with the Master. But Jesus, how He loves to mess with our well-defined theological assumptions. Social convention was the first reason for Peter's refusal. Tradition had determined that the Messiah must be served, however Peter and forgot the part that speaks of Him as the servant. Second, the breaking of convention was a thing of shame. What would his friends say about Jesus if they came in and saw the Master washing their feet? Maybe Peter was ashamed for Jesus (note I did not say ashamed of Him but for Him). How many times do we hold others from rendering service because we think it will demean them? We think, "He should not be talking to those people in the street, they are below him" or "She should stay away from her because she is less than her." Of course Peter did not want Jesus to wash his feet.

What was Peter saying about the disciples who let Jesus wash their feet? "Hey Jesus, these others may let you wash their feet, but I know better. They are not true disciples, I am." Did Peter think that this had to do with who is clean and who is dirty? Maybe so. However, Jesus says to him, "if you do not let me wash your feet you are not a part of me" (John 13:8). In other words, "How can you let me minister to others if you will not let me minister to you?" When we do not let Jesus serve us in our time of need, how can we be open when He seeks to serve others? Peter, you must let Jesus wash your feet if you are willing to let Him wash the feet of others. If you have not been washed by Him, how can you accept those whom He has washed? Peter, like many of us, finally sees that it is important to be washed by the Master and goes to the other extreme. At first, he would not let Jesus wash his feet because He was the Lord, now he wants the Lord to wash him all over because He is the Lord. Again, Peter seems to show that part of human ego that says, "I am closer to the Lord than the others." It all derives from the human misunderstanding of divine service.

Why don't you let Jesus serve you? Is it because you think that the service you need is beneath Jesus' dignity? One day I had no money, I had lost the keys to my car and was locked out. There were no spares. A man came to help me look for them. Since I did not have any money in the bank at that time, I began to pray, beseeching the Lord earnestly to help me find the keys or provide me with the funds to get my transportation working. The man turned to me and said, "I think God has more important things to do than find your keys." But here is the good news, Jesus is willing to serve me in my time of need. He would bow down low and help me. Yes, even with keys. Oh, what good news that the Lord of the universe would serve me! His amazing humility, it paralyzes my untempered tongue, that my Saviour came down and served an unworthy sinner like me. Good news it is indeed that we can serve in His name. Good news it is that He entrusts us with this service.

Serving His disciples as He did not diminish Jesus' Lordship. For as we read, Jesus resumed His place at the table and said, "Do you know what I have done to you? You call me Teacher and Lord; and you are right, for so I am. If I then, your Lord and Teacher, have washed your feet, you also ought to wash one another's feet. For I have given you an example, that you also should do as I have done to you. Truly, truly, I say to you, a servant is not greater than his master; nor is he who is sent greater than he who sent him. If you know these things, blessed are you if you do them" (vv. 12-17, RSV). Jesus does not rebuke His dis-

ciples with harsh words but asks them if they grasp the significance of His action for their own future actions. "Do you
know…?" He says. The One of highest position—the Lord and
Teacher—had humbled Himself to serve the needs of others.
Not only is this an example, but it is also an act showing the true
greatness of Jesus. He was, indeed, the Teacher of authority and
truth; He was indeed the Lord who deserved obedience.

Jesus then argues, "If I *being the Lord and Teacher* have served you in this act of foot-washing, how much more ought you to serve one another?" (v. 14, paraphrased). He shows them that His ideal of Lordship is to serve—even as He was about to become the Suffering Servant on the Cross (see Isaiah 53). The one who claims to follow Jesus must be like Him and serve as the true expression of love and greatness. We might ask: Should we, as Jesus' disciples, practice actual foot-washing today? Though some do and experience great blessing from such action, the Scriptures do not seem to indicate that Jesus was establishing an ordinance, like baptism or the Lord's Supper.

He is not commanding the disciples to do *what* He has done, but *as* He has done. In other words, His action is an example— one of many possible actions—of showing the humble service of love. To do *as* Jesus did means we must have the inner attitude of humility and love that moves us to perform actions that truly serve our Christian brothers and sisters. Jesus is our example. We must ask Him how we can express our service today.

Servanthood is girded by the divine command of love (vv. 34-35). The "new" command that Jesus gave is not unknown in the Old Testament (Leviticus 19:18) or in ethical literature. It is new in terms of its freshness, beauty, and desirability—the command to love has never become worn out or marred throughout the ages. Jesus' command is new in another sense. The newness of the precept is set forth here in the sense that Jesus requires that His disciples love one another as *he loved them!* His example of constant, self-sacrificing love must be *their* attitude and pattern for relating toward one another. The kind of love which goes to the extreme (see John 13:1), serves with a humble spirit (v. 5), and eventually dies a sacrificial death for undeserving sinners, is the kind of love Jesus commands for His disciples.

You may wonder how love can be commanded. Perhaps we could best understand it as a precept—a guideline for life. For love is not an attitude or feeling. Love is a matter of the will. Love seeks and acts in the best interest of the other person. The Lord showed His disciples this kind of love by washing their feet. Love, therefore, can be properly commanded if understood as an action. Feelings may come with or after the action, but the feelings must never be confused with *agape*, the self-sacrificing love spoken of here.

In verse 34, the command is repeated. No doubt, this is done to stress its importance for the spiritual welfare of all the Church. Jesus goes on to explain that love among the disciples is also important to the non-Christian world: "By this all men will know that you are my disciples, if you have love for one another" (v. 35, RSV). Love is the identifying trait for Christian brothers and sisters. Attitudes of selfishness and bitterness among Christians deny the Lordship of Jesus Christ and cause unbelievers to mock and ridicule His name. We must go on obeying this commandment of love to honor our Lord who loved us so much that He gave Himself to us.

The servant must have the heart for moving beyond minimalism—doing the least one can do. Do you have a servant spirit? When asked to help or when you see a need, do you go beyond the minimum? One who will serve the Lord God or even serve others ought to avoid excuses and complaining in the process of serving. For when we serve in obedience to God, God will be with us (Judges 6:14-16). In fact, the strength of God will help to overcome the obstacles in the way of our service. Sometimes it is easy to see all of the obstacles to service. Seeing mainly the obstacles may lead us to make excuses. Many great men and women have learned how to serve God while serving their fellow human beings. It is hard sometimes when we have a vision of greatness or we are convinced that we have a call on our lives to continue to serve until our time comes. We may be called to open doors or even clean the furniture of church. Our service may be to sweep the floor; but whatever it is, we must see it as service to God. For when we serve in little things, we are indeed preparing our souls for greatness. In all that we do, we are God's servants in training. When we serve our brothers and sisters, yes, and even our enemies—even when carrying out tasks that some may deem beneath our dignity—we indeed are serving God because ultimately in the kingdom of God all our serving is God-directed and should be God-informed. There are many other examples of service in Scripture resulting in praise and good news. (See 1 Chronicles 11:15-19; Genesis 24:18-21).

We must also serve one another. It may have been easy if Jesus had said "so serve the Lord" but He said "do as I have done" indicating that we ought to serve others with the same posture the He had demonstrated for us. But given the assortment of theological perspectives in our world, many would find it difficult to decide on any specific pattern of service. I can just hear some people, maybe even you reading, saying "That does not mean you ought to be a door mat." But who said anything about a door mat? The way we come up with these sort of statements when a simple demand of service is made of us almost suggests that Jesus could never in a thousand worlds have thought about them. Our faith demands that we serve one another.

Service derives from Christian piety. There are some common features to Christian service. One is that it is done with a humble spirit. This is humility informed with hope. Christian hope is not only historical, it deals with present human conditions.

Christian hope is also eschatological, that is, it is informed by a strong belief in the power of God working through the Christian to transform the future. Service transcends our rationalistic approach to life; for in our human rationality the least should serve the great, which has been the reason for so much bad news. Most of such service derives not from free, uncoerced, and willing action but from pure necessity and straitness. But the kind of serving required by the Lord Jesus is good news in that all who serve do so willingly. It is good news in that the greater willingly serves, the powerful willingly bows, and the righteous willingly loves.

Something else happens when we serve as Jesus commanded. It brings good news to those served, first because it affirms their connection to the divine. From this point of view, service still must be underpinned with divinely-informed motivation. Christian service not only affirms the humanity of the person to whom it is rendered, it also instructs the inner landscape of one's spiritual geography. Serving, as it passes from the server to the served, becomes a teaching mechanism to both and makes both learners. This is affirmed by the passage in Hebrews which says that "Jesus learned obedience from the things he experienced" in His service to God and for humanity. We also learned from his service how to serve God and one another (5:8). Thus, if Jesus learned from His willingness to serve humanity, we must also learn and serve. Based on Jesus' authority we must acknowledge the power of service and the importance of servanthood.

We are not justified in our modern view of service as negative. Yes, it is true that people do take advantage of those with a servant's heart, but it is also clear that Jesus sees our serving as an intrinsic part of our relationship with Him. Some need proof or evidence that they will not be hurt by those whom they serve or seek to serve. Others may want assurance that those whom they serve will at all times remain grateful and acquiescing. But Christian service requires that instead of focusing on potential negative results, we depend entirely on God for the outcome of service. Serving then in the mode of Jesus is not an opportunity for self-glorification. It is action meant for God, for His glory and honor. In service Jesus-style, we offer ourselves as vessels unto honor. In spite of the fact that our world remains deeply entrenched in the strange habit of taking service and trampling upon it and the server, we must, like Jesus, still serve, for serving in the name of Christ is good news. Through our Christian service, the Lord comes near to those for whom He may have seemed far and distant. In service, we can become for the disheartened a manifestation of God's care.

In our act, God becomes not God-against-them but God-for-us and indeed may continue to be seen as God-with-us. Serving is the place where our faith takes on our human body and the Word which now sits in spiritual realms comes down again and becomes flesh and blood. Christian service allows people see the love of God in reality rather than waiting for the esoteric philosophical flight of sinful imagination. Serving is then the matrix that generates passionate witness. It is the medium whereby our faith becomes continually incarnated and the Word and life of our Lord Jesus Christ becomes enlivened. In service, we share our physical, psychic, and pneumatic (spiritual) cells with a dying world, infusing it with the same life which the service of Jesus gave us. Here in service, our faith moves from mere rational head knowledge professed to people who are with us within the proverbial four walls, to a clear active statement reflecting the presence of God in people's situations. When Jesus says to His disciples "do as I have done," He sets for us a clear direction of service for other human beings. He shows us that it is in both the willingness to serve others and the actuality of doing so that we speak directly to the powers that grip our brothers and sisters. In truth, Jesus comes alive in all of His glory in our lives when we embrace humble serving as He did (Philippians. 2:1-8).

The service which Christ gave is good news, and the service which Christ commands of us is good news. It is action–oriented good news. It is good news to serve one whose cynicism has so eaten them that they no longer believe that anyone cares and then to watch their life transformed by a simple act of obedience. How different this world would be if every professing Christian took time everyday to serve someone. That would be good news. There is a joy that infuses the human soul when they receive service for what they pay for, but how much better to give and receive the joy which infuses a soul who for the sake of the Gospel gets served. What good news it is to serve those who may not deserve it but are in need, and then to watch as the light from God's face breaks forth upon their face. Lord God, help us to embrace in our day the good news of serving You and serving one another. May we never be too great to pull up our sleeves, adorn a towel, and wash the feet of the least of our brethren and so make Jesus come alive for our sleeping world.

Chapter Six

GOOD NEWS: JESUS BREAKS BOUNDARIES

BASED ON MATTHEW 8:5-13

Matthew 8:5-13

And when Jesus was entered into Capernaum, there came unto him a centurion, beseeching him, ⁶ And saying, Lord, my servant lieth at home sick of the palsy, grievously tormented. ⁷ And Jesus saith unto him, I will come and heal him. ⁸ The centurion answered and said, Lord, I am not worthy that thou shouldest come under my roof: but speak the word only, and my servant shall be healed. ⁹ For I am a man under authority, having soldiers under me; and I say to this man, Go, and he goeth; and to another, Come, and he cometh; and to my servant, Do this, and he doeth it. ¹⁰ When Jesus heard it, he marvelled, and said to them that followed, Verily I say unto you, I have not found so great faith, no, not in Israel. ¹¹ And I say unto you, That many shall come from the east and west, and shall sit down with Abraham, and Isaac, and Jacob, in the kingdom of heaven. ¹² But the children of the kingdom shall be cast out into outer darkness: there shall be weeping and gnashing of teeth. ¹³ And Jesus said unto the centurion, Go thy way; and as thou hast believed, so be it done unto thee. And his servant was healed in the selfsame hour.

Jesus came to break down barriers between human beings. The world is full of problems that cause us to burn within like a fire. There are many things which can easily create a wall of division between us and other human beings. The church continually preaches the good news about Jesus to all, yet there seems to be more barriers raised up between people than ever. Some even use the Gospel in emphasizing the division among human beings. In fact, we do not have to look too far back in history to see how some have used the Gospel to create nearly unbridgeable chasms between groups. And others wonder why people can't get together. It has been said that the "11 o'clock hour is the most segregated hour in America." It can also be said that Christendom as conceived has been the most divisive thought system since the balkanization of ancient Greek philosophical systems. We see division and separation in the synagogue and in the marketplaces of the world. Great discussions are often held to understand this phenomena of division. But in many cases, these conversations forget about the good news of Jesus which is meant to tear down walls and break down boundaries.

We may be able to characterize our age as very religious. If one were to walk around our cities and observe the devotions and worship of Christians, one may be tempted to think, because of our division and our unwillingness to get together and even they way we talk about each other, that in our temples, churches, altars, shrines, and various monuments that we do indeed worship separate gods. It is one thing for us to state that worshiping God ignorantly has led to more division than inclusion. But the so-called knowledgeable of the world continue to enhance their divisiveness with their philosophical jargon. The solution is proclaiming the true God through Jesus Christ His Son.

The Scriptures are clear that God is the Creator of all things. As Christians, we must desire to know the true God. This Hebrew-Christian description of God contradicts our tendency to box everything and package it for marketing. Clearly, the true God did not create the world and everything in it then leave it to be controlled by fate or circumstance. It is impossible for God or His creation to be circumscribed by human invention. Not only is God greater than we are, He is beyond our grasp. He is to be worshiped, we are to be worshipers. He is the adored, we are the adoring.

Even though our awesome God is Creator of all things and infinitely greater than we are, He desires to come near us. However this closeness is breached when we choose not to worship Him according to His nature but instead to worship the work of our own hands. We seem to forget that the living God, the Great Creator of all things, is not dependent on us for His well being. For He is the One who gives to all people life, breath, and everything else. Humans have nothing; but what we have been given, we received from the hand of our Maker.

We know that God also made people, for He "made of one blood all nations of men for to dwell on all the face of the earth, and hath determined the times before appointed, and the bounds of their habitation" (Acts 17:26). "One blood" refers to the creation of the first humans, Adam and Eve. From Adam, God made the nations of all people to live on the earth. Since no person or group originated independently from other human beings, this contradicts the boast that certain people are superior to other people. Every person is made by God and is a descendant from a common ancestor. God has also appointed the time and place in which every person lives (v. 26b). He has wisely given to everyone their place to dwell. God created all humankind in order "that they should seek the Lord, if haply they might feel after him, and find him, though he be not far from every one of us" (v. 27). God desires that every person from every nation should seek Him. He wants everyone to know of His existence and His character. God has made it possible for all nations, though living in different regions and climates, to have the opportunity to know God the Creator. By design, God created all people and we all are responsible for seeking Him. We cannot be whole unless we know and have a relationship with God.

Even though God is transcendent and it is beyond our ability to completely understand Him, He seeks to enter into relationship with us. But we have broken our relationship with God. A wall has gone up. A demarcation has been instituted. There has developed a chasm which we cannot cross on our own. We cannot bridge this gap by the flight of our imagination. We cannot mend this rupture by our religious superstitions. No, we cannot by the mere effort of our own searching, as Job said, find God (Job 11:7). We have been left on the other side. As human beings, even our prayers fail to reach God. For as Isaiah says "the Lord is not deaf that he cannot hear your prayers but your iniquity has separated between you and your God" (Isaiah 59:1-2, paraphrased).

It is true that ". . . in him we live, and move, and have our being" but without Him we move as beings separated from our very center. It is true that our natural life would not exist without God; but the fact is that we live naturally separated from the supernatural source of our being. Though God formed us and continually sustains us, we drift in a sea of separation because we have fallen. We are like a trickling spring cut off from its original fountain. Our lives continue from moment to moment only by the sheer power of His original mercy, adrift upon the murky sea of our iniquity and rebellion. We live, move, and have our being, but we fail to have "His being." In the words of the prophet "we are like sheep that have gone astray, we have turned every one to his own way" (Isaiah 53:6a). We are lost. Even our human righteousness which many humanists seem to emphasize places us more in need of God's cleansing (Isaiah 64:6). For instead of making us whole and drawing us to God, it serves to divide and separate us from God. We are divinely created, but our prodigality has left us without a homebound anchor. There is barrier between us and God. There is a boundary.

Our sinful nature separates us from God because we have become fundamentally flawed in our divine character. In our world today, many modernists and even post-modernists, as some call themselves, think that we have come so far that we do not need to talk about humanity's separation from God. Some think that because modern human beings do not set up idols of wood in worship at their homes that somehow we are closer to God than those who do. But our separation from God is seen in our worship of creation in place of the Creator. Our very inventions may serve to separate us from God. Our modern idols, like the idols of the ancients, continue to cause separation between us and our divine destiny. We, like our fore-parents, have set up our limited rationality in place of divine wisdom. Some people seem to worship ignorance, while others worship rationalistic intelligence. Thus, we continue to be separated from our God. Unless this gap is bridged, we are headed for serious eternal trouble.

In the past, our ignorance may have led us to walk away from God, but God demands that we change our way of thinking because there is now a way back to Him. Yes! There is a force that pulls our isolated stream upward. A life-line has been thrown into our murky sea to draw us into life. This is good news. Now those who turn around can see the light. Those who repent can now be reoriented. The good news is that this reorientation comes from God's own self. God is commanding all people to come back. The bad news is that they cannot come on their own; the good news is that God has provided a way for them to come. The bad news is that humanity is subject to judgment for separating from God; the good news is that God knows that and has made a way. Neither you nor I have to suffer the judgment of God, if we will only lay hold of God's life-line thrown into this murky turbulent waters of destruction. Our life-line is Jesus, the Messiah. He is the Saviour from our prodigality, the fountain which re-energizes our streams. By His resurrection, God has conquered the greatest sin affecting our separation and even death. By His own death, He broke the barrier between us and God. Not only did Jesus die for the sins of all people, He rose again to show that no longer should you and I be on the other side of chasm, unable to get back to God. Ephesians. 2:11-19 states:

Wherefore remember, that ye being in time past Gentiles in the flesh, who are called Uncircumcision by that which is called the Circumcision in the flesh made by hands; [12]That at that time ye were without Christ, being aliens from the commonwealth of Israel, and strangers from the covenants of promise, having no hope, and without God in the world: [13]But now in Christ Jesus ye who sometimes were far off are made nigh by the blood of Christ. [14]For he is our peace, who hath made both one, and hath broken down the middle wall of partition between us; [15]Having abolished in his flesh the enmity, even the law of commandments contained in ordinances; for to make in himself of twain one new man, so making peace; [16]And that he might reconcile both unto God in one body by the cross, having slain the enmity thereby: [17]And came and preached peace to you which were afar off, and to them that were nigh. [18]For through him we both have access by one Spirit unto the Father. [19]Now therefore ye are no more strangers and foreigners, but fellow citizens with the saints, and of the household of God . . .

The life of Jesus offers us the opportunity of immediate reentrance into the presence of God as children no longer separated from our eternal Parent (Romans 5:11; Romans 8:32; Leviticus 6:30; 2 Chronicles 29:24; Ezekiel 45:20) Will you hear Him? Will you reach out and touch Him? If we mock because we believe somehow that our being human secures our immortal bliss, we deceive ourselves. For you see, true life and peace with God is available only through the person of God's Son Jesus, the Messiah. To receive life and be reconciled with God, we must exercise faith in God's provision for us. We must believe that this One who comes from God—Jesus, who died and who rose—is for us. We must embrace Him as Emmanuel. This call is not a call to more religious politeness which results in procrastinated faith, but a call to radical faith in the good will of God towards men. This is good news that you and I no longer need to be separated from God; we can be reconciled with our very essential being. This is good news that we have our being in God. We were fenced in, enclosed by our self-imposed prison, but now that Jesus has come we are offered an opportunity to open up.

Several passages in the New Testament point to the breaking down of the barrier between God and humanity. In Romans 5:10, we read "For if, when we were enemies, we were reconciled to God by the death of his Son, much more, being reconciled,

we shall be saved by his life." Second Corinthians 5:18-19 teaches us "And all things are of God, who hath reconciled us to himself by Jesus Christ, and hath given to us the ministry of reconciliation; To wit, that God was in Christ, reconciling the world unto himself, not imputing their trespasses unto them; and hath committed unto us the word of reconciliation." The good news is that God's love has overtaken our passive and active hatred. Through Him, we are no longer enemies with

God divided by our pugnacious orientation but children of the Most High.

But it is not just between God and human beings that a barrier exists. There is also a barrier which has developed between human beings. As in the case of the God, we have developed many superstitions which have divided one group from another. This opposition which some people have toward one another comes from our inability to relate to God. Having been given an open invitation into peace with God, we must not hesitate to accept, for this peace with God also is the key to peace with humanity. How many times are people ready to hear the Gospel, but some old wound distorts the new message and thus they turn away? Most of the time, this wound results from our distortion of the nature of God and His relationship with other human beings. Some think that their religious activities give them a special relationship with God which allows them to persecute others. Ignorance of God often leads to ignorance of humanity. This ignorance of God leads us to categorize others as non-beings and then to persecute, and sometimes add to the sin of persecution, murder. Thus, we find that as we are separated from God, we are also separated from each other. But the simple fact is that because Jesus has brought the good news of reconciliation with God there can be reconciliation between human beings. Because God is the One who gives life, breath and all things, to all creatures, it follows that God has already created the material basis for breaking down all the boundaries between human beings.

While the Bible does call us God's handiwork or workmanship, it lumps all of us together in sin thus equalizing us at our high and at our low (Ephesians 2:10; Romans 3:23). Therefore, there was and is no justification in the claim that some groups are inherently superior to others. The Greeks are not superior to the barbarians, nor the Romans to the Carthaginians, or the Egyptians to the Ethiopians, or the Jews to the Gentiles. Similarly, there is no justification in these beliefs of superiority today. Consequently, whether in the ancient times or present day, there is no room for the idea of racial superiority at all. The same Creator, the Almighty God, created us all equally. Our separation and division one from another is the result of sin. Not only does superstition and ignorance create a demarcation between us, greed separates us one from another. Because we misplace our priorities by putting things before God and human beings, we thicken the walls which divide us. By seeking to become popular with people or focusing on things which we think will preserve us, step over each other and thicken the boundaries. The more distant human beings feel from one another, the more resentful we seem to become as we plot to get rid of them.

In Matthew 8:5-13, Jesus took the opportunity to break not only the boundary that separates one group from another and human beings from God, but also the barrier which blocks humanity from physical wholeness. This story takes place as Jesus comes to a place named Capernaum. The name is Hebrew in origin and is a combination of *kaphar* and *nachuwm*. The first word refers to a walled in place or a place of silence; the second part of the name *nacham*, pronounced **naw-kham'** simply means to breathe a sigh of relief. It can also mean compassion and consolation. Thus, as Jesus was going to the walled place a man met him, a centurion to be exact. The centurion symbolized the division between the people of Israel and their colonial masters the Romans. This man was part of the group that was meant to attack the people if they thought about freedom. Matthew places this story right after the story of the leper who beseeched Jesus to heal him. Like the leper, this man was separated from the community in which he lived; one by birth, the other by circumstance. The centurion represented all of that which caused Israel pain. The wall was up; it was cultural, religious, racial, professional, and political. The boundaries between this centurion and the people among whom he lived was as thick as the wall which protected Jerusalem.

The very presence of Jesus serves to soften the walls we have built up. This proud Roman who probably saw the people of Israel as troublemakers now turns to Jesus for help. His servant was sick. Sickness is our common human condition. It is one of those things that transcends class and gender, race and culture, and religious orientation. Yet, many times it may serve to divide even the most committed from each other. But here, it is this need which brings this man to Jesus. Interestingly it is not his own sickness but that of someone dear to him. One of his servants. We read that he came near to Jesus. He invited Jesus through imploration to cross his built up walls and meet his need. Some people are just too proud to reach out for help, even in the midst of the need for consolation. This centurion had a servant which was probably epileptic or paralyzed. At least the use of the Greek word *ballo*, pronounced **bal'-lo** meaning throw and the word *paralutikos*, pronounced **par-al-oo-tee-kos'** which refers to the dissolving of the muscles implies that this sickness was terribly excessive. The state of the patient as servant was probably painful and tormented. How many times do our boundaries keep us from getting the help we need? How many times do the walls we have built through pride keep us from going to each other? How often do the philosophical walls we have built even keep us from coming to the Lord for our needs.

But thanks be to God for Jesus Christ who breaks walls.

To break down our boundaries and walls, we must be willing to come to Jesus. But notice that Jesus was already on His way into the city before this man came to Him. As a Jew, Jesus could have refused to become involved in this man's problem. He could have come up with all kinds of wall-building reasons why this Gentile and Roman could not be helped. Instead, Jesus used the opportunity to break down the walls between this man and his God, and between this man and his Jewish neighbors. When the man pleaded with Jesus, He responded immediately making this outsider a priority in God's work.

Note the words of Jesus "I will come and heal him." Jesus seems to be saying, "I see your wall but I will come to you anyway. I see the walls that traditions have built between you and I, but I will come to you anyway. I see the walls that you have put up for fear of being hurt, but I will come to you anyway. There is boundary between you and your neighbour, I am willing to come near and heal that breach." This is Jesus, the breaker of boundaries, the One who bridges gaps. He said, "I will come and heal him." Watch this. Not only is Jesus healing the breach between this man and God and between this man and his Israelite neighbors, He is breaking the walls between this man his servant. He is walking through the wall, speaking through the wall, reaching through the wall into this man's heart. That is Jesus for you. That is the Son of the living God. Note that Jesus does all of this before the man even makes an explicit statement of what he believes about Jesus.

What are the walls around you, your family, your friends, your co-workers? Hear Jesus as He says, "I will come and heal you." I will come and remove the walls which have developed in your relationships." Can you hear Him beside you as He whispers, "I will come over and heal you." He will come over your walls. He is willing to come over your walls and meet your need. There may be walls in your life that have kept you on the outside. There may be walls that keep you from developing a lasting relationship both with God and other people. Listen, if Jesus can break down the walls between human beings and God, He can surely break the walls between you and your environment, between you and your hope, between you and your loved ones, and yes, between you and your enemies.

In verses 8 and 9, the centurion looks at Jesus and says, "Lord, I am not worthy that thou shouldest come under my roof: but speak the word only, and my servant shall be healed. For I am a man under authority, having soldiers under me: and I say to this man, Go, and he goeth; and to another, Come, and he cometh; and to my servant, Do this, and he doeth it." It is true that lack of self-esteem does build walls between us and our future. Jesus came to give us back our self-confidence based on God's power, not on some sort of arrogation of power. But in this man's case he is not writhing in self pity. Rather his response derives from a proportionate understanding of himself. People in high places usually allow their pride to build up walls of separation between them and others.

For example, those who were your friends may change when they get a promotion. Maybe you have put up walls between you and your friends and all of a sudden they do not want to be seen in your company anymore. This is not the case here. Here, we see a man who has been stripped of all his human pride in the presence of the Lord Jesus Christ. Oh, how humility will help tear down the walls in ourhearts. First, he knew that he could not break this barrier. Second, he realized that only the word spoken by the eternal Son of God, One with divine authority could break his walls. The word of Jesus can heal our breaches. See this man say "speak the word and my servant shall be healed." Jesus alone has this authority to speak to the spiritual forces which fragment and divide us. In order for the boundaries between this man and his God and the people to be healed and for the wall between his servant and health to brought down, he had to come to Jesus, acknowledge Jesus in humility, and affirm the authority of Jesus.

In response, "When Jesus heard it, He marvelled, and said to them that followed, 'Verily I say unto you, I have not found so great faith, no, not in Israel" (v. 10). The use of the Greek word *thaumazo,* pronounced **thou-mad'-zo,** means to be filled with wonder. Remember that as a human being Jesus was Jewish. The idea that a Gentile can have genuine faith was not easily accepted among the people of Israel. But to God, faith is a wonderful thing. By implication, this passage is saying that Jesus was filled with admiration for this Gentile, this outsider. Imagine how this expression of admiration may have affected the disciples who have been taught to loathe the Gentiles. Surely this expression of admiration from the divine One in their midst must have served to break down the barrier which existed between them. But note that it was not just empty admiration, it was wonder resulting from the man's expression of faith. In one sweeping statement, Jesus broke down what may have been their highest religious wall. This man's faith was stronger than theirs. The stereotypes of Gentiles being unable to express genuine faith was brought to the ground. There is nothing like faith to bring down barriers. Faith can move the highest mountain dividing us one from another. Faith can bridge the dividing sea between us. Faith can cut across cultures, gender, class, and even enemy lines. Why shouldn't believers continue to strive to eliminate those barriers and things in human life that continue to separate us from God and from one another.

This presents a clear picture of the result of faith expressed in the Person of Jesus. Faith in Jesus Christ is our key to dealing with our warnings and tendency to alienate others. It is this man's faith expressed in Jesus that becomes the basis of breaking down long held stereotypical traditions. The man's faith gave him entrance into the very heart of God's Son. "Everything," said Jesus, is possible to those who have faith (Mark 9:23). We, as Christians, are called to have faith, not just for our own salvation but for the salvation of this world; we are called to believe that Jesus has the power and the authority to make things whole. By faith, we could have all that we need then move beyond ourselves reaching and touching God for someone other than ourselves. This is good news that faith in Jesus can break boundaries.

Finally, Jesus uses this man's faith to teach a lesson which His life illustrates. He says, "And I say unto you, That many shall come from the east and west, and shall sit down with Abraham, and Isaac, and Jacob, in the kingdom of heaven (v. 11)."

Through Jesus Christ, the kingdom of heaven has come down to everyone. Everyone who comes to Jesus, whether they be from the east or from the west, from the south or from the north, will sit in the divine reign with God. This is good news that breaks down boundaries.

GOOD NEWS: JESUS IS COMPASSIONATE

BASED ON MARK 7:32-37; 10:46-52

Mark 7:32-37

And they bring unto him one that was deaf, and had an impediment in his speech; and they beseech him to put his hand upon him. ³³ And he took him aside from the multitude, and put his fingers into his ears, and he spit, and touched his tongue; ³⁴ And looking up to heaven, he sighed, and saith unto him, Ephphatha, that is, Be opened. ³⁵ And straightway his ears were opened, and the string of his tongue was loosed, and he spake plain. ³⁶ And he charged them that they should tell no man: but the more he charged them, so much the more a great deal they published it; ³⁷ And were beyond measure astonished, saying, He hath done all things well: he maketh both the deaf to hear, and the dumb to speak.

Mark 10:46-52

And they came to Jericho: and as he went out of Jericho with his disciples and a great number of people, blind Bartimaeus, the son of Timaeus, sat by the highway side begging. ⁴⁷ And when he heard that it was Jesus of Nazareth, he began to cry out, and say, Jesus, thou son of

David, have mercy on me. ⁴⁸ And many charged him that he should hold his peace: but he cried the more a great deal, Thou son of David, have mercy on me. ⁴⁹ And Jesus stood still, and commanded him to be called. And they call the blind man, saying unto him, Be of good comfort, rise; he calleth thee. ⁵⁰ And he, casting away his garment, rose, and came to Jesus. ⁵¹ And Jesus answered and said unto him, What wilt thou that I should do unto thee? The blind man said unto him, Lord, that I might receive my sight. ⁵² And Jesus said unto him, Go thy way; thy faith hath made thee whole. And immediately he received his sight, and followed Jesus in the way.

The St. Louis Post Dispatch newspaper reported on the sad death of an elderly woman living in a large apartment building. The woman died from malnutrition. Apparently, she had cried out for help a day or two before her demise because two neighbors reported hearing faint cries coming from her apartment. They did not bother to investigate because the woman had a reputation for complaining and seeking attention. Unfortunately, this time she was not pretending.

This story could be repeated many times in other cities around our country and the world. Millions of people are hurting and crying today because of pain. Divorce, marital separation, accidents, hospitalization, sickness, sorrow, child abuse, wife abuse, alcoholism and drug addiction, living in rat-infested apartments, inadequate funds for basic needs, hunger, discrimination, disappointments, unemployment—all constitute the discordant notes of a sad song. Why is there so much suffering and sorrow in our world today? Why do people experience pain? We can gain some insight by studying the Old Testament, especially the "acts of God." Since God gives us the gift of life and existence, we can cherish this and learn to accept the struggles which come with the gift. In other words, if we are going to question God about our struggles and sorrows, we must also question Him about our moments of joy, exuberance, and happiness. The two questions of "Why pain?" and "Why joy?" must be asked together in order to get a balanced perspective on life. Students of the Christian faith know that such questions are not without answers. We have hope. It is embodied in the Person of Jesus Christ, the Son of God, the Master Teacher, the Divine Healer. He is in a unique position to both hear human cries and to respond to them. Those of us who are participants in the life of Jesus know that our God is compassionate. Our God experiences something of the pain we feel when we as God's people are hurting. As we learn more about His compassion may we determine to become more compassionate toward others in need.

William Barclay, an English commentator, explains that Mark did not hear or see the things our Lord said and did. Peter did, and Mark stayed very close to Peter acting as his interpreter and scribe. Mark wrote down much of the detail Peter shared with him. Mark was a very sensitive young writer. Apparently, he was impressed with the action narrative of Peter's stories. His Gospel is sometimes called the action Gospel. More than 15 healing incidents involving Jesus are told in his Gospel. The earliest of all the Gospels, Mark was written about A.D. 65. Mark helps us grasp a vivid portrait of Jesus' life. He helps us understand the Master's divinity and humanity as well as God's compassion and concern. In this Scripture Lesson we see how Jesus expresses compassion toward a deaf man (Mark 7:32-37). We also see how Jesus shows compassion toward blind Bartimaeus (10:46-52).

The moving and exciting story of Jesus and the deaf man (Mark 7:32-37) demonstrates the compassion and concern of Jesus. "A deaf man with a speech impediment was brought to

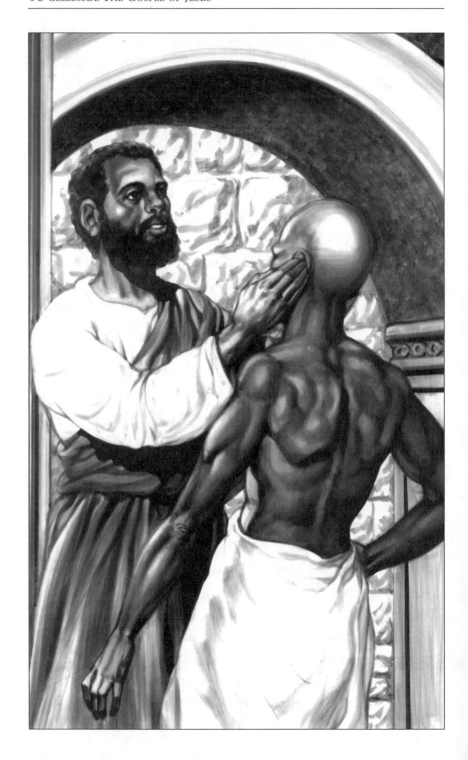

him" (v. 32, LB). We do well to bring people to Jesus through the medium of prayer. Our task is not to evaluate their worthiness, question them, judge them, or check out their credentials. Our assignment is to bring people to Jesus. Leave them with Jesus. He can help them. Somebody was sensitive to this deaf man's plight and said, "Let's take him to Jesus."

"Jesus led him away from the crowd and put his fingers into the man's ears" (v. 33, LB). Here is an act of tender consideration on the part of Jesus. Perhaps Jesus put His arm around the man's shoulders and gently led him to a private place. Like Jesus, we need to learn how to be gentle with people. A wise preacher once said, "Life has a way of beating up on people, church folks should not add to others' injuries." An unlearned and unskilled worker once prayed, "Lord, help me to be gentle and kind to everyone I meet today. Let them feel that in meeting me and talking with me, they are meeting and talking with You. Amen."

"Then (Jesus) spat and touched the man's tongue with the spittle" (v. 33, LB). In those days, people believed spittle had a curative quality. Jesus did not really need to follow that custom because He possessed all power. Nevertheless, the text demonstrates again Jesus' sensitivity to people, their customs, traditions, hang-ups, and quirks. As we go our way witnessing about the love of God, we should remember to accept people just as they are. If we love the sinner and hate the sin, we can hear the cries of people just as Jesus did. The Holy Spirit can open our ears so that we can be sensitive to the lost, dying, confused, and discouraged people of the world.

"Then looking up to Heaven, he sighed and commanded, 'Open!' Instantly the man could hear perfectly and speak plainly!" (v. 34, LB). Jesus was always interested in staying in touch with the Father. It's as though He did not want to depend on His own strength. How about you and me? Do we stay in touch with Christ? When we deal with people and their problems, we would be far less frustrated and anxious if we would remember to look to Jesus. That's where our resources are located. Jesus Christ is the source of our strength.

This story closes on an exciting note—the eyewitnesses' testimony. "Everything he does is wonderful; he even corrects deafness and stammering" (v. 37, LB). This is a solid promise that we can hold out to people who need healing from physical, emotional, and social diseases—God is wonderful, and He can cure whatever ills befall us.

In Mark's account of Jesus' compassion toward blind Bartimaeus (10:46-52), Jesus, His disciples, and the crowd of people were on their way to Jerusalem. No doubt this crowd consisted of pilgrims on their way to worship in Jerusalem as well as others intrigued by Jesus' power to perform miracles. Bartimaeus begged along the side of the road, as many other destitute people did, since there was no welfare system to assist the indigent. Certainly the throng of people passing would have gotten his attention. But he discovers an even greater reason for excitement—Jesus of Nazareth was passing that way. He doubtlessly had heard of Jesus and the miracles He performed. He apparently had heard enough about Him to conclude that He was no ordinary prophet.

Bartimaeus was convinced that this Jesus must be the promised Messiah descended from David. He cried out to Jesus, "Jesus, thou son of David, have mercy on me" (v.47). Even though those around him attempted to shut him up, he kept pleading. Perhaps they thought Jesus was too busy—that He had more important business to take care of. But how wrong they were! That kind of passionate cry to a compassionate Christ will not be denied. Jesus stood still and commanded him to be called. Bartimaeus threw away his outer garment and rushed to Jesus. Blind, dirty and poorly dressed, Bartimaeus was now the center of attention. Such physical conditions and a needy heart evoked the deepest compassion from Jesus.

"What do you want me to do for you?" asked Jesus. "Lord, I want to see—more than anything else, I want to see" (v. 51 paraphrased). No small request, but the beggar knew He was asking no ordinary person. Jesus granted his request. He was healed. Does this not teach us that we may ask large requests from the Lord and receive them when the conditions of asking are met? In this case the man made a request for his sight. Because he immediately joined the others in following Jesus rather than running off to his own business, we can be sure here was a deeply appreciative man; he wanted Jesus to have the glory rather than himself. Selfish requests to make us look good may not get the attention of God like unselfish ones would do.

The compassion of our Lord cannot be missed in these two accounts. He went about doing good. And to those of us who would be His followers, He turns, looks us dead in the eyes, and challenges us to show compassion to others as He has shown it to us.

Chapter Eight

GOOD NEWS: JESUS FORGIVES

BASED ON MATTHEW 18:21-35; MARK 2:1-12

Matthew 18:21-35

*T*hen came Peter to him, and said, Lord, how oft shall my brother sin against me, and I forgive him? till seven times? [22] Jesus saith unto him, I say not unto thee, Until seven times: but, Until seventy times seven. [23] Therefore is the kingdom of heaven likened unto a certain king, which would take account of his servants. [24] And when he had begun to reckon, one was brought unto him, which owed him ten thousand talents. [25] But forasmuch as he had not to pay, his lord commanded him to be sold, and his wife, and children, and all that he had, and payment to be made. [26] The servant therefore fell down, and worshipped him, saying, Lord, have patience with me, and I will pay thee all. [27] Then the lord of that servant was moved with compassion, and loosed him, and forgave him the debt. [28] But the same servant went out, and found one of his fellow servants, which owed him an hundred pence: and he laid hands on him, and took him by the throat, saying, Pay me that thou owest. [29] And his fellow-servant fell down at his feet, and besought him, saying, Have patience with me, and I will pay thee all. [30] And he would not: but went and cast him into prison, till he should pay the debt. [31] So when his fellow-servants saw what was done, they were very sorry, and came and told unto their lord all that was done. [32] Then his lord, after that he had called him, said unto him, O thou wicked servant, I forgave thee all that debt, because thou desiredst me: [33] Shouldest not thou also have had compassion on thy fellow servant, even as I had pity on thee? [34] And his lord was wroth, and delivered him to the tormentors, till he should pay all that was due unto him. [35] So likewise shall my heavenly Father do also unto you, if ye from your hearts forgive not every one his brother their trespasses.

Mark 2:1-12

And again he entered into Capernaum after some days; and it was noised that he was in the house. [2] And straightway many were gathered together, insomuch that there was no room to receive them, no not so much as about the door: and he preached the word unto them. [3] And they come unto him, bringing one sick of the palsy, which was borne of four. [4] And when they could not come nigh unto him for the press, they uncovered the roof where he was: and when they had broken it up, they let down the bed wherein the sick of the palsy lay. [5] When Jesus saw their faith, he said unto the sick of the palsy, Son thy sins be forgiven thee. [6] But there were certain of the scribes sitting there, and reasoning in their hearts, [7] Why doth this man thus speak blasphemies? who can forgive sins but God only? [8] And immediately when Jesus perceived in his spirit that they so reasoned within themselves, he said unto them, Why reason ye these things in your hearts? [9] Whether is it easier to say to the sick of the palsy, Thy sins be forgiven thee; or to say, Arise, and take up thy bed, and walk? [10] But that ye may know that the Son of man hath power on earth to forgive sins, (he saith to the sick of the palsy,) [11] I say unto thee, Arise, and take up thy bed, and go thy way into thine house. [12] And immediately he arose, took up the bed, and went forth before them all; insomuch that they were all amazed, and glorified God, saying, We never saw it on this fashion.

A young man and his father were having a conversation and in the midst of the conversation the young man asked his father, "Daddy, why does Jesus talk so much about forgiveness?" Of course, in his view forgiveness was for the weak. His father thought for a while and then said, "Son, why do you ask?" The son told him of the things evil people do to those who walk in the way of forgiveness. "It is easy to run over those who believe in that kind of stuff" said the young man. While the father paused, the young man continued, "People will think twice before attacking you if they know that you will not think twice to fight back." The father looked at him and asked, "Do you think it takes a stronger person to hurt someone back or to forgive?" The son, of course, had no doubt that the strong fight back and the weak forgive. The father continued, "Son" he said, "I think Jesus speaks so much of forgiveness because it's something we all need." In fact, the father proceeded to point out that the forgiver is stronger and the greater. He then proceeded to tell his son that if forgiveness was for the weak, then God must be the most weak being in the universe because God forgives over and over again. Not only is forgiveness a sign of strength, it is a divine characteristic. It is here in forgiveness that we as human beings approximate the divine more closely. For in forgiveness, mercy, love, compassion and peace coexist. In fact, in the act of forgiveness the seed of righteousness is planted that grows into peace and life.

The story is told of a young woman who cursed out her parents and left home. She wandered in many places all over the country. Eventually, she became destitute and wandered into a city mission where she heard the Gospel, repented of her sins, and became a Christian. She then wanted to return home and beg forgiveness of her parents, but she did not think they would accept her. Finally, getting enough courage, she made her way back home. When she arrived, she found a big sign out front which read, "All is forgiven, daughter. Welcome home." In this act, the parents of this young woman displayed the strength of God in them. They participated in the divine miracle of forgiveness which God performs everyday.

Forgiveness is a divine act based on God's grace. In the act of forgiveness, God chooses not to remember the sins of God's people who come to God in faith. When the Lord God forgives us we are no longer judged for sins which we have confessed. Such sins are removed by God's own self-giving act. This self-giving act is seen more clearly in the life, death, and resurrection of our Lord Jesus Christ. From His divine act of sacrificial self-giving and mercy grows the imperative for human forgiveness. Knowledge of this divine magnanimity must create in human beings the willingness to release others from the guilt and penalty of offenses already confessed. Offenses committed by our fellow human beings then become opportunities for the display of this divine characteristic of forgiveness.

There are two sides to forgiveness as it relates to our sins against God. There is a divine and human side. First from the divine side, it is something which God bestows upon us who follow Jesus the Messiah. Divinely speaking, it is the act of God's mercy and grace. This act of forgiveness moves us from our constant warring with God to friendship with God. We move from being at odds with God to entering into a peaceful and righteous relationship with our God. Forgiveness then is that act of God which results in our being moved from bondage and condemnation to freedom and righteousness which is radiated from the heart of an infinitely loving God. Through the act of forgiveness, God works in us to free us from both sin and guilt.

Forgiveness cannot be forced or coerced. It must grow from an intrinsic sense of freedom of the forgiver. Forgiveness is an act of free-will. Through a free act, one releases another from their obligation. One who is forgiven no longer has to repay a debt. Through this free act of forgiveness, one no longer has to restore what has been destroyed. When one is forgiven one may not be required to reconcile a wrong committed against the one who has been affronted. Forgiveness does not imply denial of an offense. Rather it is the ability to acknowledge the offense with all its pain, yet to be willing to let it go and refuse to enact punishment for it. It's the willingness to let healing supercede hurt. It is the act of refusal in which the offended will not allow a barrier to develop between him and other persons who have done him wrong. Forgiveness is a divine attribute that God shares with people everywhere. Healing energies are released when forgiveness is accepted and passed on. The other side of this thing we call forgiveness is that it has to be received. God forgives human beings, but the human person must reach out to receive and experience this forgiveness before it becomes efficacious in his or her life.

The Hebrew and Greek languages have several words that translate into English as "forgive." Some of the Hebrew words mean to pardon, to cover, to let pass, take away, wash, hide, and purify. Some of the Greek words mean to send away, leave, omit, and to let go. It is noteworthy that divine forgiveness is distinctively a biblical concept. The gods of the Greek and surrounding nations were unforgiving and vindictive. They had no understanding of what it meant to forgive each other, neither did they even conceive of forgiving human beings. When they did, it was laden with so many conditions that one might as well not be forgiven. The idea is more prominent in Judaism and

Christianity than in any other religions of the world. The Bible places great emphasis on the importance of and the need for forgiveness. The Hebrew Christian tradition not only speaks of the need for divine forgiveness but also underscores the need for horizontal forgiveness—human to human. This divine attribute of forgiveness is seen in the way God forgives Israel in the wilderness over and over again. The fact that Israel was not destroyed in the wilderness can only be attributed to the fact that forgiveness is rooted in the very nature of the Lord God revealed in the Bible.

Jesus, the Son of God, embodies the meaning of divine forgiveness. At several points in the Gospels, Jesus illustrates the principle of forgiveness. In Matthew 18:21-25, he uses the forgiveness of financial debt as example. It is not surprising that Jesus uses money to teach us the true meaning of forgiveness. Indeed, money is the one major barrier to our ability to forgive others. At another point, He uses the return of a prodigal son to his father as exemplification of the principle. In all of these examples, Jesus show us that forgiveness is essential to any true understanding of the kingdom of God.

The principle of forgiveness speaks directly to the human tendency to offend and the ever-present problems of misunderstandings resulting from harsh words, or even the physical abuse to which we subject one another. What is unique about the scriptural ideal of forgiveness is that it is fundamentally a quality of God's personality that those who follow God must also possess.

The Bible is very clear that we as human beings are constantly living in opposition to God's creative good-will, holiness, righteousness, and justice. Our human tendency to rebel continually affronts God. Even God's efforts of merciful outreach meets with human tantrums and God's intention for divine restoration and fellowship is rejected. From the beginning, we have turned to our own ways. We, by our very nature, are creatures in need of forgiveness. Our need for forgiveness manifests itself in various ways. In Genesis 3, Adam and Eve deliberately go against the command of God their Creator. They choose to walk in their limited intellectual capacity rather than walk in divine wisdom. They choose self-will and self-satisfaction instead of divine pleasure. This act of disobedience results in guilt, and the guilt in turn saturates their very nature, forcing a separation between all human beings and God. Thus, human beings lose the capacity to have true fellowship with God (Genesis 3:8; 23-24). Because of Adam and Eve's original sin, their progeny now live under the wrath of God.

Various passages of the Scripture paint the picture of our need for forgiveness. The truth is that we have become unholy (Psalm 51:2; 7; 10) by virtue of the fact that our very nature is saturated by sinfulness (Psalm 51:5). We as natural born sinners cannot be right or holy without God's help. As sinners, we are cut off from the very source of true life, even our God. We need forgiveness in order to be restored to our God. But this affront upon God does not only affect how we relate to God, it also affects how we relate to one another. We take the same pugnacious orientation we have towards God into our relationships with one another. We hurt, we kill, and we maim each other in self-centered acts. We even go so far as to spite those who are dearest with us. Thus, we need forgiveness not just from God but also from our fellow human beings.

The primary means of obtaining forgiveness in all known religions is through sacrifice. In the Hebrew Christian tradition, the sacrifice seals a covenant relationship established by God. In fact, from the beginning we can find this sacrificial principle. Some scholars of the Bible find the first example of this sacrifice in the fact that God clothed Adam and Eve with animal skin. We find this more explicitly illustrated in the Passover before God brought His people out of Egypt. The sacrificial system expressed the dynamics of the sinful human condition. The bringing of the animal to sacrifice showed the sense of need, the laying of the hands on the living sacrifice symbolized identification of the person with the sacrifice, as did the releasing of the life of the animal through the sacrificial slaughter. Emphasis on an unblemished sacrifice stressed the holiness of God contrasted with human sinfulness. The forgiveness of God, channeled through the sacrificial offering, was an act of mercy freely bestowed by God, not purchased by the one bringing the offering. The one needing forgiveness had no merit in himself but must depend on something or someone provided by God.

The one who needs forgiveness must also act in a repentant way. Repentance as requisite to divine forgiveness can be seen in various passages in the Scripture (Psalm 51; Isaiah 1:10-18; Jeremiah 7:21-26; Hosea 6:6; Amos 5:21-27). Someone might argue that this idea of repentance nullifies the need for sacrifice. However, this concept of repentance as the principle that activates forgiveness in one's particular circumstance deepens the understanding of the sacrifice. While forgiveness was present in the Old Testament, it seems mainly associated with acts committed by human beings rather than with the idea of human beings as natural sinners. Thus, repentance could not provide the "once-and-for-all forgiveness" later provided in the Person of the Messiah. In fact, the New Testament insists that the fact that it had to be repeated over and over means that it was not efficacious (Hebrews 10:1-4).

Jesus Christ as the Son of the living God mediates forgiveness perfectly (Romans 3:25; Hebrews 10:11-12). Jesus indeed sees Himself as one whose task and being involved in the act of effecting forgiveness. It is important to Him that He be seen and understood in terms of the provision of forgiveness. Jesus declares that He can forgive sin (Mark 2:1-12; John 8:2-11). Furthermore, He speaks of His death as the means of providing the one thing that human beings needed most. Forgiveness—true forgiveness—must come from the very being of God. It is provided for the sins of humanity by God Himself in Christ Jesus (Hebrews 9:14; Romans 3:25; Acts 13:38). Divine forgiveness is available freely to everyone who truly repents (Luke 23:39-43; John 8:2-11). This is the good news of the promised new age: that God has provided a permanent way to forgiveness and peace (Acts 2:36-39; 3:13-19, 26; 5:31).

It is not a question of God's ability or desire to forgive, but rather a matter of human willingness to meet the conditions for forgiveness. The background of the saying was the controversy between Jesus and the religious leaders of His time. The Pharisees refused to see the merciful hand of God in the work of Jesus, and rather attributed His miracles to the power of Satan. For such who deliberately closed their minds to the work and invitation of God through Christ to draw near, repent, and receive forgiveness, there is no hope. But the fault lies with them, rather than with God.

As a part of His teaching about the human need for forgiveness and the means of receiving it, Jesus speaks of the human dimension of forgiveness. A firm condition for the receiving of God's forgiveness is the willingness to forgive others. In the Lord's Prayer (Matthew 6:12; Luke 11:4) and the parable of the unforgiving servant (Matthew 18:12-35), Jesus clearly indicated

such is the case: "But if ye forgive not men their trespasses, neither will your Father forgive your trespasses" (Matthew 6:15).
The forgiven life must become the forgiving life. Human forgiveness reflects our experience and understanding of divine forgiveness. Love, not wooden rules, governs forgiveness (Matthew
18:21-22). Jesus powerfully demonstrated this teaching on the
cross, as He asked for forgiveness for His executioners (Luke
23:34). Paul reminded the church at Ephesus of both the
grounds of their forgiveness and the basis on which they must
forgive one another (Ephesians 4:32).

Peter raises the question of the limit to forgiveness. Perhaps,
prompted by the teaching of forgiveness, Peter approached Jesus
and asked a follow-up question about forgiveness, using a practical example. In the four listings of the names of the twelve disciples, Peter's name is always first (Matthew 10:2-4; Mark 3:16;
Luke 6:14-16; Acts 1:13). So it is not surprising that he asked
Jesus the question that provides the setting for today's parable.
And we can suppose that he was asking for at least some of the
other disciples as well. They had probably already discussed the
"forgiveness question" and decided that forgiving somebody
seven times was actually more than could be expected.

The issue was not referring to the decision of the church, but
personal forgiveness (compare Matthew 6:14-15; Mark 11:25;
Luke 17:3-4). "How oft shall my brother sin against me, and I
forgive him?" Peter asked and interjected, "Till seven times?" In
the rabbinical community, the agreement was that a brother
might be forgiven for a repeated sin three times. After that,
there was no forgiveness. Why did Peter come up with seven?
Was he trying to be magnanimous by suggesting seven times?
Alternatively, was he following a common thread of the use of
seven in the Bible? It is generally suggested that the number

seven indicates completeness, using the Genesis creation account as the basis (Genesis 2:1-3; compare Leviticus 4:6; 26:21; Numbers 19:4; Joshua 6:4; Proverbs 24:16). The Greek phrase translated "my brother" is *adelphos* and could be a blood-related sibling or anyone of the same religious society, as in verse 15. Jesus then said not "seven times," but "until seventy times seven." In Luke 17:3b-4, Jesus said, "If your brother sins . . . against you seven times in a day, and seven times comes back to you and says, 'I repent,' forgive him."

What does Jesus mean by seventy times seven? Reading it with a Greek or English understanding, it equals 70x7 (or 490). But with the Roman numerals LXX, which has a rendering in the Hebrew understanding, it means 70+7 (or 77). Jesus alluded to Genesis 4:24, transforming Lamech's revenge into a principle for forgiveness. In this context, Jesus is not setting 490 or 77 times as the upper limit for forgiveness, but teaches that frequency or quantity should not qualify regarding forgiveness. The parable that follows vividly illustrates the extent, rather than the frequency, of forgiveness. It further shows that we are forgiven far more than we can ever forgive.

It is common knowledge that in rabbinic literature the idea was "three strikes and you are out." According to some ancient rabbis, an act of affront can only be tolerated three times. The disciples had already learned that Jesus usually required more of them than the rabbis did. So they doubled the official figure, added one more time and arrived at seven as a good maximum number. Peter presented the question to Jesus, probably expecting Jesus' total agreement and a compliment for his wisdom. Peter's question was, "Lord, if my brother keeps on sinning against me, how many times do I have to forgive him?" And then before Jesus could answer, he presented the number he and the disciples had probably discussed and agreed on. "Seven times?" (v. 21, TEV).

To their utter amazement, Jesus said, "No!" The disciples probably felt puzzled and relieved. Had they overestimated? Maybe Jesus agreed with the rabbis. Or maybe four, five, or six times was enough to forgive. Then Jesus put their minds at ease or at greater unease. He said that seven times was not enough times to forgive. In the kingdom of God, forgiveness must not be denied because of the frequency of the offense. According to Jesus' principle of forgiveness, if a brother from the 'hood stole something out of your house every week for a year, four months, and five days, you were supposed to forgive him each time. If the "brother" stole your radio, CD or video player, television set, and whatever else he could get his hands on, and you caught him with the goods, and he said, "Man, like I'm sorry, please forgive me"—as a disciple, a Christian, a follower of Christ, the disciples and we, as believers are supposed to forgive the brother (or sister)! Can you see the disciples standing there? Amazed. Speechless. Flabbergasted! Looking at Jesus with blown minds and open mouths?

Jesus saw their dismay and said, "Let me tell you a story." Jesus went on to illustrate His point with a parable. Since Jesus required His disciples to forgive those who offended them, the kingdom of heaven could be compared with a king who dealt with his debtors. "The kingdom of heaven" means the sovereignty of God over the universe and is paralleled with the kingdom of God. The kingdom of heaven is personified by God, who was represented in the parable by an earthly king. Those in the kingdom are the servants (*douloi*, literally slaves) serving a great king. The servants may include high-ranking officials in a huge colonial empire, since the amount of money was a huge sum (v.

24). The king decides to take account (Greek *sunairo*, literally means to compare accounts). (Compare with Matthew 25:19.)

Jesus explained how the principle of forgiveness operates in the kingdom of heaven that He had talked about before (v. 23). Jesus said, "Once there was a king who decided to make an audit of his accounts receivables. His bookkeeper discovered that the king had loaned 10,000 talents or about ten million dollars" (v. 24, LB). The king told the bookkeeper to send the man a statement telling him to come in and bring this account up-to-date or prepare to go to jail. And the king instructed, "Tell him if he can't pay he must bring in a list of everything he owns, along with his wife and children, because they are going to jail too" (v. 25, paraphrased). The servant followed the king's instructions and appeared before the king with his account books and his wife and children.

Some people have estimated the dollar value of one talent (Greek *talanton*) of gold to be about $29,085 and that 10,000 talents would be approximately $290,085,000. A talent of silver is estimated at $1,920 and 10,000 would be $19,920,000. An idea of the size of the debt can be grasped when compared with the donation for the construction of the temple where David gave 3,000 talents of gold and 7,000 talents of silver. The princes donated 5,000 talents of gold and 10,000 talents of silver (1 Chronicles 29:4, 7). In today's currency value, with the rising price of precious metals coupled with inflation, these figures would run into billions or trillions of dollars. However, the amount was used in Matthew 18:28 to compare the extent of the forgiveness and mercy shown to the servant-debtor and the amount owed to him by his fellow servant for whom he showed no mercy.

The servant appeared before the king and was not able to pay the king what he owed. The king decreed that he and his family (his wife and children), with all their possessions, be sold into slavery in order to recover the debt. The practice of being sold for a debt was consistent with the practice in the Old Testament (Leviticus 25:39; 2 Kings 4:1). It was the most severe and humiliating punishment for anyone to endure. The aim of selling the entire family was not to recover the full the amount owed, but to punish. If top price for a slave would fetch one talent or less, as some suggest, then the total price of the family would not be enough to cover the debt. This was a punishment and such slaves, therefore, must be freed in the year of jubilee, every 50 years (see Leviticus 25:10, 28).

The servant, desperate and hopeless, fell down on his knees and pleads for time. "Be patient with me, I will pay back everything," he said. The phrase "fell down, and worshipped him" (Greek *prosekunei*) is the imperfect tense of the Greek

verb *prosekuneo*, which is to go on one's knees, to kneel before someone, or to prostrate or.eself in homage (Matthew 18:27; 20:20). The servant falling down and worshiping him, served a

dual purpose: paying homage was a sign of a desperate plea to his lord (master). This honor was reserved for kings and people of higher positions in the society. The king looked at him and was "moved with compassion" (8:27) seeing his desperation, help-lessness, and his inability to pay such a huge amount, his lord forgave him the whole amount he owed. To be "moved with compassion" (Greek *splagchnistheis*) is to have sympathy or to pity. The lord was moved with pity, and he forgave the "debt" (Greek *daneion*), which is better-translated "loan." The lord treated the debt as a bad loan and wrote it off. The servant did-n't have to pay it back. He was totally freed from any obligation.

The phrase, "loosed him" (Greek *luo*) is to untie, and suggests that he was arrested and bound when they brought him before the king, and now had been completely released (set free) when the lord forgave him. In this case, the debt was treated, at first, as embezzlement; but then the king canceled it, as a bad loan, and forgave the servant. Verses 28-30 give a complete opposite picture of verses 24-27. The servant who received mercy from his master for the huge amount of "money" owed, showed no mercy to his fellow servant who owed a few talents. Jesus linked the preceding story with the conjunction "but," which immedi-ately struck a note of contrast with and introduced the next phrase of the parable.

Having been forgiven his debt, the servant probably rushed out of the king's court with a celebration of joy. He found anoth-er servant, lower in rank than he, in the outer courtyard, who owed him 100 "pence" (i.e., 100 denarii, NIV). According to Drake's Annotated Reference Bible, one pence is equivalent to 17õ; one hundred pence is $17.00. The amount might be high in their standard, but very insignificant compared with the amount forgiven him. Immediately, he mercilessly grabbed the servant by the throat choking him, and demanded that the debt be paid. His fellow servant pleaded that he be patient with him, saying he would eventually pay him everything he owed. The similarity of the plea (v. 29) to his own plea to the king (v. 26) did not move this unforgiving man. Rather than show mercy, he had him thrown into debtor's prison and ordered that he be remanded there until he paid the amount in full. The other ser-vants, who witnessed what had happened, were distressed because of such cruelty, and went out to report to the master. The phrase "they were very sorry" is the Greek phrase *elupethe-san sphodra*, which means "greatly grieved." They were not merely sorry, but were severely touched in the heart to the point of grieving. They were not merely sympathetic, they empathized with the fellow servant, and showed it by reporting it to their master. The word rendered "told" (*diesaphesan* from *dia-saphew*) is a strong verb which means to explain, or to narrate, and is used only twice in the New Testament, here and in Matthew 13:36 as the word "declared." They explained in detail what the unforgiving servant had done.

On hearing this report, the master called in the unforgiving servant, reprimanded him, denounced him for what he had done, and called him a "wicked servant." He asked him why he could not forgive his fellow servant as he was forgiven. Of course, he had no answer, and the master expected no answer. There was no amount of explanation that would exonerate him for his wicked action. The master was so upset that, instead of selling him (v. 25), he turned him over to the tormentors. In the Greek language *basanisteis* means torturers, not merely "jailers" (NIV). The word refers to jailers who have charge of the pris-oners and who torture them when asked to do so. The servant was to be tortured in prison until he paid back all that he owed, which was impossible.

Jesus concluded the parable by comparing the reaction of the master to the unmerciful servant with what God would do to those who did not forgive others their trespasses. This parable demonstrates the necessity of forgiveness and how we should treat one another. Jesus advocates that we forgive from our "hearts" those who have wronged us. "From the heart," here means genuine and sincere forgiveness. Concluding His teaching on prayer, Jesus told His disciples that they ought to forgive others as they have been forgiven, lest our "Father will not forgive your sins" (Matthew 6:12, 14-15). This parable does not deal with frequency, but illustrates the extent of forgiveness we have received from our heavenly Father through the death of His Son. We are forgiven far more than we can ever forgive.

Certain questions arise from this parable. When do we forgive our brothers: before or after they have confessed? Do we have to forgive whether they repent or not? What does it mean to love your enemies and do good to those who hate you? As Christians, we have been forgiven much, and we should forgive much. Jesus' parable points to the fact that we all owe God an unpayable debt. We have all been big spenders with the graces and talents God has given us. We have taken from God but have not been willing to pay. Some of us tend to think that we owe God very little. Whether we think we owe God little or much, we all have one problem: we cannot pay back the debt we owe God. There are not enough resources in the world to cover the account developed by our continuous affront as individuals and as a race in the presence God. We must turn then to the mercy of God. God will then have to reach out to us in mercy.

You Are Forgiven

The story of the paralytic illustrates the willingness of the Lord to forgive those who come to Him. It is true that the four who carried their sick friend to Jesus were definitely looking for a physical miracle. They were probably a part of the huge crowd that gathered in front of Mrs. Mother-in-Law's house where Jesus might have stayed when in Capernaum (Mark 1:3-34). All of a sudden they looked at each other, remembered their friend, and all headed at the same time in the same direction. They were going to get their friend to Jesus. They got to his house, picked him up—sleeping mat and all—and took him to the house where Jesus was. When they got there they couldn't get in. There were "wall-to-wall people"—inside and outside. Jesus was telling them how much God loved them and wanted them to love each other (Mark 2:2). They perhaps tried to push their way in, beg their way in, and maybe even pay their way in, but with no success. Is it not amazing how we tend to stand in the way of people who are coming to Jesus for forgiveness? Why will we not give way so others can receive forgiveness? We tend to say you are forgiven but you must bear the consequence. How is that forgiveness? It seems that it is our need to keep others under the shackle of guilt which gives birth to such semantic nonsense.

There are those who will like to get beyond our hindrance to Jesus in order to hear Him speak forgiveness to their soul. But many inside and outside of the church would rather that the sinner keep their pain. We are often guilty of constantly reminding those who seek forgiveness of how evil they are rather than pointing to how merciful God is. Why do we suppose that God has a hard time dealing with sinners just because we do? Why is it that we think that God cannot look beyond another's failure because we cannot? But God bless the one who has people who are willing to carry them when they cannot carry themselves. Here we find a brother who, though every avenue through which he could get the place of his forgiveness was closed, found others who believed enough in his healing to carry him to the place where he could receive it.

They checked out the sides and the back. No way. Suddenly one of the Faith-Filled Four said, "Up!" "Up? The roof?" "Yes, the roof. It's the only way." So up they carried the Brother to the roof. It was flat and made out of tree-limb cross-beams covered with a kind of straw and sun-baked mud. They quickly calculated where Jesus was sitting in the room below and broke through the part of the roof above His head. Then they attached some homemade ropes to the sides of the sleeping mat and let the Brother down right at Jesus' feet. Jesus looked out at the crowd, up at the Faith-Filled Four, and down at Brother. He smiled and said, "Man, your sins are forgiven." Then after a little mental dialogue with the Law School faculty, He said to the man, "Pick up your mat and go on home." And, of course, the paralyzed Brother jumped up, did a little joy dance, and ran out of the house with his mat under his arm. The crowd went wild with delight. They praised God for caring so much for human beings that He would send Jesus to help them.

Can you hear Him say, "You are forgiven"? If it was not for fact that this is God's first statement when we approach Him, I believe we would be consumed in His presence. The man did not even have to ask. Jesus just knew what he needed. Though his body may have been battered, Jesus looked within him and saw that his soul was even more battered by the waves of human sinfulness. He could have healed his body and he would appeared to be well on the outside, but the guilt of his sin would continue to eat away at the center of his being. He needed to hear "Your sins are forgiven." Sometimes, like this man, we are so bruised and battered by our sins that we cannot get ourselves to the place of healing. We as believers must be willing to carry those who are weak and unable to reach out on the shoulders of prayer. Those of us who are strong at the present moment must be willing to bear the burden of those who at the moment may be weak. We must intercede for them until in the presence of the Master they hear the needed affirmation, "Your sins are forgiven." That four-word sentence changed this man's life forever. But here is the good news for you and I to celebrate: Even now Jesus is speaking to you, broken though you may be—"You are forgiven." He is looking directly at you and speaking His forgiveness into your soul—your lying is forgiven, your cheating is forgiven, your stealing is forgiven, your betrayal is forgiven. Others may be looking at you with condemnation, but He looks at you with compassion—your sins are forgiven.

Human beings may speak harshly to you in self-righteousness—but listen, listen to His sweet voice as He says "Your sins are forgiven." He is the lamb of God who takes away your sins. He is standing right here, right there where you are speaking into your sin scarred soul. He is speaking to spirits dehydrated by the hot sun of sin's wilderness—"Your sins are forgiven." What a relief to know that all my sins are nailed to His cross. I can hear him say to me "Your sins are forgiven." Silence! all you voices of condemnation. I hear my Lord's whisper, "You are forgiven." I, even I am forgiven, healed, and restored. Oh sweet consolation, oh comfort sublime that I stand forgiven in His presence. Jesus did not only say to me, "You are forgiven," but He took my place and acted out my pardon as He stretched His hands out upon the rugged Roman cross and said, "You are forgiven." Ten-thousand strings upon ten-thousand voices cannot express the gratitude of this sinner's relief at the sound of that sentence, "Your sins are forgiven." Yes this is good news, I am forgiven and my debt has been paid. So I go out to forgive all who owe me. Lord help me!

Chapter Nine

JESUS IS MORE THAN ENOUGH

BASED ON MARK 6:30-44

Mark 6:30-44

And the apostles gathered themselves together unto Jesus, and told him all things, both what they had done, and what they had taught. ³¹ And he said unto them, Come ye yourselves apart into a desert place, and rest a while: for there were many coming and going, and they had no leisure so much as to eat. ³² And they departed into a desert place by ship privately. ³³ And the people saw them departing, and many knew him, and ran afoot thither out of all cities, and outwent them, and came together unto him. ³⁴ And Jesus, when he came out, saw much people, and was moved with compassion toward them, because they were as sheep not having a shepherd: and he began to teach them many things. ³⁵ And when the day was now far spent, his disciples came unto him, and said, This is a desert place, and now the time is far passed: ³⁶ Send them away, that they may go into the country round about, and into the villages, and buy themselves bread: for they have nothing to eat. ³⁷ He answered and said unto them, Give ye them to eat. And they say unto him, Shall we go and buy two hundred pennyworth of bread, and give them to eat? ³⁸ He saith unto them, How many loaves have ye? go and see. And when they knew, they say, Five, and two fishes. [39] And he commanded them to make all sit down by companies upon the green grass. [40] And they sat down in ranks, by hundreds, and by fifties. [41] And when he had taken the five loaves and the two fishes, he looked up to heaven, and blessed, and brake the loaves, and gave them to his disciples to set before them; and the two fishes divided he among them all. [42] And they did all eat, and were filled.

[43] And they took up twelve baskets full of the fragments, and of the fishes. [44] And they that did eat of the loaves were about five thousand men.

Has your plant shut down? Has your company moved? Has your department been phased out? Have you been laid off? Are you wondering how you will pay the house note? The car note? How will you pay the ever-increasing utility bills? With so many federal funds having been slashed, will your son or daughter be able to go to college? Is there any help anywhere? Do you need a "multiply supply" miracle? Jesus is still in the business of meeting the needs of His people. There are those who through experience have become convinced of Jesus' ability to supply their needs, and are determined to trust Him to supply their needs consistent with His promises.

Almost all Galileans were aware of Jesus' ministry. The common people were so impressed with the miracles they had witnessed that they were ready to make Jesus their king. The Jewish leaders were very upset, and Herod had become concerned about the popularity of Jesus. The situation was critical. Christ had not yet completed His ministry. He was not ready for a confrontation. Therefore He withdrew from the limelight (*The Wycliffe Bible Commentary*, Moody Press, 1968, page 1001). John 6:4 tells us that the miraculous feeding of the 5,000 took place just before the time of the Passover. History indicates that

it was exactly one year before Jesus was crucified. The place where the people came to hear Jesus was in a "desert place" (v. 35). This is not a desert place as we know it, but a deserted place (*The Wycliffe Bible Commentary*, page 1001).

There are three main characters in this "multiply supply" drama: Jesus, the disciples, and the "crowd." Mark records that the apostles returned to Jesus from their tour (6:30). The word "apostle" is appropriately used here because the word means one sent forth on a mission, and the disciples were indeed returning from a mission on which Christ had sent them (*The Wycliffe Bible Commentary*, page 1001). Jesus could see that the disciples were tired. He suggested they get away for some rest. So they left by boat for a quieter place (v. 32). The people apparently antic-ipated where Christ and His disciples were going and went ahead of them to the shores of Lake Gennesaret. The crowd was already there when Jesus and His disciples landed. Obviously, Jesus and His disciples were not going to enjoy the rest they had planned. Christ was not annoyed; instead "He had pity on the people" (v. 34). He recognized that they did not have a spiritu-al leader (v. 34).

In this passage, we see Jesus perform the miracle of divine pro-vision (Mark 6:30-43). The message of the miracle is still the same as it was for the Children of Israel in the wilderness. God is the source of supply for all the needs of those who trust in divine providence. May we learn to apply the truth of this mir-acle in our everyday life.

This miracle is often referred to as "The Feeding of the Five Thousand." Matthew 14:21 indicates that only the men were counted, but women and children also were present. When allowance is made for the possible number of women and chil-dren, the total number fed could exceed ten thousand (*Victor Handbook of Bible Knowledge*, V. Gilbert Beers, Victor Books, 1981.) When Jesus met the people who had followed Him to the shores of Lake Gennesaret, He recognized that they had no spir-itual leader, and "he taught them many things they needed to know" (v. 34, LB). Mark records that late in the afternoon the people became hungry. When the disciples discovered that the people had "nothing to eat," they wanted to send them away to buy food. But Jesus commanded the disciples to feed the people (v. 37). The disciples immediately inquired of Jesus, "With what?" (v. 37, LB). The disciples objected to feeding the people because Jesus' request did not seem practical to them. "It would take a fortune to buy food for all this crowd" (v. 37, LB).

Jesus, perceiving their helplessness, asked the disciples to do what He knew they could do—take an inventory of the food available and ask the people to sit down in groups. The disciples brought the two fish and five loaves of bread to Jesus and asked the people to sit in groups of 50 and 100. Now Jesus did what only He could do—He took food which would normally feed only a few people and fed 5,000 men plus women and children. Does Jesus ever expect us to do something He knows we cannot do? The food that Jesus provided (fish and bread) was common food. The Bible has promised those who trust Him will be fed (Psalm 23; 37:3; Matthew 6:31-33). He has not promised a feast—just food.

This miracle was not only an expression of Jesus' compassion toward the hungry. Some Bible teachers believe it was also intended to teach the disciples some deeper truth. "The state of righteousness in the life to come was pictured by the Jews as a great banquet presided over by the Messiah (Isaiah 25:6; Luke 13:29; 14:15; 22:16, 30). Jesus may have desired this 'feast' to be envisaged as an anticipation of that banquet." A slightly different meaning is given in John's Gospel. John depicted Christ as the Bread of Life offering Himself as "food" to the famished world to which He had descended from heaven.(A *New Testament Commentary*, G. C. D. Howley, F. F. Bruce and H. L. Ellison.)

The feeding of the five thousand is considered by some Bible scholars to be the turning point in Jesus' career. Jesus performed this miracle in the Spring—the time of Passover. This was exactly the time of the year the Jews expected the Messiah to manifest Himself. Also, the Jews expected the Messiah to repeat the Old Testament miracle of feeding them manna; they expected a second Moses at a great apocalyptic feast. Consequently, when Jesus miraculously fed the crowd, they were ready to make Jesus their king (*A Survey of the New Testament*, Robert Gundry). Jesus knew that this was not the purpose of the miracle. He dismissed the crowd and sent the disciples across the lake. He went into the mountains for private devotions (v. 46).

This parable suggests three important questions. The first question is, "What do you have?" In the miracle, Jesus knew how much food was available, but He wanted the disciples to determine how much food they had. Jesus asks us "to go and consider how little we have, that we may properly estimate the greatness of His help" (F. B. Meyer, p. 424). Have you taken inventory? Do you know what and how much you have?

The second question is, "What do you need?" The disciples took inventory, they knew how much food they had. What they didn't know was how much food they needed, but they were sure they needed more than they had. When the disciples told Jesus how much food was available, they did not ask Jesus to explain or discuss with them how He would feed so many with so little. They simply gave the two fish and five loaves of bread to Jesus and waited for Him to act. Have you given your need to Jesus? Have you asked Him to supply *whatever* is needed? Have you given what you have to Jesus so He can multiply your gift for the benefit of others?

The third question is, "When do you need it?" Note that the disciples did not ask for food until food was needed. And Jesus met the need *when* the need occurred. Jesus taught His disciples to pray, "Give us *this day* (emphasis added) our daily bread" (Matthew 6:11). Opinions about the meaning of the word "daily" vary. Some Bible scholars define it as necessary for existence; others define it as for the coming day (*The Wycliffe Bible Commentary*, page 939). Either definition implies supply will arrive *when needed.* Are you asking Jesus to supply needs you *think* you will have sometime in the future?

Dr. E. V. Hill a noted pastor and lecturer, related the story of how God performed a "multiply supply" miracle for him. He recalls the time when his mother took him to the Trailways bus station, gave him $5, and sent him off to Prairie View College. As he boarded the bus, his mother said to him, "I will be praying for you." Tuition was $80. When it was time to pay tuition, E. V. Hill's $5 had dwindled to $1.90. But he got into the tuition payment line anyway. While in the line, E. V. Hill recalls that the devil said to him, "Get out of the line, you don't have the money to pay your tuition." But he remembered the words of his mother, "I'll be praying for you." So he stayed in the line. Before it was his turn to pay his tuition, Dr. Drew, the president, touched him on the shoulder and said, "We have been looking for you all morning. We have a four-year scholarship for you with an additional $35 a month for spending."

Sometimes Jesus Christ does not supply just enough. "He is able to do exceeding abundantly above all that we ask or think" (Ephesians 3:20). There were 12 baskets full of food left after the feeding of the 5,000 plus. E. V. Hill received $35 more than he needed for tuition. Note that E. V. Hill did not receive the money he needed in the mail at home, at the bus station, nor even after he arrived at the school. He received the money when it was due—as he stood in the tuition line. Do you need a "multiply supply" miracle? Have you taken inventory of what you have? Have you brought what you have to Jesus? "Ye have not, because you ask not" (James 4:2). Have you *asked* Jesus to take care of your needs? Has the *time* arrived for the need to be met? "Rest in the Lord; wait patiently for him to act" (Psalm 37:7, LB).

Chapter Ten

JESUS IS THE LIGHT OF THE WORLD

BASED ON JOHN 9:1-11, 35-41

JOHN 9:1-11

And as Jesus passed by, he saw a man which was blind from his birth. ²And his disciples asked him, saying, Master, who did sin, this man, or his parents, that he was born blind? ³Jesus answered, Neither hath this man sinned, nor his parents: but that the works of God should be made manifest in him. ⁴I must work the works of him that sent me, while it is day: the night cometh, when no man can work. ⁵As long as I am in the world, I am the light of the world. ⁶When he had thus spoken, he spat on the ground, and made clay of the spittle, and he anointed the eyes of the blind man with the clay, ⁷And said unto him, Go, wash in the pool of Siloam, (which is by interpretation, Sent.) He went his way therefore, and washed, and came seeing. ⁸The neighbours therefore, and they which before had seen him that he was blind, said, Is not this he that sat and begged? ⁹Some said, This is he: others said, He is like him: but he said, I am he. ¹⁰Therefore said they unto him, How were thine eyes opened? ¹¹He answered and said, A man that is called Jesus made clay, and anointed mine eyes, and said unto me, Go to the pool of Siloam, and wash: and I went and washed, and I received sight.

John 9:35-41

Jesus heard that they had cast him out; and when he had found him, he said unto him, Dost thou believe on the Son of God? [36] *He answered and said, Who is he, Lord, that I might believe on him?* [37] *And Jesus said unto him, Thou hast both seen him, and it is he that talketh with thee.* [38] *And he said, Lord, I believe. And he worshipped him.* [39] *And Jesus said, For judgment I am come into this world, that they which see not might see; and that they which see might be made blind.* [40] *And some of the Pharisees which were with him heard these words, and said unto him, Are we blind also?* [41] *Jesus said unto them, If ye were blind, ye should have no sin: but now ye say, We see; therefore your sin remaineth.*

One of the things we take for granted as human beings is light. We walk into a room, flip on a switch, and instantly the room is bathed in light. Light is important in our modern world because it helps us to see and, in some cases, would be impossible to live without. Scientists tell us that if we lost the light of the sun our earth would soon freeze and all life would die. However, as important as the sun, florescent, incandescent, and sunlight are, there is one "Light" more important than all of these—Jesus Christ, "the Light of the world" (John 9:5). Just as literal light brightens our path to keep us from stumbling, so the spiritual light from Christ enables us to know Him and walk in His paths.

Jesus is called the "Light of the world" because He "illuminates" our lives and helps us "see" spiritually where we are and where we need to be in God. Without Jesus, we are spiritually blind and grope around in the darkness of sin, which leads to destruction. With Jesus, we can find the path of righteousness and truth. He can take the "blinders" off our eyes and point us in the right direction. In this text, we will see two contrasting views of people who encounter the "Light of the world": those

who are physically blind and know they need Jesus' help, and those who are spiritually blind and think they can see. Jesus knows both very well and has a remedy for each.

In this chapter, Jesus makes another very bold assertion pertaining to His identity. Jesus tells His disciples "I am the light of the world" (John 9:5). He then proceeds to heal a man who had been born blind to demonstrate His statement. John chapter 9 has one of the most interesting episodes in the Gospels. Here, we find Jesus telling a blind man to wash in the pool of Siloam, and when he does, he receives his sight. After this miracle, the

blind man is seen by some who knew of his blindness but cannot believe that he is the same person. When the Jewish leaders
got wind of this, they were outraged, supposedly because the
healing was done on a Sabbath (John 9:14). What followed was
like a courtroom drama, with the Pharisees bringing one witness
after another before them to prove whether the formerly blind
man was actually born blind. They did not want to believe that
this could be true (John 9:13-24). So they brought the man
before them a second time to question him. The man did not
care about all the issues important to the Jews. His answer to
them was, "Whether [Jesus] be a sinner or no, I know not, one
thing I know, that whereas I was blind, now I see" (v. 25). This
should be our attitude as believers when doubtful situations
arise. We don't know all the whys and wherefores, but we do
know the One who has helped us through many adverse situations.

When Jesus heard all that had taken place, He revealed
Himself to the man as the Son of God (v. 35). The NIV has
"Son of Man," a name which was understood by many to refer
to God's anointed, the Messiah (Daniel 7:13). The man
believed and worshiped Him.

The lesson today takes up at the end of the previous one. Jesus
has just left the temple after "insulting" the Jews by claiming to
be "older" than Abraham (see John 8:51-58). They were so outraged they wanted to stone Him. But He left the temple "going
through the midst of them" (John 8:59). Somewhere near the
temple Jesus encounters a blind man. Even after such an ordeal
as being confronted by religious leaders, Jesus could not pass up
an opportunity to glorify God and manifest His power through
service to the less fortunate.

As Jesus and His disciples were walking along, they encountered a man who had been blind all of his life. When Jesus' disciples saw the man, they immediately questioned Jesus as to who sinned, the man or his parents, that he was born blind. The disciples assumed that sickness and suffering were directly attributed to sin. Therefore, if no one sinned, how could this man be born blind? Many times when we are confronted with challenges, we seek to find out the cause. People with disabilities often ask themselves what possible wrong they could have committed. We seek to account for all the mishaps in our lives as though our finite minds can actually understand them.

The thought of living in perpetual darkness and hearing others wonder what or whose sins caused his malady must have tormented the man. He, like many of us, needed light in his life to be free from guilt and despair. The disciples' ignorance led them to conclude that some crime must have been committed to warrant such cruel punishment. Jesus was always ready to teach and had an apt answer. "Neither hath this man sinned, nor his parents: But that the works of God should be made manifest in him" (v. 3). God, of course, knew before the world was created that this encounter of Jesus with the blind man would take place. Now the disciples were about to see a display of God's power through the hands of Jesus. If punishment were God's only aim, He would, undoubtedly, find justification in the sins of all humanity. But there are times when providence provides that God show Himself to His people.

While Jesus made it clear that neither this man nor his parents had sinned to cause this man to be born blind, we should not conclude that sin is never a cause of a malady. Jesus told the man whom He healed at the pool of Bethesda to stop sinning or else something worse would happen to him (5:14). When people abuse themselves with drugs or alcohol, they sometimes pay the high price of children being born with physical defects. However, the fact is we do not know whether some parental sin or genetic dysfunction is the basis of a malady, so we should never judge people who are born with defects. We should treat every person God created with respect and compassion.

Jesus was very focused on what He was about to do. Having finished His brief discourse, He healed the blind man to glorify the Father. Everything Jesus did during His earthly ministry had an instructive value to it, even the miracles He performed. Jesus prepared an eye salve made from clay and spittle, anointed the man's eyes with the salve, and then admonished him to go wash his eyes in the pool of Siloam (9:6-7a). The pool is located at the southeast corner of Jerusalem, where Hezekiah's tunnel channeled water inside the city walls from the Gihon Spring (*The Bible Knowledge Commentary*, Vol. 2, 1984, p. 307). When he did as he was told, the Gospel writer tells us that he returned to the place where he first encountered Jesus. Only now he could see.

Several principles are at work here. One is that God's ways are past finding out. A salve made from clay and human saliva would probably harm a man's eyes, not open them! Another principle is of hearing from God. The man could have been like some of us, so consumed with how we feel God should move in our lives that we can't hear Him when He speaks. A third principle is one of obedience. The man did not hesitate to do as he was commanded, no matter how unusual it may have seemed to him. When we follow the Light of Jesus and do as He commands us, we can't help but "see."

The man must have encountered some of his neighbors who were used to seeing him sitting around begging. Now he was up and about, and able to see those who may have made fun of him before. They subjected him to questions because they were not willing to accept the truth of his miracle. Whenever we are blessed unexpectedly, questions come from our "neighbors." First there may be disbelief that something miraculous could have occurred, and then there may be questions about whom or what is responsible for the change. The blind man's neighbors were no exception. How callous the man's neighbors must have been to question his identity and integrity. The way we sometimes view those with mangled bodies or disabilities was exemplified by the neighbors. Yet this man was not too proud to admit that he was once blind and a beggar. He eagerly admitted, "I am he" (v. 9). Those who have been touched by God in a special way are so absorbed by His mercy, love, and grace that they cannot keep these things to themselves. They don't mind letting the world know how their lives have changed.

The next issue for the onlookers was "How were your eyes opened?" (v. 10) People are always searching for answers but often cannot accept that which is true. If truth is not consistent with their beliefs, it is usually rejected. The man had a limited revelation of Jesus. He only heard His voice when he was told to wash in the pool, but he spoke what he knew to be true at the time. "A Man called Jesus made clay and anointed my eyes and said to me go to the pool of Siloam and wash. So I went and washed and received my sight" (v. 11). The man stated the facts as he knew them, no more and no less. Yet he received his sight because he did not hesitate to follow Jesus even though he could not see Him. If we would act on what we know of Jesus, we would receive much from Him ourselves. It isn't necessary to always have full knowledge of the Son of God. We should trust and obey what we do know of Him.

When God begins to enlighten us and we begin to receive

from Him, we can always expect opposition from the enemy. The world can never comprehend the light that Jesus brings us. They also cannot rationalize it away. But they will always try to hinder what God is doing in us. Because of the man's testimony about the miracle in his life, he was cast out of the synagogue by Jesus' enemies, the Pharisees (see John 9:24-34).

Jesus heard about the man's troubles and asked him if he believed in the Son of Man. The man was not sure who the Son was but he wanted to know His identity so that he could believe in Him. He seemed to have the faith and desire to believe. He needed divine revelation from Jesus to build up his faith. Once Jesus enlightened him spiritually, the man believed and worshiped Jesus (v. 38). Jesus is always willing to reveal Himself to those who would first express faith in Him. Then Jesus revealed His role as the One who had come to judge the world. He had come to reveal the hearts of people, to shed light where darkness had reigned. Jesus explained Himself by using a metaphor drawn from the blind man's miracle. Those who thought they had sight would be made blind by the truth of His doctrine. And those who were lost by man's standards would be able to see because of the illuminating presence of Jesus (v. 39).

There were some Pharisees who no doubt questioned the man standing nearby. They overheard Jesus' words and wanted to know if He felt they were blind. According to Jesus, if they had accepted Him as the Saviour, as the man did, they would not be blind to the truth. Because they held onto their doctrine (vv. 28-29), their sins of disbelief and rejection of Jesus would remain with them forever and they would have the greater condemnation (v. 41). We must allow Jesus' light to shine in our hearts so that no sin remains in us. He gives sight to the blind and lights every person's way so that no one will ever be in darkness again. Jesus is the Light. Aren't you glad you can "see"?